The American Poetry Recovery Series

Collected Poems

EDWIN ROLFE

COLLECTED POEMS

Edited by
Cary Nelson & Jefferson Hendricks

INTRODUCTION AND NOTES
BY CARY NELSON

UNIVERSITY OF ILLINOIS PRESS
Urbana and Chicago

The poem by Langston Hughes is copyright by and
used by permission of the Langston Hughes Estate,
George Huston Bass, Executor-Trustee

Illini Books edition, 1996
©1993 by the Board of Trustees of the University of Illinois
Manufactured in the United States of America
P   5   4   3   2   1

This book is printed on acid-free paper.

Library of Congress Cataloging-in-Publication Data
Rolfe, Edwin, 1909–1954.
    [Poems. Selections]
    Collected poems / Edwin Rolfe ; edited by Cary Nelson
and Jefferson Hendricks ; introduction and notes by Cary Nelson.
        p. cm. — (The American poetry recovery series)
    Includes bibliographical references.
    ISBN 0-252-06640-5 (pbk. : alk. paper)
    I. Nelson, Cary.   II. Hendricks, Jefferson, 1953– .   III. Title.
IV. Series.
PS3535.047A6   1993
811'.52—dc20   92-42324
                                                        CIP

CONTENTS

1ˢᵗ called Two Wars, then The Eternal Field, then
First Love
self published

sections marked by Lia Nickerson's illustrations

First Love and Other Poems (1951)

PREFACE

What was rare about Edwin Rolfe was this:
that everything he wrote about in his clear and
pungent lines he also fought for. . . . He was a poet
who could translate into verse the intense emo-
tional impact of his experience which he knew to
be the most vital experience possible to the men of
his generation, their dedication, even to the point
of death, to the common good.
—*The Contemporary Reader*, January 1955

Edwin Rolfe's *Collected Poems* brings together the body of his work that we be-
lieve will be of greatest use to those readers with a general interest in American
political poetry and with a specific interest in Rolfe himself. It gives people for
the first time a comprehensive view of one of the more inventive political poets
of the Great Depression, of the writer Americans who fought in the Spanish
Civil War regard as their poet laureate, and of a writer who used poetry as a
weapon against the reactionary politics that dominated the United States in
the 1950s.

Rolfe's *Collected Poems* includes the complete texts of his three published
books, *To My Contemporaries, First Love and Other Poems,* and *Permit Me Refuge.*
These are supplemented with three groups of uncollected or unpublished
poems, placed after each of the published books to keep the arrangement of
the main body of the *Collected Poems* roughly chronological. These sections sig-
nificantly increase one's sense of Rolfe's range and add to the body of his work
the very strong but unpublished poems written toward the end of his life. Fol-
lowing Rolfe's own practice, we have supplied titles for poems when necessary.
Although Rolfe often left poems untitled in manuscript and sometimes pub-
lished them that way in journals, he always titled poems in his books. Rolfe
also occasionally provided dates of composition with his published poems. We
have supplied that information for additional poems whenever the information
was available in his archive.

This *Collected Poems* does not, however, reprint all the poems Rolfe pub-
lished, and it includes only a few of the substantial number of unpublished
poems in the Rolfe archive. As it happened, many of his unpublished or un-
collected poems were written either when he was in his teens or before 1932,
and we felt it would be counterproductive to overwhelm the book with poems
written before Rolfe had matured as a writer. Yet we wanted readers to have
a few examples of his first revolutionary poems ("May Day Song" and "Any

Slave"), his less political modernist experiments ("Sunday Evening Revery"), and voices he took up briefly and abandoned, such as the distinctly Frost-like "Barn in Wisconsin." All these poems are in a section called "Early Poems" placed at the end of the book; the last two poems give us a sense of the very different poet Rolfe might have become if he had lived in a different time or history had presented him with other options. We have also added two appendixes—one honoring the somewhat separate life Rolfe's poems have had in Spanish translation and one reprinting "The Sixth Winter," a well-known depression-era poem that Rolfe collected only in severely condensed form. Readers should consult the Bibliography for detailed information on Rolfe's publishing history; for the biographical and historical background most relevant to the poems the Introduction and Notes to the Poems should be helpful. The Introduction also quotes a number of interesting fragments and unfinished poems that will not be found elsewhere in the book. An earlier version of the Introduction was published in a special, multigenre issue of *Modern Fiction Studies* on the politics of modernism.

This book would not have been possible without help from a number of people. Our greatest debt is to Mary Rolfe, who preserved Rolfe's papers for the decades since his death and then entrusted them to us. Several people gave full and careful readings of the manuscript: Michael Bérubé, Karen Ford, Philip Levine, Reginald Gibbons, Robert Parker, Mary Rolfe, Paula Treichler, and Alan Wald. Edward Brunner, Leon Chai, and Michael Thurston were helpful with specific advice. There is no question that this is a better book because of their efforts. Rolfe's archive was purchased by the University of Illinois Library with the assistance of the Chancellor's Office, the Research Board, the College of Liberal Arts and Sciences, and the English Department. We would like to thank everyone who made that purchase possible. We would also like to thank both Centenary College and the University of Illinois for continuing support of this project. Finally, we note that several of Rolfe's poems are scheduled to appear in 1993 in *TriQuarterly* and in the second edition of *The Heath Anthology of American Literature*.

INTRODUCTION

Lyric Politics:
The Poetry of Edwin Rolfe

Cary Nelson

Sometimes I wake at night
out of completest sleep
and see their remembered faces
luminous in the dark.
Ghostly as tracer-bullets
their smiles, their hesitant speech,
their eloquent hands in gesture
and their smiles belying fear:
Antonio, Catalan,
eighteen years old . . . Hilario, filling
his lungs with power and purpose.

If there's any place in the world where I could be dropped
from an airplane, alone, blind-folded, in pitch darkness,
and yet know from the very smell and feel and slope of the
earth exactly where I was—that would be the hills and
valley just east of the Ebro, in Spain.

These two previously unpublished fragments come from notebooks that Edwin
Rolfe (1909–54)—poet, journalist, and veteran of the Spanish Civil War—
kept during the late 1940s and early 1950s.[1] The first recalls some of the young
Spanish soldiers who filled out the depleted ranks of a group of mostly Ameri-
can volunteers—the Lincoln Battalion—in the spring of 1938; the second
recalls the last great campaign that Rolfe and the other Lincolns fought when
they crossed the Ebro River that summer. It was on the hills and in the valleys
east of the Ebro, a day's travel southwest from Barcelona, that Rolfe and other
members of the International Brigades trained in during the spring and sum-
mer of 1938. And it was just east of the river that they assembled their forces
before crossing to engage Franco's troops that July. Although he completed
a number of poems about Spain both while he was there from 1937 to 1938
and in the decade that followed his return to the United States in 1939, Rolfe's
body of work includes as well a continuing (and significantly less finished) dia-
logue with himself and his culture about the meaning of this most passionate
of all 1930s commitments.

Spain was the focus of the second of the three books of poems Rolfe gathered for publication, *First Love and Other Poems* (1951), so it is thus literally at the center of his career. But it was also for him, as for so many of those who fought in Spain, an experience that became in some ways the fulcrum of his life. The experience in Spain provided him with a way of thinking about much that was admirable in the revolutionary Left of the twenties and thirties as well as a contrast to the dark decade and more of national repression that followed World War II.

If I begin with Spain, then, it is, first, to acknowledge what was for Rolfe the most fulfilling political moment of his life; but it is also to give current readers the point of entrance that is most likely to win sympathetic attention. That is likely to be true for two reasons: first, because *First Love* is Rolfe's most overtly lyrical book. It is there, then, that readers who feel hailed by Rolfe's language and his passion can discover part of what is most distinctive about his poetry—that in Rolfe's work the lyrical voice becomes a politically positioned subject. Second, of all Rolfe's political engagements, Spain is the one many contemporary readers can most readily honor. That was not the case in the twenty years following Franco's 1939 victory, a period when the Americans who aided the Spanish republic were regularly demonized by more reactionary politicians. Now it is possible once again to recognize that, at the largest narrative level, the Spanish Civil War was the historical event that set the tone for the whole subsequent struggle between democracy and fascism. It was also a unique moment when men and women across the world came together to give their lives for a cause in which they believed.

To read Rolfe's first and last books, *To My Contemporaries* (1936) and *Permit Me Refuge* (1955), on the other hand, is for many Americans to take up periods of our history—the Great Depression and the long postwar inquisition that culminated in the McCarthy era—whose social and political realities we would now rather forget or disguise. It is not, to be specific, the depression itself that Americans would as well forget but rather the critiques of capitalism and racism it occasioned and the broad and sometimes revolutionary Left alliances that accompanied those critiques. What we would like to forget about the anticommunist hysteria of the forties and fifties is how long it lasted, how many people lost their jobs, how many institutions were involved in these purges, and how deeply cold war psychology penetrated people's lives. To the degree that poetry can testify to and reflect on those matters, Rolfe's poetry does so without compromise.

The Great Depression, the Spanish Civil War, and the long postwar inquisition are not the only subjects addressed in Rolfe's work, but they do dominate his three books of poems. I raise this problem at the outset to make explicit and self-conscious the issue of the politics of contemporary taste. For no effort to make Rolfe's poetry an appropriate subject of historical inquiry can avoid asking whether his work represents a past that remains usable now. If a democratic international socialism is to remain available as a cultural and political resource in the decades to come—and it would be foolish to assume now that the future is so readable that we know when and whether people will want to draw on those traditions of progressive thought—then the visionary Marxism that recurs throughout *To My Contemporaries* needs to remain part of our cultural memory. More immediately, if we are to resist repression in the future, we need to know its role in our own history. And we need to know as well that, contrary to the story that dominates existing literary histories, American poets of the late forties and early fifties did not only write about family life and classical myth; the poems of *Permit Me Refuge* help recover poetry's more critical role in the culture of paranoia, terror, and conformity that reigned in the postwar years.

Rolfe himself began to focus on the fragility and necessity of historical memory—on its key place in maintaining an informed and viable politics—almost immediately upon returning from Spain in 1939. Despite the massive loss of life typical of modern war and despite the special anguish of a civil conflict, the effort to aid the elected Spanish government in its struggle against fascism represented a triumph of internationalism, whether in support of democratic socialism, the ideals of communism, or the common interests of the working classes. It was in part the selflessness of that commitment that was recognized when the International Brigades held their farewell march through Barcelona on October 29, 1938. Unique in history, it was a parade to honor brigades that were part of what many realized would likely soon become a defeated army. As Rolfe would write nine years later in an unfinished poem, "Even the day of defeat / Exalted us." As part of the parade—in what must seem an improbable gesture by our contemporary political and poetic standards—printed poems commemorating the occasion were passed among the crowd.

Rolfe was there, and he saved some of those poem cards and brought them back to the United States. It was yet one more lesson about what role poetry might play in alerting readers to the crucial matters of their day. Poetry was to be at once a call to witness—a sign of where it mattered to stand and an example of the voice one might assume in standing there—and the essence of the historical record, its most succinct and telling form of testimony. In a few months Rolfe returned to his own country, where those who stood with Spain were scandalized as "premature antifascists." In less than a decade, many began losing their jobs in the massive postwar purge of the Left. As Rolfe wrote in an unpublished stanza he revised repeatedly, to remember Spain in those days was to stand against the dominant culture and against the national madness:

> Let the callous and secure, who have so much to lose,
> Forget Spain's passion and agony. Memory's an encumbrance,
> Embarrassing, even dangerous at times. For myself I
>   choose—
> Because to forget is to betray—the pain of remembrance.

The cost of forgetting would be paid both in our collective public life—in a curtailed knowledge of political possibilities, resources, and consequences—and in each one of us. Rolfe describes some of the individual cost in another unfinished postwar fragment:

> This is the age of the made-over man
> Name changed, perhaps,
> whose life is cut in half as by a knife
> (and, like the worm, each half goes on living)
> who must, if he is clever and cautious, forget
> the first and passionate years in favor of
> his made-over self, which must suppress
> all memory; his made-over self
> which is cunning at last, and uninvolved,
> and slyly garbed in protective colored-suit
> which he dare not divest himself of, even for a minute,
> not even for sleep, if he wants to feel safe.
> Not even for sleeping, lest his true history
> rise in his dream to confront him.

Rolfe's career opened with the "first and passionate" commitments commemorated in this fragment. The strong political statements in most of these early poems came fairly naturally to Rolfe; although they reflect his own experiences and political activities, they also flow partly from his family background.[2] His father was a Socialist and an official of a union local in New York. His mother was active in the birth control movement, pitched in during the famous 1913 silk workers' strike in Paterson, New Jersey, and later joined the Communist party. At the flat on Coney Island in New York where they lived for much of Rolfe's childhood, they let rooms to other people to help cover the rent; one such tenant was a red-headed Wobbly from the West—a member of our most irreverent, disruptive, and populist union, the Industrial Workers of the World—who used to give Rolfe and his younger brother Bern rides on his motorcycle and tell them stories of IWW organizing. Rolfe himself joined the Communist party (and was assigned to the Young Communist League) in 1925, when he was fifteen.[3] When he published his first poem in the *Daily Worker* in 1927, "The Ballad of the Subway Digger," it was a newspaper he already knew well at home.

Rolfe was born Solomon Fishman; his parents Nathan and Bertha emigrated from Jewish communities in Russia early in the century and met in Philadelphia, where they lived for the first few years of Rolfe's life. He began using pen names in high school, adopted the name "Edwin Rolfe" on some publications in the late twenties, and by the early thirties had effectively become Edwin Rolfe. Changing his name was a gesture that signaled at once his chosen identity as a writer and his conscious decision to commit himself to political activism.

After working intermittently in the already selectively depressed New York economy of the late twenties, Rolfe wanted relief from the city and a chance to read and write in a less-interrupted way. He was also ready to break with the Communist party, some of whose functionaries neither then nor later did he find sympathetic figures. Left politics, moreover, had been frequently disputatious during the twenties; indeed, in one such dispute his parents had aligned themselves with different groups, and thus the political conflicts of the period also played themselves out in Rolfe's family.[4] In the fall of 1929 he quit the party and left New York to enroll in the Experimental College at the University of Wisconsin at Madison. As his advisors noted, he retained strong loyalties to the working classes,[5] but for most of the next year he avoided politics and instead read widely and wrote relatively nonpolitical poems, including three written in 1929 or 1930 and published in *Pagany* in 1932. As the depression deepened, however, he was drawn to politics again and left Wisconsin in the middle of his second year there.

Rolfe rejoined the Communist party in New York and, after a variety of temporary jobs, began working full time at the *Daily Worker*. This was the period when the party was beginning to move toward becoming part of a mass movement. In the midst of massive unemployment, vast dislocation, and widespread hunger—and little faith that capitalism would recover—many in the United States and in Europe were radicalized. For a time revolutionary social and political change seemed possible. Dozens of radical journals sprang up not only in large cities but also in small towns and rural communities across the country. Radical theater drew audiences from all classes. Political art appeared in public places. Despite considerable suffering, the midthirties were thus a heady time on the Left. Much of the poetry of the period combined sharp social critique with a sense of revolutionary expectation. More than simply reflecting the times, however, the "proletarian" poetry of revolution sought to define a new politics, to suggest subject positions within it, and to help bring about the changes it evoked.[6] Far from a solitary romantic vocation, moreover, thirties political poetry was a form of collaborative rhetorical action, as poets responded to one another by ringing changes on similar revolutionary themes and metaphors.

It was largely from his poetry of the midthirties that Rolfe finally selected the poems that went into *To My Contemporaries*. At first he planned a longer and more comprehensive collection, tentatively titled *Also to Bear Arms*. But Horace Gregory convinced him to shorten the book and simplify its structure. It is clear that Rolfe also had doubts about the quality of both the early political poems he had written during and after his teens and the conventionally humanist poems he published in 1930. In the end, from the years 1927–32 he chose only two of the twenty-nine poems he had published. "Asbestos," published in the *Daily Worker* in 1928, indicates what he was already capable of; a stunning, if gruesome, conceit transforms a worker's body into his deathbed:

> John's deathbed is a curious affair:
> the posts are made of bone, the spring of nerves,
> the mattress bleeding flesh. Infinite air,
> compressed from dizzy altitudes, now serves
>
> his skullface as a pillow. Overhead
> a vulture leers in solemn mockery,
> knowing what John had never known: that dead
> workers are dead before they cease to be.

The exploitation of workers, we learn, literally impresses itself on their bodies. Those bodies are the fulcrum, the point of application, of all the power relations in which their lives are embedded. Yet the poem's very fluency, its metaphorical bravado, embeds political resistance within social tragedy. Rolfe was only nineteen when he wrote the poem, but he had learned a lesson that would help carry him through the rest of his career. It was first of all a lesson about class relations and about how they play themselves out in the industrial workplace. But it was also a lesson about how political poetry can take up traditional lyric forms—here the rhymed quatrains of the ballad stanza—and give them fresh social meaning. Both the *abab* rhyme scheme and the character's generic name (John is a common name in ballads and folk poems) might lead us to expect a conventional folk tale, but the power of the central conceit and the recurrent enjambments disturb the potential for predictability. The partial echo of the ballad form, then, creates a context that the poem's content violates, though the generic form also reminds us that the poem's unique metaphor points to social relations that are anything but unique. For the poem demonstrates that the popular imagination of the time must encompass the culture's exploitation of the ordinary worker; John *is* the everyman of the twenties and thirties industrial state.

During the period when he was writing the poems of *To My Contemporaries,* Rolfe also wrote his one long narrative poem, *"Cheliuskin,"* as well as this unpublished satiric description—very much in Kenneth Fearing's manner—of an unemployed depression businessman:

> Your Sunday sleep calls you from the banquet table:
> the feast recedes, the mulligan goes dry,
> the tin can cup rots with rust that held your coffee
> and you, Jeff Meredith, Virginian, forty-four, walk with
> rheumatic legs, broken steps, swollen arches, gangrened
>   toes,
> painfully to the dried grass dump beyond the fire's glow
> to take your final Sunday evening nap . . .
> After the day's
> battle with the bulls, after the long-shot try
> for the agency job, where the man with the buttonhole
>   flower
> stared you cold with his one green eye; after the leap for
> the last steel rail when the Memphis express went by,
> and the man who said Sorrybuddy
> when you shouldered him in the crowd,
> this is your revenge:
> whoopensacker for the guts and brain,
> rugged individual restless sleep
> on spiked beer-barrel hoops in the sunfried garbage heap;
> snoring among bluebottle flies that soar and settle on your
>   eyes.[7]

This passage—with its ironic recitation of the benefits to be gained from individual enterprise—can be linked, on the one hand, with Rolfe's more anguished poems about working-class life and, on the other hand, with the many published and uncollected poems about revolutionary collective action.

Rolfe was writing such poems, it is important to realize, in 1927 and 1928, months before the stock market crash in 1929 and years before the worst of the depression. He had grown up on the Left, and among his strongest influences as a young man were two notable friends from the older generation of the Left of the twenties, Joseph Freeman and Mike Gold. He took a writing class from Gold and was among the young people who often gathered at Freeman's house for conversation. Gold later wrote the introduction to *We Gather Strength* (1933), a collection of poems by Herman Spector, Joseph Kalar, Rolfe, and Sol Funaroff. Rolfe also knew other people associated with *The Masses* and *The Liberator;* Floyd Dell, for example, wrote Rolfe a recommendation for college. Rolfe was among those whose evolving political sensibilities prepared him to understand the depression in a particular way and to act on that understanding. He entered the thirties with deep sympathies for working people; by the time the collapse of the economy seemed irreversible, Rolfe was thoroughly devoted to international socialism as the only real alternative to continuing economic misery, destructive nationalist rivalries, and the basic racism of American culture. Lest we think such convictions quixotic, we might, for example, remember that in 1932 some fifty-three writers and artists—including John Dos Passos, Langston Hughes, and Edmund Wilson—signed the pamphlet *Culture and Crisis* that urged people to support the Communist party in that year's presidential election.

Rolfe's own commitments began earlier and continued longer, but the special force and coherence of *To My Contemporaries* grew out of the historical context of the Great Depression. "They who work here know no other things," he wrote earlier, "only heat and smoke and fumes of baking bricks." Now he offers a vision of "America today: its / fields plowed under . . . its wide / avenues blistered by sun and poison gas." "They who have reaped your harvest," he warns, merely "offer you the stalks." "This is the season when rents go up: / men die, and their dying is casual"; "their blood is dust now borne into the air"; "you see the dead face peering from your shoes; / the eggs at Thompson's are the dead man's eyes":

> This is the sixth winter:
> this is the season of death

Figure 1: The cover to *We Gather Strength* (1933), poems by Herman Spector, Joseph Kalar, Edwin Rolfe, and Sol Funaroff. The workers' tools rise serially together—wheel, book, pick, hammer, sickle, and shovel. Poetry is thus figured as an integral part of the revolutionary class movement.

> when lungs contract and the breath of homeless men
> freezes on restaurant window panes . . .
>
> The forest falls, the stream runs dry,
> the tree rots visibly to the ground;
> nothing remains but sixteen black
> bodies against a blood-red sky.

But if we "admit into our lands the winds / blowing from the east" and learn "the miracle of deeds / performed in unison," then we will see "the way / men act when roused from lethargy" and "the withered land will grow—purged." If *To My Contemporaries* opens with Rolfe's call in "Credo" to "renounce the fiction of the self" in order to "welcome multitudes," the book closes with the title poem's admission that it is difficult "to surrender / the fugitive fragments of an earlier self." He calls on his fellow poets on the Left—mentioning Sol Funaroff and Alfred Hayes by name—to join with him in a collective project of witness and transformation. Their task in part will be to encourage one another to combine conviction with the intricacies of technique. In the first stanza above, for example, we read the first two exclamatory lines—"This is the sixth winter: / this is the season of death"—each in a single breath—for the lines are perfectly cadenced and pointedly terse. Rolfe achieves this effect with the internal assonance of the repeated short *i*'s, the sibilance of the alliterated *s*'s, the initial "this is," and the controlled dactyls. But in the third line he lets his breath out; a medial caesura falls, the meter degrades, and we must draw breath as do the homeless men.

In the end, it is in that way that *To My Contemporaries* must be read, as Rolfe's contribution to a dialogic chorus of voices. Though Rolfe's poems tend to be finished and coherent in the way many readers have come to expect poems to be, a full reading of them in context would qualify their independent existence as aesthetic and political objects. None of the poems of that time stands alone. They are voices answering one another amidst a passion for change. The depth of these beliefs can only be gauged if we try to place ourselves back in those paradoxically desperate and hopeful times. Of course we cannot actually recover the felt reality of the depression. But in the effort to do so we can mark some of the differences between the sense of political possibility then and now; then perhaps we can begin to understand Rolfe's yearning, in what may be the most defamiliarizing metaphor in the book, to "live within the heart's vast kremlin."

While *To My Contemporaries* concentrates on the suffering and aspirations

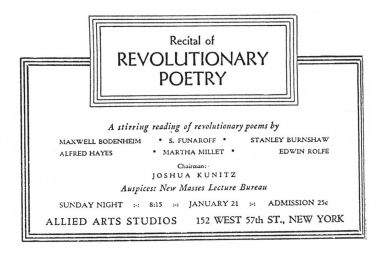

Figure 2: The interactive environment of 1930s political poetry was not only textual but also theatrical and social. *Above:* a *New Masses* notice for a 1934 reading of revolutionary poetry. *Below:* the printed invitation for the 1936 party celebrating the publication of Rolfe's *To My Contemporaries*.

of the depression and *First Love and Other Poems* is centered on Spain, Rolfe's final book, *Permit Me Refuge,* published posthumously from a manuscript in progress by the California Quarterly in 1955, takes the long postwar inquisition and the McCarthy era as its primary subject. Rolfe's focus throughout his career was thus political and historical; he believed that we live in history and that it is within and to history that even the supposedly more transcendent arts speak. Yet Rolfe's poems are also in their own way strikingly personal. For history to him was never the object of a disinterested gaze but rather the substance of his daily life: the context of his memories, the ground of current struggle, and the basis—when hope was possible—of any actions aimed toward the future. His life, then, is intricately woven into these poems; indeed he based many poems on his and his friends' personal experiences. Sometimes the personal context is partly or wholly elided; when we could, we have supplied those contexts because we believe they make the poems richer and more complex, rather than restrict their meaning to "merely" autobiographical references. They let us see some of what is at stake for Rolfe in transmuting personal experience into poems that are politically and historically useful. For Rolfe's poetry disavows the lyrical belief that anything personal can be wholly exceptional; both he and his friends lived extraordinary but in some ways representative lives. Whether struggling to find work during the depression, burying a dead comrade in Spain, or resisting the anticommunist madness of the postwar decades, Rolfe and the other people written into these poems acted in response to the times in which they lived. These poems are therefore not simply Rolfe's legacy but rather history's legacy to us. They are a testimony to what history gave to us, demanded of us, and took away from us in the decades in which Rolfe lived. And they urge us to reexamine our national past if we are to have any chance of acting responsibly and progressively in the present. To take up a position and act in relation to the cultural struggles history imposes on us is, finally, a major part of what it meant to Rolfe to be alive.

It is perhaps only in black poetry since the Harlem Renaissance and in feminist poetry since the sixties that one finds so consistent a claim that the personal is political. That is not, of course, a phrase that was available to Rolfe in the thirties and forties, and he would in any case have had in mind something rather different from more recent formulations of how personal life is politically inflected, but it is a phrase that we can use to help understand the way Rolfe's work reformulates and repositions biographical incidents. In some cases this means that only a few friends are likely to understand the personal source of a poem. In other cases those who need to know—and can position themselves productively in relation to the knowledge—will understand the exact historical reference. Rolfe published his individual poems and his books as interventions in the social and political processes of his day. He had in mind the audiences of his time; indeed, at times he withheld poems from publication or decided not to reprint them in his books because he thought they would either be counter-productive or politically ineffective as a result of historical events or changing political conditions since the poems were written.

A few examples of the most fragile sort of autobiographical reference—the sort that can easily be invisible to succeeding generations—can demonstrate how this kind of information can open up these poems without exhausting their meanings. These examples also suggest a good deal about the relationship of personal experience to Rolfe's process of composition.

"Room with Revolutionists" is dedicated to "J.F." (Joseph Freeman) and in fact is based on a conversation between Freeman and the Mexican painter David Alfaro Siqueros. That much is confirmed both in Rolfe's letters to Free-man and in Freeman's own correspondence.[8] Rolfe describes Freeman in the poem as "brother, Communist, friend, / counsellor of my youth and manhood." The focus of the poem, however, is on the mix of similarity and difference in revolutionary commitments in Freeman's and Siqueros's respective cultures. One man is most known for his writing, the other for his painting. One works on behalf of the Mexican "poor who burrow / under the earth in field and mine," the other on behalf of American working people. But they are also bound together by a vision that "transcends all frontiers." It was possible then, in the midst of the thirties, to grasp an international solidarity that overrode national differences. Knowing that Rolfe had specific people in mind helps us realize that he was reflecting on the political implications of actual practices, not on some unrealizable internationalist utopia. Yet the elimination of their identities from the poem also reinforces the idea that these and comparable roles can be filled by a variety of people. And the poem demonstrates that, even before Spain, Rolfe was drawn to the idea of an international revolutionary movement.

"Epitaph" is dedicated to Arnold Reid, who died on July 27, 1938, at Villalba de los Arcos in Spain. In fact, when Rolfe published the poem in *New Masses* in 1939 he called it "For Arnold Reid." What we know from the poem is that Reid was a friend of Rolfe's and that he was among the American volun-teers who gave their lives in the Ebro campaign that summer. There is a great deal else about Reid and Rolfe's relationship with him, however, that the poem holds at a distance. Much of this is not "in" the poem at all, but it is arguably part of what Rolfe negotiated in order to write the poem. In putting all this material back into an active relationship with "Epitaph," I may be burdening its three stanzas with more than they can easily carry. But this exercise gives us a clear opportunity to establish some of what can be at stake in the complex negotiations between poetry, autobiography, and history, relations we have ignored for too long.

What we might not know without reading about the war itself is that Reid was a political commissar in Barcelona and did not have to leave and go into battle.[9] Like Rolfe, who left his post as editor of *Volunteer for Liberty*, the English-language magazine of the International Brigades, so that he could join his comrades in the field, Reid chose to leave Barcelona and put himself at risk. Rolfe was thus in a sense acknowledging that double commitment—first to go to Spain and then to take up active duty when there was an alternative readily available.

Rolfe actually met Reid nine years earlier, in 1929, when they were both students at the University of Wisconsin. At the time Reid was still Arnold Reisky, though he was already a committed Communist and was soon to change his name to make it easier to be a party organizer among people who were more comfortable with names that sounded conventionally American. Reisky was Rolfe's first good friend in college, and they often debated the virtues of political commitment. Rolfe had quit the party and in May 1930 wrote to another friend that "Reisky has found me guilty of being a renegade from the Holy Cause."[10] Standing over his grave—"we buried him / here where he fell"— some of this history no doubt came back to him. It was certainly in his mind earlier in July when he talked with Reid about their Wisconsin days and again a few months later when he wrote "His Name Was Arnold Reid: An American on the Honor Roll of the Ebro's Dead," a prose piece published in the October 4, 1938, issue of *New Masses*. There he acknowledges that they were classmates at Wisconsin and talks briefly about their friendship.

"Epitaph" was written on July 30, 1938. Three days after Reid was killed, Rolfe returned to his battlefield grave to write an elegy on the spot where he died. Reid's blood, Rolfe imagines, will now nourish the vineyards and olive groves of the surrounding hills. Yet it will also run "deeper than grave was dug / ever," deep enough to feed those fields "no enemy's boots / can ever desecrate," fields sown in honor of Spain's democratic revolution and its devotion to equality for all people. These are not, therefore, for Rolfe the conventional fields of heaven, for he is not that sort of believer, but rather fields of historical memory and witness, fields traced by the camaraderie of shared commitment, the mutual recognition of historical understanding, and the record of things done. Those too are the fields of Spain—fields that for Rolfe represent the material history of an ideal—and thus they are fields no enemy can capture.

Perhaps Rolfe had in mind the 1937 antifascist portfolio, *Galicia Martir,* done by the Spanish artist Alfonso Rodríguez Castelao, which he had with him in Madrid the year before. One of Castelao's sketches is captioned "It is not corpses they bury, but seed." Since Rolfe saw Rafael Alberti regularly in Madrid, and since they exchanged poems with one another, Rolfe would almost certainly have known Alberti's "You Have Not Fallen" ("It is not death, this sowing. / There is a birth pang in your anguish"). And perhaps Hemingway in turn, whom Rolfe met and became close friends with in Spain, would have had all these texts in mind when he adapted the metaphor for a piece he did for the February 14, 1939, issue of *New Masses.*[11] So may have Langston Hughes, whose poem "Tomorrow's Seed" was later published in the 1952 anthology *The Heart of Spain.* The metaphor has a longer history, of course, but it grows distinctively in Spanish soil. In any case, in a gesture that echoes through the poetry of the war, Rolfe concludes that this is, after all, no grave but a "plot where the self-growing seed" reaches out to turn the soil over, "ceaselessly growing."[12]

In this, as in everything else in the poem, Rolfe writes Reid's epitaph in the light of his representative sacrifice. What testifies to their personal history is not the recitation of intimate detail—for there is none in the poem—but rather the decision to write the poem at the site of Reid's freshly dug grave, the choice of Reid as the embodiment of the commitment to Spain. Late in 1938 Rolfe wrote to Joseph Freeman, who had published a letter about Reid in *New Masses* in September: "Your letter on Arnold was good. I wish I hadn't felt that I had to throttle all personal feeling in my own dispatch."[13] Yet Rolfe's *New Masses* "dispatch" is actually relatively personal, very personal, certainly, in comparison with his poem "Epitaph." No such second thoughts, notably, occur about the poem in any of his diaries or letters; he simply does not think of poetry as an appropriate vehicle for autobiography or unmediated self-expression. It is rather the place where personal experience is to be transmuted into epiphanic historical testimony.

"Political Prisoner 123456789" is from the dark days of the postwar suppression of free speech in America. The title's serial recitation of the first nine numbers signals several things at once: the relentless accumulation of the inquisition's victims, the way that incarceration obliterates their individual differences, and the paradoxical interchangeability of their personal suffering. It is

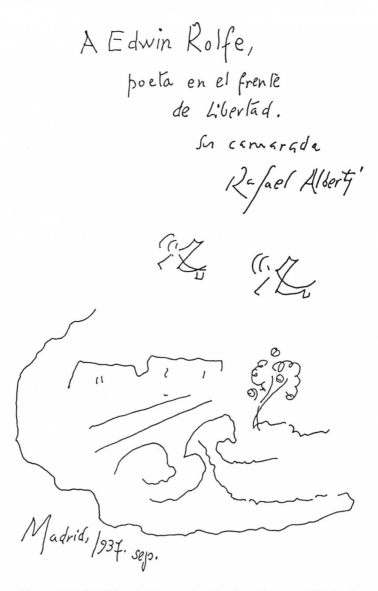

Figure 3: Rafael Alberti's illustrated dedication of a copy of his book of poems *De un momento a otro*, which he presented to Rolfe in Madrid in 1937.

the shared, characteristic, but individually felt and lived reality of their stories
that the poem itself then takes up. "I have heard this man called traitor," Rolfe
writes, "I saw him shamed / before his friends . . . the walls of his few rooms
torn wide for all to see." Although we can read the poem as speaking for all
the political prisoners of its time and read it so that it continues to speak for
the political prisoners of our time as well, it really addresses those who have
been unjustly imprisoned. There is a risk, then, in overly idealizing and uni-
versalizing its referent. Hidden beneath the anonymity of the poem's object,
moreover, is a different and more specific form of testimony. For it was the
Hollywood Ten, several of them close friends of Rolfe's—in federal prison for
standing up for their constitutional rights—that he had in mind.[14] The title in
fact was to be "Political Prisoner 12345678910." But one of the ten, Edward
Dmytryk, recanted and cooperated with the House Un-American Activities
Committee.[15] He was thus effectively excluded from the poem's title. And the
poem testifies—by that silence—to the shock of that betrayal and to the moral
standards incumbent upon victims of oppression. As Rolfe makes clear here
and in other poems, it is not, finally, his position that there can be no traitors,
rather that these nine men were not:

> I heard this man called traitor . . .
> —yet knew the deed was a lie, the accusations false,
> the men whose mouths uttered them not fit to tread
> the same earth he walked, nor able to oppose him
> by other means than falsehood. They lied to save
>   themselves.

If all these poems are about Rolfe's friends, if they are all written out of per-
sonal experience, their testimony on that level is either indirect or elided. For
both Rolfe and the people who became subjects of these poems are positioned
primarily as subjects of history. Part of what one can regain by recovering some
of the biographical background to the poems is a sense of how Rolfe typically
dealt with material from his life; writing a poem for him was partly a matter
of deciding how to handle biographical materials at the politically pertinent
distance. The people in Rolfe's poems most often live as agents within history,
and when they act—because action *is* possible—they often pay the price the
times exact for their agency. The ways contemporary history plays itself out
in people's lives and the ways people take up public issues in their beliefs and
actions were Rolfe's most pressing subjects. Of course he sometimes wrote
about himself, but generally he treated himself as a historical subject as well.

Even a poem addressed to a former girlfriend takes as its occasion her journey to "a happier continent than this"; the poem is titled "Letter for One in Russia." None of this should suggest that the poems are impersonal or dispassionate. For when he wrote poems about key events of his times—about the Great Depression, the Spanish Civil War, and the McCarthy era—he addressed these topics out of political conviction and lived experience. History at every point mattered in his life.

Not all his poems include the sort of largely hidden personal references I have noted above, though it is now too late to know for certain how many do. One would not know from his poem on Chaplin, "The Melancholy Comus," that Rolfe and Chaplin were friends. And one would not know that when Rolfe was in the hospital after Chaplin had left the country, he dreamed once that Chaplin visited him there. The poem takes up the public Chaplin with obvious affection—"Because he is what we would be / we love him"—and it does so in part because Rolfe felt Chaplin's public trial by the media as the harrowing of a friend. But Rolfe aimed to draw on those personal feelings to augment and deepen the public Chaplin we all can know:

> The poem finds in the figure of Chaplin an embodiment of physical and emotional contradictions—the tiny hat perched awkwardly on his head, the too-small vest, the overlarge pants, and the enormous shoes are external manifestations of the complexity of the character's psyche. These are the contradictions that define us. When the speaker says "our own feet ache in his comic shoes," he reminds us we are like Chaplin, an "authentic mystery." "Our loneliness from which there is no escape" is in this vision both what makes us individuals and part of what ties us to each other as a society. It is a subtle joke to say that our own feet ache in his comic shoes, since the problem of Chaplin's shoes is that they are too large, not too small. What "pinches" us in our subjectivity is not its narrowness but its wideness; the ache is nothing less than the self's social relations. Chaplin symbolizes a certain reconciliation of all these discontinuities: "In him, blended perfectly, are man, woman, child." Our feet ache in his shoes, ironically, because they are so hard to fill.[16]

In the case of "The Melancholy Comus" Rolfe carefully wrote a public poem grounded in unacknowledged personal affection. Yet personal associations are not the only kinds of information virtually erased in Rolfe's work. One might conclude from the overridingly clear and consistent thematics of his three books that Rolfe's historical references are readily available to the reader. Often they are. Certainly long descriptive or narrative poems like "The Sixth

Winter," "*Cheliuskin*," "Entry," and "City of Anguish" give a rather full sense of the historical conditions they seek to evoke. The poems in each of his books, moreover, reinforce one another and fill out each other's historical contexts. But Rolfe's poems also contain a significant number of almost fatalistically abbreviated historical references. How many readers will remember the German anarchist writer Erich Muehsam when they read the phrase "Nazi faces murdering Muehsam" in the poem "May 22nd 1939"? How many will catch the allusion to the czarist-era Pale of Settlement in the phrase "the colorless Pale" in "Now the Fog?" Will anyone not knowledgeable about the Spanish Civil War be aware of the extraordinary story behind the reference to "the words that Unamuno spoke" in "Song for a Birth Day in Exile?" In a very real sense the poems themselves are written in exile from their proper audience, an audience for whom all these references are resonant.

Rolfe thus knew that many of these allusions would pass unrecognized. Superficially, the tactic of including fragmentary historical references in a modern poem seems Poundian. But with Pound we know that every historical reference had been taken up in the synthesis effected by one idiosyncratic ego; the only real significance of these bits of history lies in what they meant to Pound. Rolfe, however, often testified instead to the pathos of the now culturally decathected material facts themselves. It is almost as if the more fragmentary references can testify only to their absence from common knowledge; by the time we read the poems certain names have been cast already into a void of forgotten time. Rolfe knew he could not keep all these names within a network of shared meanings; all the poem can guarantee is their audibility. They are thus, in effect, vanishing citations, testimony at once to the forgetfulness that dominates historical memory and to a fatalistic recognition that a poem can never contain everything we need to know in order to interpret it.

Not uncommonly, writing such poems for Rolfe was partly a way of coming to terms with difficult historically representative experience and of asking what can be learned of it that might be useful for the rest of us. Thus when Rolfe was unjustly slandered at the *Daily Worker* in 1934 and fired as a result, he turned to poetry to make some sense of the experience.[17] The result is one of his most well-known early poems, "Definition," in which he acknowledges that some who are underhanded and some who are fools will choose to be called comrade, but argues that the ideals underlying the word cannot be compromised that way. Hailed as a comrade by one deficient in these values, he will nevertheless "answer the salutation proudly," thereby honoring the ideal. Nearly twenty years later, in May 1952, he turned on the radio and learned that his friend

Clifford Odets had just betrayed himself and his friends by testifying before the House Un-American Activities Committee. Rolfe turned from the radio and in a few hours drafted a new poem, first calling it "Ballad of the Lost Friend" and later retitling it "Ballad of the Noble Intentions," thereby again making the poem more representative than personal.[18] It is a ballad structured as a dialogue, a kind of witty and anguished mock interrogation, as Rolfe adopts the committee's question-and-answer method with different aims—to search for the truth rather than for lies. "What will you do, my brother, my friend, / when they summon you to their inquisition," he asks, "And what will you say, my brother, my friend, / when they threaten your family's food instead?" The form, of course, has obvious risks, since the speaker is effectively conducting another interrogation. It works only because Rolfe also enters into the inner world of painful self-justification that unwilling witnesses had to create for themselves:

> *I engaged them in skilful debate, since I felt*
> *   that mere youthful defiance was unrealistic.*
> *I told what I knew, or thought, to be true;*
> *   it was harmless, anachronistic. . . .*
>
> *And there were some living men too that I named.*
> *   What harm could it do them, after two decades?*
> *Besides, as I've reason to know, it was all—*
> *   after all—in the records.*

The answers are not sufficient to save this speaker's honor—indeed, Odets, as it happened, unlike some other witnesses, tortured himself about his testimony—but it is only in the last four stanzas that Rolfe's judgment is set: "Your act of survival betrayed *not* your friends, / but yourself. . . . And *that* was your crime; in the noon of your life / you resigned from the living."

At every point Rolfe imagined such poems not simply as detached comments about events but as events themselves, as interventions in social and political life. He wanted poems to empower readers who shared his beliefs—giving them language and speaking positions they might need but be unable to articulate on their own—and to challenge and persuade those who disagreed with him. Both groups, moreover, were asked to take on complications not always typical of political dialogue. Rolfe also clearly believed that poetry had distinctive cultural work to do. For him, poetry was not interchangeable with other forms of persuasion. More than any other kind of writing, it could succinctly capture what was most critical in the dynamics of lived history. If poetry

A Poem for The Amusement of My friend, Who Like to Laugh (handwritten title)

That was the year
the birds committed suicide against the Empire State,
having, in some still-unexplained manner,
lost, or disregarded, their aerial radar.

That was the year
when men and women everywhere ceased dying natural deaths:
the aged, fac_ing sleeplike death, took poison,
the infant, facing life, died with his mother in childbirth.
And the whole wild remainder of the population
crashed their cars horribly in auto accidents
on roads as clear and uncluttered as ponds.
More people, reported the National Safety Board,
perished in traf fic than in war.

That was the year
all ships on every river, lake, habor, ocean
vanished with out trace; and even those docked at quays
turned over and sank on their sides like wounded Normandies.

That was the year
even the civilian transport planes
found, like the war-planes, the airxlines crowded,
and crashed like baby-Oedipi to earth in flames.
(The average carnage in each wreck was half a hundred.)
Others, mild stay-at-homes, slipped in bathtubs,
others, confined to indoors, descending stairs,
and some were eve_n killed playing musical chairs.

Figure 4: Rolfe's revisions to a draft of "A Poem to Delight My Friends Who Laugh at Science-Fiction."

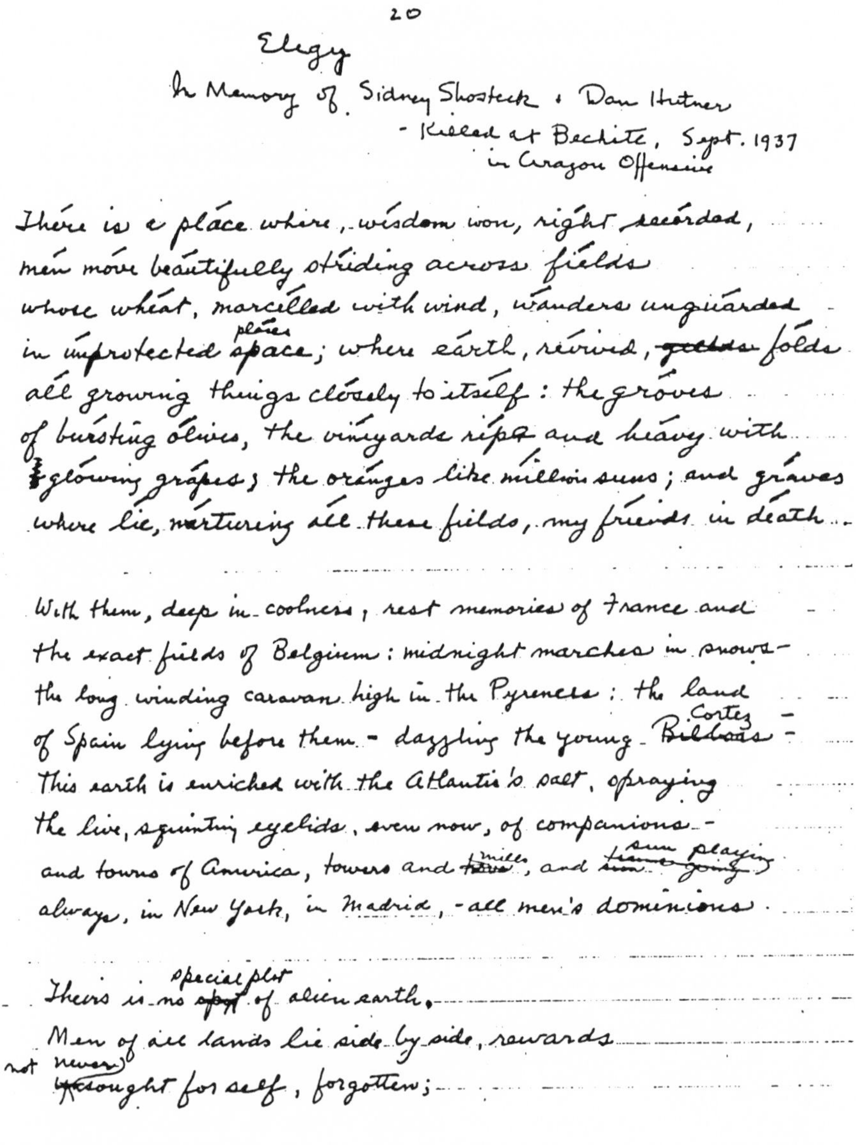

20

Elegy
In Memory of Sidney Shosteck & Dan Hutner
— Killed at Bechite, Sept. 1937
in Aragon Offensive

There is a place where, wisdom won, right recorded,
men move beautifully striding across fields
whose wheat, marcelled with wind, wanders unguarded
in unprotected space; where earth, revived, folds
all growing things closely to itself: the groves
of bursting olives, the vineyards ripe and heavy with
glowing grapes; the oranges like million suns; and graves
where lie, nurturing all these fields, my friends in death.

With them, deep in coolness, rest memories of France and
the exact fields of Belgium: midnight marches in snows—
the long winding caravan high in the Pyrenees: the land
of Spain lying before them — dazzling the young Cortez —
This earth is enriched with the Atlantic's salt, spraying
the live, squinting eyelids, even now, of companions—
and towns of America, towers and mills, and sun playing
always, in New York, in Madrid, — all men's dominions.

Theirs is no special plot of alien earth,
Men of all lands lie side by side, rewards
not sought for self, forgotten;

Figure 5: A manuscript version of Rolfe's "Elegy for Our Dead." Note that Rolfe has marked the stresses in the first stanza.

Honor in this lies: that theirs is no special
plot of alien earth: Men of all lands here
lie side by side, at peace now after the crucial
torture of combat, bullet & bayonet gone, fear
banished from those who, knowing it well,
were willing and
clothe the vision with flesh
despite it to fight, to live, to die. Their rewards,
not sought for self, show in live faces, smiling,
Remembering what they did: Deeds were their
final words.

Madrid
Sept. 20,
1937

for Rolfe was effectively the soul of an age, that means it could record the essential character of history, not that it could exit history and transcend it.

Accomplishing this sort of work meant taking on poetry as a deliberate craft. These poems are not for the most part composed of the sort of political rhetoric that can come easily in daily speech. Although Rolfe sometimes wrote and published poems immediately after the events they describe, he also revised poems extensively, occasionally working on them for years, and his revisions consistently sharpen his language and make his metaphors more distinctive. In some ways, indeed, his methods are quite traditional; a number of his drafts, for example, have been carefully scanned, the stresses noted and counted. If the image of a revolutionary poet studiously monitoring rhyme and meter is surprising, so be it. If it seems improbable or contradictory, perhaps that is because we have forgotten what social and political functions poetry has served in the past and may yet serve again in the future. For the last five decades in America many of us have held an image of political poetry as automatic and unreflective. Yet the historical record is actually quite different from that.

For a time, Rolfe had some real cultural support in the role of revolutionary poet. He rarely had much time to write poetry, to be sure, since he generally earned his living as a journalist, but at least he was recognized as a notable young poet. When *To My Contemporaries* was published, it received some of the attention it merited as a distinctive contribution to a major cultural movement. Horace Gregory provided the book's jacket blurb and selected Rolfe as the lead poet of the social poets issue he guest edited for *Poetry* in May 1936. A few months later, in the July issue of *Poetry*, Harriet Monroe described him as "the best among these inflammatory young men and women." That year the *New York Times Book Review* reviewed Rolfe along with Kenneth Patchen and Stanley Burnshaw under the heading "Three Young Marxist Poets" and declared him "one of the best of these younger poets." Rolfe's photograph was published on the first page of the review. The *New Yorker* declared him "If not the most flowery, perhaps the most readable and sincere of the poets of the Left." Morton Dauwen Zabel, in an omnibus review in the *Southern Review,* ranked him the best among five radical American poets. More detailed commentaries appeared by Joseph Freeman in *New Masses* and by Kenneth Fearing in the *Daily Worker*. It was partly that reputation—as well as his credentials as a Left journalist—that led Bennett Cerf to sign him on two years later to do the first history of the Lincoln Battalion. Yet *To My Contemporaries* would be the only time Rolfe received widespread attention for one of his books of poetry. Ironically, his later work was more rhetorically accomplished, but by then the dominant culture had scandalized and excommunicated everything that mattered to him, and Rolfe's subsequent books of poetry went mostly unnoticed in the major reviewing media.

In the months after publishing *To My Contemporaries* Rolfe spent much of his spare time working to complete a novel based on the experience of joining the Young Communist League. His correspondence suggests he may have finished the novel in the summer of 1936. At that point Rolfe had been living with Mary Wolfe for two years, and they were married that fall. Mary had also grown up in New York on the Left and was also a party member, so they shared not only their personal lives but also the social and political life of the next two decades. As for the novel, no copies of the manuscript have survived. In any case, that was also the summer when the Spanish Civil War began, and Rolfe's thoughts soon turned to Spain. He also abandoned writing revolutionary poems about the Communist party, something he had been doing since the late 1920s.

No cause in the thirties had quite the power and purity of the international effort to come to the defense of the Spanish republic. From the outset, when a group of right-wing army officers revolted against the elected Popular Front Coalition government in July 1936, it was clear that Spain was to be at once the real and symbolic site of the growing struggle between democracy and fascism. Mussolini's Italy may have begun to work on behalf of the army officers even before the revolt began, and Franco secured the cooperation of Hitler's Germany within a week. The Western democracies, unfortunately, assumed a noninterventionist policy, partly on the deluded hope that such a stance would discourage German and Italian participation and partly because some in the West were more comfortable with a fascist government in Spain than with an elected government whose policies were disturbingly progressive. Only the Soviet Union regularly made limited arms available for sale to the Spanish government. As a result the Loyalist troops were often undersupplied and poorly armed. But their cause drew support from the broadest possible international coalition. "Spain," Rolfe proclaimed in "Entry," a poem written during the war, "is yesterday's Russia, tomorrow's China, / yes and the thirteen seaboard states."

At first there was no organized effort to solicit foreign volunteers. But people recognizing the great danger of fascism and people sympathetic with the Left soon began crossing the border into Spain to offer what help they could; most entered Spain through France, but they came from Britain and from all across Europe. This remarkable phenomenon—a mixture of selfless idealism and historical insight—helped galvanize the international Left. Soon the Comintern (Communist International) decided to organize groups of international volunteers and to make travel arrangements for them; Spain in turn set up a formal training base at Tarazona, a small town northwest of Albacete, which was the administrative center for the brigades. By that time some volunteers had already seen action, but the first battle in which the International Brigades themselves made a major contribution was the historic struggle for Madrid that November. Franco attacked the city in force, hoping to take the capital and end the war swiftly. But the people of Madrid built barricades, organized to fight, and the city held. The fascist offensive was broken in dramatic battles that included hand-to-hand combat in the city's suburbs. For five months Madrid and the surrounding towns were the main strategic goal of the rebel troops.

It took Rolfe some time to get permission from the Party to join the volunteers, but in June 1937 he hiked across the Pyrenees Mountains and was shortly in training at Tarazona. By that time the International Brigades were issuing a regular newspaper in several languages out of their Madrid offices. The novelist Ralph Bates, who was editing the English-language version of *Volunteer for Liberty,* was scheduled to leave Spain. After training for a month to join a fighting unit, Rolfe was offered Bates's job. Rolfe refused, but his extensive experience as a journalist made him an obvious choice, so the offer was soon changed to an order. The job of editing the newspaper brought him back to the front regularly, and he assumed other responsibilities as well: serving as political commissar in Madrid and organizing shortwave radio broadcasts. The broadcasts become the subject of his unpublished poem "Radio Madrid—1937," which he first called "Voice of Spain" when he wrote it on August 18.

With the front only two kilometers away, Madrid was very much a city under siege. Food was limited and several times a week the rebel guns on Mount Garabitas shelled the city. In the downtown section hundreds of civilians were regularly killed or wounded. Consistent with the paradoxical intensity of a city at war, the experience felt alternately theatrical and terrifying. At night, Rolfe and other Madrileños sometimes watched the bombardments from rooftops. But there was also continual surreal violence and appalling human tragedy. The bombings took their places in the poems he began to write. It took some time to complete his long poem "City of Anguish," first simply called "Madrid," but on August 3 he began working on it, writing four pages about the previous night's bombardment:

> The headless body
> stands strangely, totters for a second, falls.
> The girl speeds screaming through wreckage; her
>   hair is
> wilder than torture.
>   The solitary foot,
> deep-arched, is perfect on the cobbles, naked,
> strong, ridged with strong veins, upright, complete . . .
>
> The city weeps. The city shudders, weeping.

Exploiting the literariness of poetic language, as Rolfe does here, has obvious risks when the subject is violence. If the ironies of a violence transfigured, beatified by literariness, cannot be entirely controlled, however, they can at least be clearly bound to their context. After "Season of Death," "City of Anguish" is Rolfe's most elaborate effort in that direction. Here he makes it clear that part of the city's anguish is the transfiguration of its mental life. He specifies not only the violence that he sees but also the violence he imagines. Madrid is a city where "soil and stone / spilled like brains from the sandbag's head." "The mind," he writes, "calculates destruction" whether we will it to or not. Part of what he commemorates here, just as he commemorates heroism in battle in other poems, is the special beauty of Madrid under siege. Yet in Rolfe's poetry it is possible to be drawn to the surreal beauty of these images without feeling that their horror is undercut.

At other times, like some of the other poets who wrote about Spain, Rolfe preferred a more straightforward polemicism. At such points he did not want his moral aims subverted by the duplicities of explicit metaphorization. He was also, however, capable of taking on the ambiguities of metaphoric language while retaining clear moral and political perspectives. "Come for a joyride in Madrid," he urges us, but don't count yourself as having had the full experience until you've heard "the zoom of / planes like a ferris wheel strafing the trenches": "War is your comrade struck dead beside you, / his shared cigarette still alive in your lips."

As these lines suggest, while Madrid suffered Rolfe also had to deal with another kind of death, not so visible as the bodies he saw in the streets, but because of that distance perhaps still more painful—the deaths of his comrades in the battalion. Sometimes he simply sat down to record the names of the dead and wounded in his diary. A September 13 entry includes the lines "Sidney

Shosteck dead—shot between eyes by a sniper's bullet while bringing a tank in. Danny Hutner also dead." The same day he wrote home about Shosteck's death, reporting that they had met during training and that Shosteck visited him in Madrid. A week later, on September 20, he wrote "Elegy for Our Dead," which he dedicated to Shosteck and Hutner and eventually published in *The Volunteer*. A number of the poems written earlier still remained in unfinished drafts; this was the first finished poem about Spain that fully satisfied him. And it is his effort to make an enduring historical statement about what was distinctive about these comrades he had lost there. As he noted in his diary, the "poem was not meant to be, but turned out to be," at least in part, "an answer to Rupert Brooke's 'corner that is forever England' "; this time the dead honor something larger than nationalism:

> Honor for them in this lies: that theirs is no special
> strange plot of alien earth. Men of all lands here
> lie side by side, at peace now after the crucial
> torture of combat, bullet and bayonet gone, fear
> conquered forever.

That August and September of 1937 in Madrid he also drafted several of the other poems he used in the opening section of *First Love and Other Poems,* including "Entry," a poem about the journey through the French countryside at night and across the Pyrenees into Spain, and "Eyes of a Blind Man," which he wrote on September 6 after meeting Commandante Fort of the Franco-Belge Battalion; Fort was blinded at Brunete in July. Several unpublished or uncollected poems come from the same period, including "Not Hatred" and "Eyes of a Boy." "Death by Water," a poem about a steamship carrying volunteers that is torpedoed off the coast of Malgrat, is of special note because of its explicit reference to Eliot. Although Rolfe's first title was "City of Barcelona," his direct quotation of Eliot's phrase "the cry of gulls" in his first line makes it clear that he had the fourth section of *The Waste Land* in mind from the outset. "Death by Water," is, of course, the shortest and most unqualifiedly mythic section of Eliot's poem. So Rolfe's poem—which is about real people who die within history because of their political commitments—directly confronts the mythic tendency within high modernism with his own convictions about historical specificity. The second stanza invokes Coleridge's "The Rime of the Ancient Mariner" to reject another kind of allusive mythologizing as well: the albatross is superseded by "the vultures descending on an Ethiopian plain," recalling Mussolini's invasion of North Africa. All this sets us up for the sudden shock of the torpedo exploding against the steamship in the next stanza.

Throughout this time Rolfe felt deeply troubled at being relatively safe in Madrid. The raw character of his feelings at the time is apparent in another unpublished fragment from 1937:

> Being neither writer nor soldier
> Despite ten years at one trade, a month at the other,
> What can I do, here in safe Madrid
> When I hear the death of Paul, my brother?
>
> He died at Fuentes, struck in the belly;
> The fascist bullets got him on the road
> That runs by the river Ebro. And I
> Am safe, ashamed to be alive, in Madrid

In January 1938, the International Brigades offices were moved to Barcelona. That spring the order came through for all able-bodied men to leave for the front. It was not supposed to apply to Rolfe, but he decided to act on it anyway and joined the battalion in the field in April. He participated in the Ebro campaign, which included the largest battles of the war, and soon after that was asked to take over for Joe North as Spanish correspondent for the *Daily Worker* and *New Masses*.

Ten years later Rolfe gathered together these poems, written in Spain and in the midst of its Civil War, to form the first section of *First Love*. He added to them one poem only, "To Thine Own Self," that may at first seem almost to contradict his Spanish experience. No cause, the middle stanza seems to argue, can ever be counted constant in its own right; one needs to hold to an inner sense of aims and values:

> No words men speak are really, finally, true.
> No friend can know nor understand completely.
> No woman means everything. No one pursuit
> captures the spirit to exclude all others.
> And no single star is ever faithful;
> the mariner must lean on compass more than sky.

But of course Rolfe placed this poem there in the desperate days of the postwar inquisition. If he is now "to count deeds / well-done which otherwise might fall behind / meaningless," he will have to seek the memory of Spain within, there being little public honor in the name for Americans now. No pure abstraction will guide him through the current nightmare. No "single star," not even the Soviet Union's red star, can prove unwavering. He must instead use that inner compass that points toward Spain and all it meant. The inner compass points toward the lessons of lived history; the self one can rely on takes shape in an engagement with its times.

It is Rolfe's general habit to measure subjective experience against history, to turn the situated individual into a measure of historicized values. Indeed, in truncating Polonius's famous dictum ("This above all, to thine own self be true") for his title, he turns it into a dedication to a subjectivity that is here wholly embattled and secured only by uneasy assertion. The quirky diction in the last line above—"lean" rather than, say, the more obvious "rely"—diction that puts forward an unworkable choice of physically leaning on a compass or the sky—underlines the fragility of that self-dependence in "these days that . . . haunt us too deeply." As a result, the tone of the statements in the poem's central stanza becomes unstable, wavering among anguish, resignation, and calm certainty.

By the time Rolfe put this poem at the end of the sequence of wartime Spain poems he had learned that none of the causes he served was always faithful. The Communist party, certainly, had erred often enough and often enough acted badly. Not all who served Republican Spain served it well; André Marty, for example, a leader of the International Brigades throughout the war (and whom Hemingway savages in *For Whom the Bell Tolls*), Rolfe describes in a notebook as "a devil on the side of the angels." But the goals and values represented by Republican Spain and international socialism merited his loyalty. Some of those principles, indeed, he had formulated in an unfinished, untitled poem either written in his teens or shortly thereafter, a poem that adapts Shylock's famous speech from act 3 of *The Merchant of Venice*:

> We ought to dream, said Lenin. We ought
> to dream of a world transformed, project
> our wills above the motion-throttling mesh:
>
> And we do! Comrades, in the soot-smeared day
> of coaltown—here to show these men
> the way to wisdom, we risk the bayonet
> in light; at night we plan and dream again:
> at dusk, when coal blurs the falling sun,

when dark heads rise from countless pits,
we lead our somber brothers, one by one,
to secret meeting place:
                    The million dots
you see, flecking the hillsides, these are the men
we came here to revive: these their wives and sons
emerging from raw-planked huts, and all descend
to a thousand meeting halls.
                    This is the beginning
and the end! This is broken spirit come to life
in broken bodies: and the spines bent under tunnels
straighten up here. They know we bring them life!

And we? Who are we? We are the communists.
Men and women like you; like you we bleed
when bullets pierce us: like you we hunger
when we lack food: like you we groan
in the torture chair, cringing under blackjack,
but we remain silent: all blood from our veins
will drain before our lips will utter sound.

When the Rolfes returned from Spain in January 1939 the Loyalist cause
was already under attack. Martin Dies had begun congressional hearings on
Communist activity, and people who had worked on Spain's behalf were under
suspicion. Rolfe's brother Bern, a federal employee who had raised funds for
Loyalist Spain, was among those who came under scrutiny, though he kept his
government job for a time. In any case, it was clear that the Left was in for
some difficulty, though it seemed then that the Left would be strong enough
to defend itself successfully. Still, it was deeply disturbing to watch heroes of
the war like Milt Wolff harassed in front of the House Un-American Activi-
ties Committee. For much of the next two years, then, Spain remained at the
center of Rolfe's life. He signed a contract to write a history of the Lincolns,
and late in 1939 Random House brought it out under the title *The Lincoln
Battalion*. That July he also finished the striking but uncollected poem "Paris—
Christmas 1938," first calling it "Lullaby," and later that year drafted a version
of "Brigadas Internacionales," his brief, ringing proclamation of the justice of
the Spanish cause, a poem that should be read in its context, as a principled
defense of a cause under assault:

To say *We were right* is not boastful,
nor *We saw, when all others were blind*
nor *We acted, while others ignored or uselessly wept.*

We have the right to say this
because in purest truth it is also recorded:
We died, while others in cowardice looked on.

One of the more notable poems of that year, however, remained unpublished. Two copies of "Munich" are dated, one "May 1939" and the other "May-August 1939." Since the copies are the same, it is likely that the poem was actually completed in May but redated in the summer as a way of extending its effective historical testimony. May 1939 was the month Hitler and Mussolini met to plan the conquest of Europe, but Rolfe focused on the impotence of the Western democracies in the face of fascist support for Franco and on the policy ,of appeasement that permitted Hitler to overrun Austria and Czechoslovakia. Munich, of course, was the site of the September 29–30, 1938, meeting between Neville Chamberlain, the British prime minister, Edouard Daladier, the French president, and Hitler and Mussolini. Hitler was granted all his territorial demands for Czechoslovakia in a meeting that the Czechs themselves were not invited to attend. As agreed, he occupied the Sudetenland immediately, but the following March his troops overran the rest of Czechoslovakia as well. Rolfe ended the poem with a recitation of the names of some of the "minor connivers, / statesmen, envoys . . . cowards" and "ineffectual saints" at work to facilitate Europe's capitulation to fascism: Lord Walter Runciman, sent by Chamberlain to inform the Czechs that Britain would not stand by them if they resisted Hitler; Edward Halifax, the British foreign secretary who helped implement Chamberlain's appeasement policy; Georges Bonnet, French foreign minister during the Munich conference. A passage on Spain makes the poem a clear warning that no compromise with fascism is possible. In that context, the revised dating for the poem, which extends its field of reference to August without altering the text itself, makes the poem also serve as a comment on the Nazi-Soviet pact of August 22. It too, however expedient, would not stand.

In the late forties, when Rolfe assembled a collection of poetry he called *Two Wars,* he included "Munich." A few years later, further into the hearings and deeper into America's fanatical anticommunism, he revised *Two Wars* and retitled it *The Eternal Field* and then *First Love,* dropping several poems from the last decade and earlier, most of which we have restored to his *Collected Poems.* In some handwritten notes for a possible preface to *First Love,* he remarks that he has left out the poems of his "Munich period," in part, as he puts it, "because I fear the praise of my enemies." He had acquired certain "Berchtesgaden allergies," making an analogy to the private mountain retreat where Hitler first met Chamberlain in 1938. It was not the time to grant an increasingly reactionary America any satisfaction in its belated stand against European fascism. Nor was it the time to fault the Soviet Union for the twenty-two months respite it bought itself by the 1939 pact. By the time *First Love* appeared in 1951, the book had different work to do.

Rolfe's life in the meantime took unexpected directions. Once *The Lincoln Battalion* was done, he had to face the difficulty of finding work again. In March 1940 he took a job as an editor at the New York office of Tass, the Soviet news agency, which employed several Spanish Civil War vets at the time. Although he managed to attend meetings of the Veterans of the Abraham Lincoln Brigade, Rolfe otherwise had to obey Tass's requirement to avoid political activities. Unfortunately, Tass also prohibited employees from publishing independently. Rolfe thus could not publish his poetry for several years, not until he was drafted into the U.S. Army and resigned from Tass in 1943.

Rolfe became ill while in training at Camp Wolters in Texas and was discharged, but not before he had a chance to see the difference between the deeply committed volunteers in Spain and the young recruits in Texas. Two poems from that spring and summer in Texas are of special importance. In May, borrowing his title from William Vaughan Moody's turn of the century anti-imperialist poem against the United States war in the Philippines, Rolfe wrote "In the Time of Hesitation." It is one of the "Munich period" poems he omitted from *First Love,* one in which he realizes that Spain is already disappearing from the popular memory but affirms nonetheless that not all reasons for going to war now are the same:

> What's in the wind? There is no wind.
> What's in the air? Dust.
> The dust hangs yellow in the stagnant air,
> oppressive on the treeless drill-worn fields
> where eager boys with ancient eyes
> master their manual-of-arms, till soon
> instead of group, they call themselves platoon.
>
> Here, under smoldering Texas sun,
> summer beginning and training ending,
> daily we read the morning headlines,

nightly we turn the dial, listening
for the words that do not come, the deeds
that hang, suspended like dust in air. . . .

And I, one among many, remember
other clouds upon other horizons,
the urgencies of other years and other deeds
. . . but somewhere, always,
hearts quicken when the word Madrid is spoken
and minds recall its lonely betrayed splendor,
the lost war but the undefeated men . . .
imprisoned in the ruins of their immortal city. . . .

Here, on these Texas plains, we simulate
all the innumerable movements of invasion:
down ropes into a hypothetic barge,
from barge to sandy beach, then uphill past
barbed tanglements we cut to let the others by;
then on to the attack. Only combat missing:
actual shell, flesh-mangling bomb, bullet with million
    eyes.
. . . And even the Texas plain
will be fertile or scorched, as the war is lost or won.

Thus Rolfe did not leave the army before historicizing his situation in a more profound and problematic way. For a series of recognitions converged on him in Texas. It was partly the sharp realization of his generational difference and partly as well the specific social and political commitments, the very distinctive camaraderie, he witnessed in Spain but missed among the young men and officers around him in Texas. Training to fight in Texas, he could not help recalling that he had fought five years earlier with very different passions and out of an articulate sense of history and history's entanglements that had little equivalent among the draftees he met. If the cultural environment he was part of was improbable and the immediate audience for his writing at best surreal, he nonetheless did begin to write again. It may be that the alternating heat and rain in Texas were not altogether unlike the seasonal extremes on the plains at Tarazona. When he left the army, he began theorizing the differences between these two wars in prose. But at this point these issues coalesced and found expression in poetry.

"In the Time of Hesitation" was the first realization of his double consciousness. There is the dust of these plains, he observes, the dust in the ruins of Spain and the dust that individual memory faces if it is not recorded. And of course, always in the background is the famous passage from the service for the burial of the dead in *The Book of Common Prayer:* "ashes to ashes, dust to dust." Rolfe concludes with a reflection on the necessity of turning these children rapidly into "men or corpses." For "the world cannot wait." Some, to be sure, await the invasion of Europe; others await the opening of that second front that will deflect some of the pressure of the German attack on the Soviet Union; it is a difference temporarily to be set aside. But Rolfe was not yet satisfied with his rendering of the meaning of Spain remembered on the possible eve of a return in arms to Europe.

Under the pressure to give witness to that renewed memory, something changed in the rhetoric available to him. His poetry underwent a shift in compression and metaphoric complexity. And in the heat of Texas he wrote what would become his signature poem, "First Love," a haunting and lyrical tribute to Spain's hold on him and a poem that, while politicizing a romantic trope, also insists that the passionate core of his politics remains a permanent resource:

> Again I am summoned to the eternal field
> green with the blood still fresh at the roots of flowers,
> green through the dust-rimmed memory of faces
> that moved among the trees there for the last time
> before the final shock, the glazed eye, the hasty mound.
>
> But why are my thoughts in another country?
> Why do I always return to the sunken road through corroded
>   hills,
> with the Moorish castle's shadow casting ruins over my
>   shoulder
> and the black-smocked girl approaching, her hands laden
>   with grapes?
>
> I am eager to enter it, eager to end it.
> Perhaps this will be the last one.
> And men afterward will study our arms in museums
> and nod their heads, and frown, and name the inadequate
>   dates

and stumble with infant tongues over the strange
place-names.

But my heart is forever captive of that other war
that taught me first the meaning of peace and of
comradeship

and always I think of my friend who amid the apparition of
bombs
saw on the lyric lake the single perfect swan.

As Karen Ford has written persuasively about this love poem to Spain, "contrary to what we might expect, the romantic suggestiveness of the title 'First Love' is not exposed in the poem as a subjective, idealized illusion that the grim brutality and grave morality of war must embarrass. Instead, the poem insists that the intense subjectivity of romantic love and the daunting generality of social struggle are connected, though their connection must constantly be scrutinized to assure that each term is held up for measure by the other."[19] As she adds about one of the poem's more haunting images,

> that war makes love central to Rolfe's ideals is expressed in the image of the Spanish girl, who embodies both love and death: "the black-smocked girl approaching, her hands laden with grapes." The girl is clearly a reaper (she carries the grapes she has picked) and probably a grim reaper (the black smock, however traditional, nonetheless suggests this), but she is also a figure of innocence (she is just a girl) and vitality (she is young and holds the bacchanalian grapes). The approach of death makes love urgent because it forces us to decide what in our lives is most important. She is Spain personified as an exotic yet innocent woman; as such, she is an instance of the poem's irreducibly inaugural and retrospective title. What Rolfe wants from this and many other invocations of romantic love is both a paradigm of human relations and a source of energy—emotional and erotic—that can be tapped for revolutionary purposes.

Here in America, then, in the heat of our southwestern plains, he found Spain present to his mind and central to his life. And there is a reason why this is true, beyond the accidents of circumstance and the politics of commitment that brought him to Madrid and to the hills above the Ebro River. For at the core of the Spanish experience were a set of values and a vision of human perfectibility within history that were quite different from the need, however real, to put an end to Hitler and Mussolini.

That is not to say that "First Love" has no relevance to other historical moments and to other people's lives. The poem would have resonance for anyone training to fight in a second war amongst younger recruits with no comparable experience. Certainly the pathos of the "strange place-names" that enter public discourse during a foreign war only to be widely forgotten shortly thereafter, meanwhile remaining resonant or even pivotal for those who fought there, is a pathos any veteran will understand—as indeed will anyone who has lived long enough to see crucial historical events become irrelevant to younger generations. Rolfe himself calls the field of battle "green with the blood still fresh at the roots of flowers" an "eternal" one. But in fact he means that field to have other connotations as well: it is the field of specific memories that hold fresh for him, and those memories are eternal not so much in their applicability to other struggles as in their singularity. The selfless gift of those international volunteers who went to the aid of the Spanish republic—a gift whose purity remains a resource to succeeding generations—is part of what justifies the assertion that there were flowers on those battlefields, flowers that thus signify more than the ordinary disruption of a pastoral setting by war or the flowers at a soldier's grave.

Despite Franco's victory, despite the subsequent red-baiting of those who went to Spain, the dream and the trauma of Spain remain unsullied. The last stanza, with its self-declared lyricism, makes that claim explicit. A biographical incident lies behind these lines, but it emerges in the poem not as autobiography but as a lyrical emblem. When a train full of American volunteers was scheduled to leave Spain, Rolfe and the correspondent Vincent Sheean were among others there at Puigcerdá to see them off. As it happened, the train arrived and left early, and it was well it did, for at the scheduled arrival two squadrons of Franco's planes flew over and bombed the station heavily. They thus missed their intended target, and that group of internationals left safely. Shortly thereafter, Sheean saw one swan on a nearby lake and remarked the contrast to Rolfe.[20] Here, however, Rolfe raises the image to a more general meaning. For it is the special justice of the Spanish cause—its moral specificity as a historical event—that justifies the lyrical vision at the poem's end. If it is thus an explicit triumph of literariness, it is not an exclusively textual one. Rolfe's point is that the poetic lyricism is historically warranted.

By the time Rolfe left the army that summer, his wife Mary had accepted a job administering the Left-oriented writer's school established in Los Angeles by the League of American Writers. Rolfe stopped in New York briefly and then headed to California to join Mary; he remained there for the rest of his life. He began to work on the manuscript of *Two Wars,* meanwhile writing a number of short stories and finding a little work on the fringes of the motion picture industry. Late in 1945 he finished a coauthored mystery novel, *The Glass Room,* the film rights for which were purchased by Warner Brothers. Industry newspapers announced that Humphrey Bogart and Lauren Bacall had been signed to play the leads, and it looked like Rolfe might finally have some financial security. History intervened, however, in the form of the blacklist, and plans for the film were dropped.

In 1947 anticommunism, in remission during the war when we were allies with the Soviet Union, returned to function much more effectively and pervasively than it had before. A vast confederation of repressive forces—from national, state, and local government to the media, business leaders, and political organizations—collected around economic and political interests that had much to gain from instituting and maintaining the cold war. Business interests found communist conspiracy theories the best way to win consent to continue the profitable war economy and the best way as well to break those unions that remained strong and uncooperative during and after the war. Opportunist politicians with little national following found theatrically staged anticommunist hearings an easy way to build reputations. A group of reactionary political organizations whose members actually believed the well-publicized stories of Communist subversion—from the American Legion to the Daughters of the American Revolution—offered enthusiastic support. In the end, some people on the Left went to jail and many thousands lost their jobs. There was a nationwide purge from all public and much private employment not only of Communist party members but also of anyone with any history of support for the Left.

Rolfe saw his friends amongst the Hollywood Ten go to prison, including Alvah Bessie, a fellow Lincoln Battalion veteran. A number of party officials also fought losing battles through the courts. Efforts were under way to deport some of his exiled comrades and force them to return to Spain and certain death, and the blacklist destroyed the careers of most of his Hollywood friends.

In this gathering atmosphere of repression, Rolfe turned one last time to write of Spain. The place of Spain in the manuscript he was calling *Two Wars* is clear in a brief statement he wrote at the time:

> The recurrent theme in many of the poems is war, and the emotion of war: the clouded and guilt-muddied emotions of World War II, during which we in the west felt (in the words of an English poet [C. Day Lewis]) that we had to 'defend the bad against the worse'; as contrasted with the emotional

exaltation of a previous war—the war in Spain (1936–1939) when justice and truth were so overwhelmingly on the side of the Republic that even its tragic defeat has never quite killed the passion and purity of its living legend.

As early as 1939 he had planned a long narrative poem about Spain focused on the international volunteers. It was to include a history of the major military actions—from Jarama through Brunete and Teruel to the Ebro—and first-person narratives of some of those who died. His typed outline begins with a definition of "the *spine* of the poem: that hope for men exists in the survival of such qualities which (whether the Spanish government is finally defeated or not) has been proved by her defenders. In this poem the stress will be on the International Brigades, and specifically the Americans in the Brigades. The qualities: courage, conviction deep enough to move men, voluntarily, from safety and comparative security to field of battle; clarity, hope, deepest kind of human dignity." He also planned a long poem from the perspective of a Spanish peasant on the Loyalist side. It was to be the young man's story of the struggle over his village, Segura los Baños, as it was captured by the enemy, freed by his people, and finally taken again by the Nationalist troops.[21] Rolfe drew a picture of the town, modeled partly on Tarazona de la Mancha (where the Lincolns had trained) and Federally, and wrote a prologue to the poem: "My village rose along the side of a hill, terrace above terrace, to a point mid-way between the miniature valley and the pine-scrub dotted peak of Sierra Pedigrossa. You would not find it on any map; it is too small—perhaps 100 clay and stone cottages for men and women and children, and another fifty stone and adobe huts for the animals. Yet my village is important—it is the exact center of all space and all time." Neither of these poems ended up being written. And there were many other fragments from during the war and after that never coalesced into finished poems:

> Last night they fought in Castellon
> Hand to hand,
> Seeking refuge later in the orange groves.
> Strange, orange trees and war.
> Oranges we peeled when young, never thinking.
> Blood oranges we called them.
> And did they come from Spain,
> Gathered by the hands that now bear rifles?
>
> Darkness, where the dark is thickest,
> Hides the bodies of my comrades

> Fallen where the barbed wire's fingers
> Cannot clutch or strangle them again.
> Only when the moon is fullest
> Are their white skulls visible.

In 1948, when he turned to Spain for the last time, it was the status of the memory within the battalion and amongst Spanish exiles that most needed retelling. A year earlier, Hemingway, whom Rolfe was corresponding with regularly, felt the need to sound similar themes. Unable to attend an anniversary dinner for the vets in New York, Hemingway went to a studio in Cuba and recorded a talk that was played there in his stead. He opened by saying: "I am very glad to be present in this distinguished company of premature anti-fascists. That is a classification that a number of us received during the last war. They don't give oak leave clusters with it, but I would still rather have it than a lot of the spinach we saw on the chests of a lot of different people in a lot of different places. Most of these places that a number of us visited in the last few years I doubt that we would have had to go to if they would have let us win in Spain. . . . It was knowing that which made a man a premature anti-fascist."

As he had with "City of Anguish," Rolfe chose again to focus on a city. There were other cities he would remember, including Barcelona, where his wife Mary joined him in October 1938, as well as "Valencia, fronting the gentle waters . . . land's end . . . sloping complacently shoreward"[22] and

> Málaga, cradled in blue, the buildings white in the
>   sun,
> the mountains rising beyond it, fir-grown, brown bouldered,
> stretching toward Andalusia, to the inland cities:
> Granada, Cordoba, Antequera, Seville.

And he would remember wartime landscapes, such as

> the cliff-capped hills, the
> Heads of these Catalan hills, where dwell
> Only the very old now
>   and where bombers drone
> The hour of rising.

But among cities, above all, like many others who stood with Spain, he would remember Madrid under siege—Madrid, where "trees became torches / lighting the avenues." As Aaron Kramer would write in a review in the *National*

Guardian, "into this love-song to Madrid, written ten years after his return, Rolfe pours all the emotion he'd been holding back for so long. . . . Paraphrasing the 137th Psalm, that unforgettable love-song to Jerusalem chanted once by the rivers of Babylon, Rolfe sings 'If I die before I can return to you . . . my sons will love you as their father did.'" Now, by the waters of an American Babylon, marginalized on a Left under increasing assault, Rolfe calls on the memory of the great city under siege that had been the heart of the world. Madrid would be a figure not only for what might have been but also for a common cause, a successful alliance politics, that only weeks before had come unraveled in America precisely when it was most needed. Thus Madrid in 1948 would be a figure for an idealism and solidarity not so much imperiled as near extinction:

> Madrid   Madrid   Madrid   Madrid
> I call your name endlessly, savor it like a lover.
> Ten irretrievable years have exploded like bombs
> Since last I saw you, since last I slept
> in your arms of tenderness and wounded granite.
> Ten years since I touched your face in the sun,
> ten years since the homeless Guadarrama winds
> moaned like shivering orphans through your veins
> and I moaned with them.
>
>   When I think of you, Madrid,
> locked in the bordello of the Universal Pimp,
> the blood that rushes to my heart and head
> blinds me, and I could strangle your blood-bespattered
>   jailors,
> choke them with these two hands which once embraced you.
> When I think of your breathing body of vibrancy and sun,
> silently I weep, in my own native land
> which I love no less because I love you more.
> Yet I know, in the heart of my heart, that until your
>   liberation
> rings through the world of free men near and far
> I must wander like an alien everywhere.

Just over 110 lines, "Elegia" was Rolfe's last great poem about Spain. It was written the year after Alvah Bessie and others were called before HUAC to testify as punishment for their long commitment to the Left. From 1936 to 1939 something like a chorus of voices called back and forth to each other about the besieged city of Madrid. In poem after poem in country after country the name *Madrid* was used as a rallying cry and an incantation, sometimes with and sometimes without an exclamation mark. The poems echoed one another across time and space and national or political difference, rang changes on the suffering and courage of the Madrileños, and established in print, in voice, and in dream and nightmare the point of articulation of an antifascist politics for its time. In 1948 Rolfe printed the name repeatedly to form his opening line. There is no punctuation in the opening line, and an extra space falls between each recitation of the city's name. Into each of those spaces ten years fall. Across each of those spaces reaches an unanswered yearning for the lost community of the Left.

The lyricism of the opening lines has won readers to the poem ever since it was published. And it would be easy for those of us steeped in the New Critical taste of the last five decades to conclude that Rolfe succeeds in such lyrical moments and fails when his language is more worldly, brutal, or hortatory. Thus among Rolfe's Spain poems the lyrical "First Love" would meet with our approval and the declamatory "Brigadas Internacionales" would not. These two stanzas provide a good place to test that sort of perspective because the first stanza is more explicitly lyrical and the second more angry and rhetorical. But the two stanzas are not mutually exclusive stylistically. The two tendencies invade one another, suggesting that these two discursive registers— lyricism and polemicism—are actually interdependent. Thus the ten years that have "exploded like bombs" cannot be purely metaphoric in the context of a city that was the scene of massive bombardment; the metaphor slips over into real violence. Similarly, the more lyrical notes in the second stanza—the reference to Madrid's "breathing body of vibrancy and sun" and the concluding reference to the enforced diaspora of the Loyalist alliance—are colored by anger at the fascist victory that keeps the speaker distant. Rolfe, we realize, was not interested in indulging himself in a transcendentalizing lyricism but rather in displaying a lyrical impulse that is itself historically occasioned and necessarily in dialogue with other kinds of language. We have become accustomed to thinking of poetry as a space where lyricism can be entertained for its own sake, but Rolfe was not willing to pursue lyricism as an independent cultural value. Even in shorter poems he was unwilling to give himself or his readers over to an unselfconscious lyricism. Indeed, whether Rolfe's different styles compete within individual poems or coalesce in poems dominated by one style or another, their effects remain relational. These styles, moreover, enable poetry to do different kinds of cultural work. Recognizing that makes it possible to value both "First Love" and "Brigadas Internacionales." Failing to recognize that, moreover, means maintaining an impoverished view of a poem like "Elegia."

Indeed, it may be that Rolfe never wrote a poem that does not in some way problematize its lyrical language. Even in "First Love" he carefully disturbs and compromises the more overtly poetic diction and rhythms. Thus the lyrical first stanza—troubled early on by the surreal assertion that the field is *green* with fresh blood, diction that may recall Lorca—is then three times abruptly terminated in its final line: "the final shock, the glazed eye, the hasty mound." These three phrases also compress a narrative sequence into three brutal photographs—a soldier is hit and killed, the glazed eyes of his corpse stare emptily at the sky; the hasty mound is a burial site in the field. He returns in the second stanza to lines more reassuringly lyrical, but even there inserts the beautiful but aurally difficult image of "the Moorish castle's shadow." Throughout, as in so much of Rolfe's poetry, evocative specific description ("the sunken road through corroded hills") sits near relatively flat abstraction ("the meaning of peace and of comradeship"). And even the most memorable lyrical effects are realized with relatively unadorned diction. In "First Love," the epiphanic final image is inseparable from a number of willfully self-conscious effects, including the insistent alliteration of "lyric lake" and the off-rhyme of "bombs" and "swan." Similar complications run through the entirety of a long poem like "Elegia."

When Rolfe wrote "Elegia" there was literally no place to publish it. Even the Communist party supported *Masses and Mainstream* refused it, in part because the biblical allusions offended the editors; religion, after all, could only be the opiate of the people. It was one more piece of foolishness from the party, but Rolfe would not break the commitment to communism he had first made in 1925. Still, it was singularly painful to have his lamentation and love song for Madrid silenced. But his friend the Spanish exile José Rubia Barcia, under attack from the U.S. immigration service, translated the poem into Spanish and sent it to the filmmaker Luis Buñuel, who gave it to a mutual friend, the well-known Spanish poet and printer Manuel Altolaguirre, living in exile in Mexico City. Altolaguirre, one of the key Republican poets during the war, was so moved that he set the poem in type and printed it as a pamphlet without charge.[23] Circulated throughout Latin America, it was read out loud in meetings of Spanish exiles in Argentina, Chile, and Mexico, one last gift from a

member of the International Brigades to his Spanish comrades. In 1950 Rolfe
sent the poem to Hemingway, who replied in April: "Got back four days ago
and just found your letter and fine ELEGIA. . . . Your fucking poem made me
cry and I have only cried maybe four times in my life which is now gone on for
half a hundred years and 8 months. If this is any value as literary criticism there
she is and how do you like it now, Gentlemen? Anyway the times (five now) I
always cried for other people and now for a fucking town."[24]

"Elegia" was not to appear in English until 1951, when Rolfe finally pub-
lished *First Love and Other Poems* himself; it had become clear that no commer-
cial publisher would touch a book whose commitments were now heretical.
The book opens with some of the poems Rolfe wrote in Spain during the war,
including "Casualty," which he wrote in Barcelona on March 17, 1938. It closes
with his most lyrical postwar tributes to the memory of Spain. *First Love* is also
effectively framed with two long poems—one placed second in the book and
one in the penultimate position—"City of Anguish" and "Elegia"—and thus
by the name of one city: Madrid.

From this point on, for the last six years of his life, Rolfe wrote largely of
repression at home. As he makes clear in an unpublished fragment, the poems
of these years serve first as a call to his country to look into its own heart:

> Yes, you, my dear friends, fellow-dwellers in my town,
> inventors of hearsay, slanderous tellers of tales,
> assassins whose weapon is nuance, betrayers of friends,
> look into the face of this poem: its features are your own.

Despite the damage done to people's lives, cooperation with HUAC became
somewhat ritualized: apologies for earlier radical activities, disavowal of all Left
positions, compliments to the committee on the importance of its work, and,
finally, and most important, the naming of names. People who were either in
the party or fellow travelers were expected to name people they believed to be
Communists or sympathetic to Communist causes. Meanwhile, paid informers
invented stories to sustain the fictional melodrama of a Communist conspiracy
to take over the country by force. In Hollywood, watching the newspapers to
see if you were named in testimony was like waiting to see if your name ap-
peared in the obituaries. Once your name was published, you had but a few
weeks to decide: hold firm to your principles or testify and name names your-
self. As he explains in another unpublished passage, it was those who sacrificed
others to save themselves whom Rolfe could not forgive:

Those I could not forgive
were not the ones who, tiring in midstream,
turned frantic back to reach their starting point,
although the desired and shining shore
was closer than the one they chose to scramble back to;
not those who, in the middle of their journey,
turned sadly back; not those who, weakening,
equated private guilt with large injustice. . . .
But those who, turning back, sucked others with them,
them I could not forgive; nor those who,
secretly accepting the bribe of coin or conscience,
sought weakly to lend their treason dignity
with soothing words, with frightened reasoning—
whose motives, too transparent, were to please
their own tormentors—
these alone
remain my own
and all men's enemies.

Several of Rolfe's published and unpublished poems take up the materiality of testimony from different perspectives, most notably "Ballad of the Noble Intentions," "Are You Now or Have You Ever Been," and "Letter to the Denouncers." Material like this, which attacked the committee directly, was almost impossible to publish. *The Nation,* for example, accepted Rolfe's "Ballad of the Noble Intentions" for its December 12, 1953, issue and then backed out, claiming the space had been taken by advertising. They promised its publication in a forthcoming issue, but the poem never appeared. Even the *California Quarterly,* one of the few magazines of the Left, decided not to publish "Little Ballad for Americans—1954," one of Rolfe's poems that takes up the general atmosphere of surveillance and betrayal. Not all the poems of this period, however, address the specific practices of the inquisition. "Words Found on a Cave's Wall" works to name the resources left to the victims of the terror: "we endured in the long darkness, sharing our warmth and our desperate hopes." Some, like "Bal Masqué," "On Rico LeBrun's *Crucifixion,*" "The Poisoned Air Befouled the Whole Decade," and "Now the Fog," interrogate the culture as a whole:

Now the fog falls on the land.
Imagination's eyes go blind. . . .

> Knaves masqued like sovereigns decree
> what we shall say, listen to, see.
> The habit of slavery, long discarded,
> becomes our normal comfortable suit.

Except for a few magazines on the Left, there were no outlets available for such poems. Even then, the harsher, more sardonic, and unforgiving poems could not be placed. He had a few mainstream successes, but only when the analogies with McCarthyism were oblique enough to be missed by many readers. "A Poem to Delight My Friends Who Laugh at Science-Fiction," published in *Poetry* in 1953, is at the outer edges of that sort of indirect critique, for some readers at the time would have easily recognized the poem's political thrust, though its appearance in numerous anthologies since suggest it is easily decontextualized. The initial inspiration for the poem came from a story on the front page of the *New York Times* on Sunday, September 12, 1948.[25] The opening paragraph read "Fog up the Hudson was held responsible for the death of hundreds of migrating birds that crashed into the Empire State Building early yesterday morning and plummeted to the street or setbacks of the skyscraper." Rolfe took the event as a figure for the times, writing to his brother Bern to say that the poem urges us to "wake up and see how closely life in our neck of the world approximates the so-called fantasies of science fiction; how we head ever-closer to a world in which the only ones left alive will be the 'sullen' soldiers, 'unwilling, puppetlike, directionless.'" In any event it is now not the building but the Empire State itself against which we sacrifice ourselves; "the small birds in their frail and delicate battalions / committed suicide against the Empire State":

> That was the year
> men and women everywhere stopped dying natural deaths.
> The agèd, facing sleep, took poison;
> the infant, facing life, died with the mother in
>   childbirth;
> and the whole wild remainder of the population,
> despairing but deliberate, crashed in auto accidents
> on roads as clear and uncluttered as ponds.

This is the poem's second stanza, and its last line—with its striking image of mortal roadways as "uncluttered as ponds"—wittily combines malice with pastoralism and reinforces the poem's recurring motifs of nature and culture gone wrong. With their "aerial radar" defective, the eerily technological birds crash like lost bomber battalions. Docked ships are discovered "turned over like harpooned whales." Nature and technology interpenetrate to corrupt one another. The culture of the inquisition is everywhere obscene. "Shrieking *I am the state*," the speaker exclaims in "All Ghoul's Night," another poem written in the midst of America's Walpurgisnacht, "Ghoul unleashed his terror."

As we read through Rolfe's McCarthy era poems we begin to see what a range of voices and styles is necessary to negotiate these oppressive years. Characterizing this period of American history is a nearly impossible task, or at least a task that cannot be done on one occasion but rather must be assayed in multiple ways, by direct assault as well as indirection. Indeed, as the first stanza of "In Praise Of" suggests, the intensified knowledge such a task requires is itself nearly disabling:

> To understand the strength of those dark forces
> phalanxed against him would have spelled surrender:
> the spiked fist, the assassin's knife, the horses'
> eyeless hooves above as he fell under.
> To understand the sum of all this terror
> would *a priori* have meant defeat, disaster.
> Born of cold panic, error would pile on error,
> heart and mind fall apart like fragile plaster.

In the end Rolfe wrote both poems indicting the inquisition and poems honoring those ruined by it. There are also poems describing the culture of suspicion—"lighted continents / where privacy is publicly outlawed," a country ruled by those with "the strength / to kill all thought," where "all the bright awards" are "bestowed by coward on his fellow coward" and "where even an innocent unguarded eye / means sudden expulsion." In many of these poems the most difficult effort is to find a rhetoric and a voice that can sustain itself in the presence of impossibly contested emotions. In "Little Ballad for Americans—1954" the wit is inseparable from rage and anguish. "Are You Now or Have You Ever Been" intervenes in the persona of a man testifying before HUAC with a relentlessly unstable mix of irony and self-abasement.

More than once in these years, as in the following fragment, he thought back to the deaths of Sacco and Vanzetti to make sense of the continuities in his own history and the history he had witnessed:

> I think of two men who were murdered
> Twenty-three years ago, this very day—
> Whose death was my first real introduction to life—

> life as my land and my century know it—
> Sacco the shoemaker, Vanzetti the seller of fish,
> the vendor of human ideas in the market place.

He pairs the deaths of Sacco and Vanzetti with the death of Federico García Lorca, "the murdered soul of Spain." With these victims linking Spain and America, linking the martyred poet Lorca—very much a people's poet but not a political figure until his death made him one—with two articulate and politically committed working-class heroes, he draws a circle that is sufficient to define the historical ground of his work.

This unfinished poem about Sacco and Vanzetti and Lorca was written in 1950 while Rolfe was in a veteran's hospital in Los Angeles recovering from his third heart attack, his first two having occurred in 1944. He was thus very much aware that he could not count on living a great deal longer, and he was inclined to think of beginnings and endings. Looking back on several decades of writing revolutionary poetry and of the lived history that occasioned it, he reflected both in prose and in numerous unfinished poems on the continuities and limits of his craft and on his own mortality. He realized that he had seen people's scattered discontent and their sense of hopeless disenfranchisement turned by poetry into an articulate anger. He had seen poetry's startling singularity—paradoxically—empower people to become part of a community. He had heard poetry focus the will to change and give lyrical voice to irremediable loss. He had known people to take up a poem's voice as their own and—at least for a moment—live as though its form were their own body. He had seen people moved by poems written in trenches, tacked to trees, passed hand-to-hand amongst crowds, sung under fire. He had known people to live and die in part by way of the meaning they gleaned from reading poems. But still there were forces poems could not muster, powers poems could not defeat. Poetry could be a force for change—it could alter consciousness, forge alliances, position people differently within the culture—but it was rarely historically decisive on its own. Oddly enough, a life given over explicitly to poetry's social meaning forced him to interrogate the very idealism that came so easily to those committed to the fantasy of poetry's transcendent self-sufficiency. Poetry, he discovered, never had the effective autonomy of a true weapon. As always, the limit case was his experience from 1937 to 1938. "If art is a weapon in the thoughtless sense that many people think it is," he wrote in an unpublished essay, "how could Republican Spain have lost?"

He had lived in Madrid in the days when it was the heart of the world. Now his own country, dominated by the inquisition, seemed to have no humanity.

And his own heart was failing. In another notebook he records a dream of Spain: "In the dream, there was the battle on the hill, amazingly vivid and formal in its movements. And none of us escaped wounding. We were all maimed (men and women alike), but we consoled one another with our love, with the fullness of our love and pity." Now, "before the hyena's laugh gathers his bowels and tongue into knots, he remembers the days of his power and ease." Among the poems that follow, some come close to meeting the standard set by the notion that art can be a political weapon. Some, indeed, become chiseled, rhymed aggression, among them such brief unpublished poems as the following two quatrains, the first comparing the Supreme Court's roles in executing Sacco and Vanzetti in 1927 and Julius and Ethel Rosenberg in 1953:

June 19, 1953
This court, supreme in blindness and in hate,
supremely flaunts its lickspittle estate;
kills Jews today, as twenty-five years ago,
it killed Italians.

Pastoral—1954
Who used to lie with his love
    In the glade, far from the battle-sector,
    Now lies embraced by a lie-detector
And can not, dare not, move.

Striking because of the abrupt, elegantly brutal economy of their wit and their controlled rhythms and varied but deliberate rhymes, these poems are, if anything, even more unsettling for displaying Rolfe's craft in the service of a politically focused anger. In the context of the times, however, that articulate anger was itself a significant political accomplishment, for the cultural resources readily available for resistance were few indeed. "Living in 1951," he wrote in a note, "is like living in the peaks of the Andes—the air is thin and tense and we must develop new adaptations to survive."

You must write, he urged himself in a notebook, "as though you lived in an occupied country." For there was increasingly only one public culture in the country, a kind of bland conformity enforced at any human cost. To get some distance from that culture, to gain control over its ideologically saturated language by fixing it in his mind, he wrote a little "Skeptic's Dictionary":[26]

CONSTITUTION—(noun)—a document, drawn up by our revered forefathers, which every American boy or girl is told about in childhood, but which, as he grows up and his blood becomes redder (vide expression:

"red-blooded American"), he would as soon use, or "hide behind," as be found dead.

THE FREE WORLD—(noun)—a hyperbolic euphemism, used by some members of the western military alliance to designate themselves. A form of incantation.

He tried to warn his readers of what underlay the nation's self-congratulatory view of itself: "Friend, in your faith so like a marvelous loom," he wrote in June 1953 in the opening lines of an unpublished poem titled "A Double Hymn," "I hear the discord of a wheel of knives." By then, however, he was ill from a series of heart attacks. He had been putting together another book, titling it *Words and Ballads,* but in the last year of his life he concentrated instead on a series of his strongest political poems, and they never made it into the plan for the book. Under pressure himself from HUAC, near the end of "A Double Hymn" he simply pleaded for relief:

> O friends and tyrants,
> O my ancestors, and you
> committee of the dead,
> judge me no more

"My great crime," he told himself in one characterization of his Left politics, "is that I still believe in the perfectibility of human nature." But there was little audience then either for his ideals or his satiric critique. "Because it is prettier to protest an unrequited love / than to protest the murder of a people," he wrote in an untitled poem in 1948, "my poems are not popular in my own land."

Still, he persisted in performing acts of witness. Ten years after he returned from Spain he wrote and left unpublished one version of such an act of witness and remembrance, an unfinished poem to Federico García Lorca. Part of the impulse behind these lines—the reference to the passage of time and the memory of Lorca's poems in Spanish bookshops—ended up in "Elegia." But the passage as a whole, like many of the quotations in this essay, has remained unpublished until now. Ten years had passed since the events he describes, but describing them places him once again in his characteristic mode of testifying to lived history:

> *A Federico García Lorca*
> Ten years have passed since I found in a book shop
> in Albacete,
> The paper-bound case of jewels which I treasure still, the
> book

Romancero Gitano,
And turned to the first poem, the "Romance de la Luna,
    Luna,"
And read and found fabulous peace in the midst of the war.

Later, in Madrid, the lads of the guerrilleros
Crossed the midnight lines from madness to the light of
    the Casa de Alianza.
And told us (Langston was there, and Rafael, and María
   Teresa)
That they came from the choked south, from your buried
    city, Granada.

And they told how they met in the streets the people who
    told them in whispers
Of the way you died, with surprise in your eyes,
      as you recognized your assassins,
The men with the patent-leather hats and souls of patent-leather.[27]

    The time that passed had not taken the edge off the emotions he felt. If anything, he felt more strongly the need to make this moment part of the lyrical historical record. At no point in his life did Rolfe write what could be said to be a poetry that denies the passions of lived history. The only reason to write poems of that sort, perhaps, would be to urge inaction in the present, to spread the notion that proper historical understanding is possible only in retrospect. But Rolfe realized that even reflections on the past are written *in medias res;* thus all historically focused poetry becomes reflective advocacy and analysis for events in process, on the pain and ecstasy of historical experience as it is taking place. Yet it is never a question of simply transcribing experience, for there is no illusion here that language simply records and expresses. Rolfe was concerned instead with what difference language—poetic language—can make in a lived present. This is not, however, the open poetry of process we would have in the sixties, for Rolfe was committed to writing finished poems and to making decisive political and moral judgments. One of the differences poetry can make, he realized, is to grant politically engaged analysis a certain formal and aesthetic resolution—and a claim on values that will have special power as a result. His *Collected Poems,* published now, nearly forty years after his death, gives us as eloquent an example as we could wish of a progressive poetry written in the midst of history, written on our behalf with our common history in view.

TO A POET ON HIS BIRTHDAY: Edwin Rolfe
Madrid, September 7, 1937

```
        Poet
        On the battle front of the world,
        What does your heart hear,
        What poems unfurl
        Their flags made of blood
        To flame in our sky——
        Bright banners
        Made of words
        With red wings to fly
        Over the trenches,
        And over frontiers,
        And over all barriers of time
        Through the years
        To sing this story
        Of Spain
        On the ramparts of the world——
        What does your heart hear,
        Poet,
        What songs unfurl?

            Listen, world:
            Heart's blood's the color
            Of the songs that unfurl
            And heart's blood's the color
            Of our banners so red
            And heart's blood's the color
            Of the dawn that we know
            Will rise from the darkness
            Where yesterdays go
            And heart's blood's the color
            Of the red winds that blow
            Carrying our songs like birds
            Through tne skies
            Urging the wretched of the earth
            To arise——
            For the red red flames
            Of new banners unfurled
            Are the songs the poet hears
            On Spain's
            Front of the world!
            The red red songs
            Of new banners unfurl█,
            Leading the workers
            At the front of the world!
```

Langston Hughes

Figure 6: A poem Langston Hughes wrote and presented to Rolfe in Madrid
in 1937.

NOTES

1. Unless otherwise noted, all unpublished work by Rolfe is quoted from the Edwin Rolfe Archive in the Rare Books and Special Collections Library at the University of Illinois at Urbana-Champaign. The collection is in the process of being catalogued. Quotations from Rolfe's unpublished poetry and prose are © 1992 by Cary Nelson.

2. Information about Rolfe's family comes from a series of interviews with Bern and Stanley Fishman (Rolfe's brothers), Mary Rolfe, and Leo Hurwitz, Rolfe's oldest friend. For more complete biographical information, see Cary Nelson and Jefferson Hendricks, eds., *Edwin Rolfe: A Biographical Essay and Guide to the Rolfe Archive at the University of Illinois at Urbana-Champaign* (Urbana: University of Illinois Library, 1990), which includes a thirty-thousand-word essay about Rolfe's life as well as a number of photographs of Rolfe and his contemporaries. I am currently at work, with Jefferson Hendricks, on a biography of Rolfe.

3. The year Rolfe joined the party comes from information supplied to me by Leonard Levenson, himself a Spanish Civil War veteran and recently editor of *Political Affairs*. Levenson has a copy of the records of many of the interviews given by International Brigades volunteers on their arrival in Albacete. They were asked such basic questions as their name, date of birth, and address, along with their political affiliation and the date they made that political commitment. Levenson supplied me with a photocopy of Rolfe's answers to these questions. The answer recorded for Rolfe was "CP and YCL 1925." Although it is possible that there was an error in transcription, the information Levenson supplied is reinforced by the fact that Rolfe published three editorial cartoons in the *Daily Worker* the year before. John Gates suggested to me in an interview that young people who sought to join the party were automatically assigned to the Young Communist League.

4. Both Stanley Fishman and Leo Hurwitz independently recalled Rolfe's parents' political differences in interviews.

5. The files of the Experimental College at the University of Wisconsin–Madison are unusually complete. They include the written reports filed by Rolfe's advisors.

6. See Cary Nelson, *Repression and Recovery: Modern American Poetry and the Politics of Cultural Memory, 1910–1945* (Madison: University of Wisconsin Press, 1989), for a general discussion of thirties poetry.

7. This passage is taken from an unpublished poem titled "Others, Too, Will Die Hard."

8. Rolfe's letters to Joseph Freeman are in the Joseph Freeman Archive at the Hoover Institution, Stanford University.

9. Interview with John Murra, Spanish Civil War veteran and later professor of anthropology at Cornell University.

10. Edwin Rolfe to Leo Hurwitz. Shortly before his death in 1991, Hurwitz kindly made Rolfe's letters to him available to us.

11. When Hemingway's piece "On the American Dead in Spain" was reprinted in *Somebody Had to Do Something: A Memorial to James Phillips Lardner* (Los Angeles: James Lardner Memorial Fund, 1939), the same Castelao print was selected to illustrate it.

12. Cf. Marilyn Rosenthal, *Poetry of the Spanish Civil War* (New York: New York University Press, 1975): "The image of Spain, of its cities, of its people, dying and destroyed, but becoming the seed of a new Spain, appears time and again among Hispanic poems. They regarded the war dead not as dead but as part of a living army, not as absent and finished but as sharing in the continuing struggle with the people with whom and for whom they had fought" (252).

13. Rolfe's note to Freeman is written on the backs of two copies of the memorial postcard the International Brigades issued to honor Arnold Reid. Since the postcards are undated and unstamped, they were presumably mailed in an envelope. The Freeman archive at the Hoover Institution at Stanford University is not yet catalogued, but the postcards are in a temporary file labeled "Arnold Reid." Freeman's letter about Reid is in the September 13, 1938, issue of *New Masses*.

14. Interview with Thomas Viertel, a close friend of Rolfe's. The best history of HUAC's impact on Hollywood is Larry Ceplair and Steven Englund, *The Inquisition in Hollywood: Politics in the Film Community, 1930–1960* (Berkeley: University of California Press, 1983). For a wider history see David Caute, *The Great Fear: The Anti-communist Purge under Truman and Eisenhower* (New York: Simon and Schuster, 1978).

15. Edward Dmytryk broke with the Ten and testified before HUAC in 1951, revealing twenty-six names in public testimony. He also recanted his earlier Left commitments in a *Saturday Evening Post* article, which Albert Maltz answered in his "Open Letter to the *Saturday Evening Post* on Edward Dmytryk," published in the *Hollywood Reporter* in 1951.

16. Karen Ford, "First Love," paper presented at a symposium on Edwin Rolfe, University of Illinois, October 1990.

17. Rolfe describes how and why he was fired in a letter to Leo Hurwitz. Mary Rolfe confirmed in an interview that "Definition" was based on that experience.

18. A number of Rolfe's friends and family members, including Mary Rolfe, volunteered the information that "Ballad of the Noble Intentions" was written in response to hearing that Odets had testified before HUAC.

19. Ford, "First Love."

20. Sheean himself wrote a poem about the incident titled "Puigcerdá," published in the October 4, 1938, issue of *New Masses*, p. 16, and in the 1938 anthology *Salud!: Poems, Stories, and Sketches of Spain by American Writers,* ed. Alan Calmer (New York: International Publishers), 41. Sheean's poem also ends with the image of the swan:

But the swan there,
the swan upon the water—
the swan's enchantment over the silver water—
moves still,
pure and proud,
disdains the shrapnel,
scorns the thunder.

The swan in beauty floats upon the lake,
serene before the choice that death must make.

21. See *The Lincoln Battalion* (New York: Random House, 1939) for Rolfe's own experience of Segura de los Baños.

22. This group of descriptions of landscapes and cities is excerpted from some of Rolfe's unpublished poems.

23. Born in Málaga in 1905, Manuel Altolaguirre was a cofounder of the influential prewar magazine *Litoral*. He also started *Poesia* in Paris and *1616* in London and was a cofounder of *Hora de España* (Spain's Hour), one of the major antifascist literary magazines of the Spanish Civil War. His book *La lenta libertad* was awarded the Premio Nacional de Literatura in 1933. In exile in Mexico he became a filmmaker. He died in a car crash on his first return to Spain in 1959.

24. Hemingway's letter is published in its entirety in Nelson and Hendricks, *Edwin Rolfe*.

25. A much shorter version of the story appeared in the *Los Angeles Times*. Rolfe saved both clippings.

26. Rolfe's "Skeptic's Dictionary" is unpublished. The other words or phrases defined are "Red-blooded American," "Satellite," and "Totalitarian."

27. Rafael Alberti and María Teresa Leon were both Spanish writers and were married to each other. Langston Hughes was in Madrid regularly in the fall of 1937. Rolfe spent a good deal of time with Alberti and Hughes while he was in Madrid editing *Volunteer for Liberty,* scheduling radio broadcasts, and serving as American political commissar. See Nelson and Hendricks, *Edwin Rolfe,* for further information about Rolfe's relationship with Hughes in Spain. Rolfe first met Alberti and Teresa Leon in New York in 1935, at which time he wrote a story on them for the *Daily Worker*. The last line of Rolfe's poem alludes to Garcia Lorca's "Ballad of the Spanish Civil Guard": "They ride the roads with souls of patent leather."

to My Contemporaries

TO LEO T. HURWITZ

Credo

To welcome multitudes—the miracle of deeds
performed in unison—the mind
must first renounce the fiction of the self
and its vainglory. It must pierce
the dreamplate of its solitude, the fallacy
of its omnipotence, the fairytale
aprilfools recurring every day
in speeches of professors and politicians.

echo of J. P. Thompson's "Union Poem" *

It must learn
the wisdom and the strength and the togetherness
of bodies phalanxed in a common cause,
of fists tight-clenched around a crimson banner
flying in the wind above a final, fierce
life-and-death fight against a common foe.

Emerging then, the withered land will grow
—purged—in a new florescence; only then,
cleansed of all chaos, a race of men may know
abundance, life, fecundity.

1931

* You cannot be a Union Man,
No matter how you try,
Unless you think in terms of "We,"
Instead of terms of "I."

TO MY CONTEMPORARIES

Winds of Another Sphere

Let us admit into our land the winds
blowing from the east and the voices wafted
with them, the voices attendant on the spheres
in which we too shall inevitably whirl;

for something in our land is dying: not the trees
nor mountain-crags nor buildings jutting through clouds
but something less permanent: the way we wearily smile,
the way we half-heartedly hail a comrade in the street,
the way we dismally work in factories and mills
and railroads spanning the land.

                              We know
the color of the hardening arteries,
their bulging through the skin of our uncertainty,
their weakening within the metamorphosis
in which we move. (America is big
and trees and crags and skies are permanent
but walls and fences crumble to dust and eyes
of blankness kindle with fire and comradeship.)

And when the last corrosion sears our land
(flames low in death, and fumes and smoke lifted)
winds of another sphere will cleanse our winds
and the voices wafted will be our voices.

                                   1931

Testament to
a Flowering Race

We are wise in ways which none has preordained.
We have captured the sparks blowing idly in the world
and harnessed them to our metallic chariots
of fancy and reality. We know
the worm imbedded in the apple's core
will, extricated, do no harm. We grow
in stature and in strength in our newfound knowledge,
creating clearer visions as the heritage
we plan to leave to our offspring, who
(more numerous than waves on seas or leaves on trees)
will live the wisdom our lives but pondered.

The many flowers that the father plants
surrender the honey for the child to suck,
knowing the evident verities: that we
toiled for ourselves and all our other selves,
transmuting stone to gold, transcribing
fantasy to actuality,
sweat to produce and earth to riches
in which our progeny may grow to Herculean stature.

1st published in the Daily Worker as
"The 100 Percenter" on Sept. 22, 1928

Asbestos

Knowing (as John did) nothing of the way
men act when men are roused from lethargy,
and having nothing (as John had) to say
to those he saw were starving just as he

starved, John was like a workhorse. Day by day
he saw his sweat cement the granite tower
(the edifice his bone had built), to stay
listless as ever, older every hour.

John's deathbed is a curious affair:
the posts are made of bone, the spring of nerves,
the mattress bleeding flesh. Infinite air,
compressed from dizzy altitudes, now serves

his skullface as a pillow. Overhead
a vulture leers in solemn mockery,
knowing what John had never known: that dead
workers are dead before they cease to be.

                                                           1928

compression, extended metaphor, meter, + rhyme
conceit of man who becomes a thing
3rd stanza — thing that becomes a man

Daily Worker June 22, 1929

Brickyards at Beacon

Here, on the rivershore, the edge of music,
of water flowing, melodious, to sea,
they work: and the rainbow is obscured;
the sunshower seen through smoke-haze seems
     unreal, repellent;
the west wind rolling across the Berkshires
     meets inferno heat here
and is absorbed into heat, becomes heat.
They who work here know no other things:
only heat and smoke and fumes of baking bricks.

Shelley, but natural
-force annihilated by
the brickyard

Early in the morning, punctual as the dawn,
they leave their hovels after a meagre meal,
follow the dusty paths that lead to the
     brickyard gates
(dusty paths that they themselves have
     grooved throughout the years);
they are stooped and bent and vaguely deathlike,
their chests are tragic parodies of chests.

Once, watching them at dawn, a wealthy tourist
     said:
"They seem completely broken, ready to fall
     back into the earth."
But he had never seen them returning at nightfall,
after twelve hours, over the same dusty paths . . .

Once, at night, I heard them singing:
slow, beautiful and melodious as the river
     when it is arced with rainbow-color.
They were sad, these songs that were outlets
     for a million pains;
sad, but soaring in the night, and powerful.

And many times (most meaningful of all)
I have heard them at their work,
bent under heavy burdens,
wet with rivulets of sweat,
utter two words, a beginning:
"Some day . . ."

1929

Faces No Longer White

Let something in through the open window.
It is dark here and the floors creak
whenever your bare feet tread on them. Go
to the eye of the crumbling house where your meek
face will be visible to air, to light,
to all that moves intangible in night.
Here is only blackness and stifling air
and a dead face no longer white in its frame
of dim gaslight and black-smudged walls. Go where
seethes the turmoil out of which you came.
Dive into it as you would into a lake
whose depths are thick with tangled stalk and weed:
plunge! Then surge upward, leaving in your wake
a path through which these faces may be freed.

TO MY CONTEMPORARIES

Somebody and Somebody Else and You

Brother, consider as you go your way,
hemmed in by houses or flanked by fields,
conjunctions of roads through midland plains
or grain, watching dried cornstalks sway
dead and cracking in the wind's running:
who spews pennies on the streets of cities?
who jams the faucet, holds rain from crops?
who carves the sagging lines in roofs of barns
      and who reverses this?

They who have reaped your harvest
offer you the stalks. They
have teeth and fangs but their breasts
are dry, sucked empty. They have seen
millions of you stretching skeletal
hands toward them. They have been
deaf to everything you've had to say.

But you go your way, brother. They will go theirs.
By the time you meet you will have gathered
mass enough to challenge their right of way.

Maybe there won't be any doughnuts and coffee,
maybe you'll go a long time before you find
a house to shelter you, a bed to sleep in nights
and somebody to lie with, closely, and feel
here at last you've a moment for breathing
easily, peacefully, without hurry.

    But when have you had a house
    for nightrest, and a place
    to sleep in without rats
    gnawing in your head, and
    somebody with everything
    vital and whole and real?

TO MY CONTEMPORARIES

You can read it in the papers every day
about somebody and somebody else found dead
in a furnished room (and think of all the bother
for the poor landlady, cleaning the mess away)
and nobody knows why they did it or who
they are or where the hell did they come from anyway
and no relations are there to claim the bodies
because their relations are far far away
in Chicago maybe, or Brooklyn, say.

The coroner will chant his Death-by-Suicide dirge
and nobody'll know
that somebody and somebody else have hit the eternal hay.

And maybe in the very same sheet you'll read
how somebody and somebody else are dead,
a couple of Mexicans this time. Headlines:
STARVING MEXICAN PEONS EAT GRASS, DIE.
You probably won't see it (it's in 12-point lightface.
Babe Ruth and Garbo rate 48-point bold)
but read it if you find it among the want ads.
Doughnuts to grass it will leave you cold.
Elsewhere in a city, Milwaukee maybe,
somebody'll say, "Isn't it terrible Mamie?"
staining the newsprint with everready tears
"and just think of it Mamie dear they died
without even an uncle around to bury them."

But you, brother, think as you go your way
reading this in papers under your flophouse mattress,
you know who pours the pennies and the lead, you know
who rots the watered crop, you know
who makes the walls of barns to sag
inward on emptiness
                    who waves a flag
and blows hot air through a star-spangled trumpet

while crops in fields and faces in streets
go slowly empty and yellow.

Georgia Nightmare

There are sixteen bodies of lifeless men
swaying a little in a slow wind,
outlines against a gray, torpid sky.
They sway gently, a little, to and fro,
black against the dull, unmoving sky.
These are no silhouettes, friend learning life:
these are men's bodies
hung against the sky . . .

I walked yesterday, in a dream,
through a night-forest where no light
penetrated, where no bright
fireflies flickered above the stream
that labored sluggishly through the night.
Through dank branches I labored, like the stream,
over dead twigs that groaned under my feet,
over muddy swampland that coveted my body
and after numberless, uncounted hours
I reached a clearing, strange in the darkness,
where a tree stood like an isolated tower,
growing purple up into a flaming sky.
And I looked up, and higher, and saw
sixteen black bodies, strung against the sky.

The forest falls, the stream runs dry,
the tree rots visibly to the ground;
nothing remains but sixteen black
bodies against a blood-red sky.

I see crazy mountains in the distance,
crazily moving (mountains do not move);
each one snowcapped, white in the distance,
peaked to a pinpoint, coming nearer—
imagine mountains moving to a man!
moving to me, alone in this weird land,
moving to me, shrinking to the sand.
Martial music rasps through a brass band

and off with the snowcaps, off with the mountains:
a million faces leering in the sun!
Then I see a gun,
then two, and three—a thousand!
RUN!

A heavy rope is flung into the skies,
a heavy rope hangs tautly from a tree,
a black man strangles above a sea of eyes.
The black man looks like me.

Kentucky

They sprang up out of darkness, shouting!
—from a womb of darkness to a black world underground—
a challenge on their lips
and in the line of their backs,
suddenly erect after ages of stooping:
     remembering *Greene*—the midnight encounters
     among the hills, the wounded that their women
     nursed back to life, back to courage;
     the solitary stand against their masters
     with only the blue grass, the trees and the hills to aid them—
     and *Daniel Boone:* the axes clearing
     the wilderness, the long alert rifles
     levelled against the dark
                      before the soft men,
the stay-at-homes, buried them
under mountains of laws and greenbacks.

Asphyxiation of years in their memory,
and a golden moment of sun remembered—
their small farms sheltered by trees and brooks,
the long grass drying in the autumn days,
crisp in the sun over the rolling hills.
And then the little soft men wrote words on paper
     and the soil was no longer theirs;
the stay-at-homes passed laws in their legislatures
     and mines ulcerated the hills;
     they built railroads spanning distant dots on the map
     and levelled the woods; the tall slim pines
     became a pattern of poles supporting a network of wires
and then the voices, the soft office voices
condemned them to underground imprisonment
for life
     and their children's children . . .

A hundred years is a long time.
Men die and their grandchildren totter on aged limbs.
But a century is long enough
for the blind to see and the sleepers to awake!

Out of darkness, out of the pits now—
foreigners only to the light of day—
claiming the mountains in the sudden glow
of battle, welded in a mass array,
shouting!
> This is our land, we planted its first seed!
> These are our mines, our hands dig the coal!
> These roads are ours, the wires across the land
> are ours! THIS IS OUR EARTH!

Under the smoke of bullets and hunger,
the gray sky reddening to dawn,
gaps appear in their ranks, but others
spring to their places! One by one
the dead awaken, the old ones quicken
with anger and life. The moving ranks
surge like the smoke of the coal they dig
in solid, unconquerable phalanx!

Assassins' bullets, bankers' laws—
these cannot stop their sure advance!
Under the blood and the lead, their feet
pound the old mountains. Under the night
of stars of a fading era, they light
the blazing signals of a world in birth.

1932

Letter for One in Russia

This is for you, Carla, and your quick
soft sudden hands, your long white groping
fingers probing the dark for certainty
or illusion of certainty. This is a letter
written in renascence, written in limbs
tired from pacing the low dark lanes
of the streets at midnight, written in lips
grown acrid with the smoke
of countless burning cigarets, smouldering,
awake with the molecules moving in my brain.
Carla, this is written in sleepless
hours that winds cannot soothe, in minutes
the empty body lengthens into hours and days,
long days that reel remorsefully.

For love was ours, Carla, and the vinculum
of the flesh in calm and tension and the spent
still moments afterward when surging stilled
the singing of your brain within my brain.
Glory was ours, Carla, and the still
throb of eternity (which few men know)
and quiet words, decipherable
only in dream, where fragments grow
within a surer logic than the mind
can ponder on, or love, or understand.

Do these words vex you?
                    Forgive me, for the world
is emptier tonight than it has even been:
too many traitorous faces smile, too many
hypocritical arms are interlocked,
too many vulgar shades are drawn
wide for the innocent, inquisitive host
(and arms and faces, shades and arms
unseen, and smiles, inquisitive,
bridge the oceans and consume the plains
that I shall never—nor can ever—know).

TO MY CONTEMPORARIES

Your message smoulders in me: time and space
have nullified all ancient wounds
and made us comrades; and your face, through words,
is changed, unknowable. Even your name
destroys in its last syllables the flame
the first ones kindled. It is strange I know
the image so well, who cannot pierce the real.
The blurred, submergent certitude eludes me,
stranger forever to the memory.

Yours is a happier continent than this:
"All that we do is play and work and sleep."
But here we do not play, we may not work
and sleep escapes us. Here we find our sun
burning upon us in the public parks,
on benches cracked by heat, on which we sit
brooding our hurts and ills;
                          and in the brain
a fiercer sun corrodes our brittle thoughts;
and in the guts—(old violin strings betray
the music of another time)—tightened
in hopelessness, the world dies.
                          Even you . . .

for a former girlfriend

The Pattern of Our Lives

The pattern of our lives was simple then,
time and place identical. No moods
plagued us for long except the vague
soon-solved pains of adolescence. We arose
each day at dawn, met each other at the grocer's,
returned nibbling hot rolls, consumed
oranges and eggs and milk, and fought
with our brothers for the biggest jellyroll.
Afterwards we trudged to school, books
strapped over shoulders. Sometimes stopped
to scale flat stones across the bay's surface,
entered classrooms late. In winter
we chose exciting, difficult ways,
shunned streets, sought the harbor shore,
leaped from rock to icy rock and sometimes
shied at chasms, descended to the beach,
trampled snow and sand. We arrived
late in winter as in summer but our lessons
were almost always done. In '24
all of us made Junior Arista.

Late afternoon and evening we played
pool in Don's cellar, smoked forbidden pipes,
listened in on Mike's cat's-whisker radio,
saved our pennies for extra earphones,
argued with Casey about God and chased
Don's kid-brother from the room when Joe
told what he'd seen in the bookroom: Billy Shane
the football coach, and Miss Reeve our Civics teacher.
None of us believed Joe's detailed story
but listened eagerly and asked, "Is that all?"

And there was always time. For Don:
handball and prayers after his thirteenth birthday,
Latin, to be a doctor. Mike stayed home
much of the time, read books, experimented
with fifty ways of making gunpowder;
quiet more than the rest of us, most

TO MY CONTEMPORARIES

often by himself. Casey left school
in his fifteenth year to get a job;
his mother was bearing her ninth child
and Casey was her first, his father a hunched tailor.

And there were others whom I loved less
but slowly learned to love their living more—
more like my own, not play at any hour
but talks that ripened to mature beginnings:
the dockyard strike, where Sigmund's father worked,
cheaper meals in the lunchroom, freedom
to write what we felt in our magazine,
to admit harshness.

        One day Sigmund and I
killed God forever in a crowded subway
and Flory, Dominic, Howard, Peter
joined us in soaring the heavens, freed of God.

Now we together through the mounting years
recall this childhood
and meet you still loitering, still inert,
coats, shoes, brains in tatters. Now no more
endless days upon the harbor shore,
lazing, playing in dream; no more
rolls in the morning. The library's
long forgotten but you dig and summon
lying fantasies to keep you living.

Three, two years ago, we would have forgiven
aimlessness, pitied your blind days;
we would have forgiven, remembering childhood
and you, companions of our early search.

But now the time's allotted. There can be
no faltering now. The night descends
on every fragment of your world to blind
those who have lived in dusk. And we,

attuned to a future your eyes ignore,
dissect beyond the visual, the core
our dreams and struggles have made clear
with painful, startling wonder. But the pain
is negligible and the wonder
tempered with knowledge. We will be
like children fresh before the first known dawn,
like men grown wise, cognizant, alive
to this, our doing.

       Weaklings, fools,
poor slow deluded—this our last
spent breath of pity. At the tools, comrades!
You who were my friends
              go under!
Send me letters from the heaven you spoke of.

Homage to Karl Marx

Here in the dim of the dusk with the wings of birds and
the noise of their cries and the slim lines of the trees
against sea and horizon
                     we the sons the fathers
have dipped in the thunder again for a final tilt with
our foes the dying enraged the angry powerless
fathers and sons of decay made strong in despair and
the thoughts that are those of any and all who die
knowing death is certain the victors smiling above them . . .

Here in the whiteness of morn with the gleam of the day on
our swords long-tempered in fire and fine with the deep
exquisite molded precision of strength and huge with
the whelmed and accumulate power of mass
                         we charge
(certain as night is here now that day is impinging
its cleansing immaculate light on our mass-arrayed army)
on to the shreds of resistance still left to the old men
their strength swiftly ebbing their eyes showing clearly they die
knowing death is sure we the victors laughing! above them.

* * *

In his great rooms, the countries of the world—his
cumulative fatherland—how many candles guttered
unnoticed? the huge sweeping movement of his brain
(rooted in poverty, love as great as deep
as he was poor) unhindered? How many hands,
dripping with blood, the torment of numberless men,
crept across boundaries at night, the fingers feeling their way
into his moments of peace? (the prophet grappling with worlds,
suspended between
                 yet rooted in both
                            the old and the new)
left him at last, broken in strength, to die—

But late, too late to check him, too irrevocably decayed
to wreck his shining pyramid, too weak with history

(the weakness of those who die knowing death is certain)
to pierce the impregnable fortress of his work.

                          And now
the world's ablaze! Into our ears and eyes,
his words! like rivets in a tower's steel,
red with sparks showering, penetrate. We feel
the imminent thunder in the charted skies
(charted by him, for us—his inheritors!)
and wonder need not overwhelm us; fear
is foreign now, as weakness from our will
to crash the rotting structures, standing still
only by our grace!
                 The hour draws near . . .

Look on the world, my comrades! It's aflame!
fire-tongues in the sky, new sword-blades at its core,
cutting the dry dead harvest that it bore
a generation gone, in all the lands of earth.

His dialectic enervates the doomed,
inspires the mass to courage: not for long
can our foes delay our unfolding destiny!

Witness the death which he foresaw: the seed
springing to flower, flinging its color, its breath,
into the long-patient channels of our need—
silent no longer! Now, fifty years since his days
met their last midnight, we—his countless heirs—
rise dauntless in all lands, his wisdom in our brain,
the added lessons of half a century,
to impregnate the earth with newer life, to win
the final battle; and, classless, to assume
the final right to our supremacy.
                         March 1933

These Men Are Revolution

1

These men are revolution, who move
in spreading hosts across the globe
(this part which is America), who love
fellow men, earth, children, labor
of hands, and lands fragrant under sun
and rain, and fruit of man's machinery.

These men are revolution even as
trees are wind and leaves upon them
trembling in a pattern which was
quiet a minute past, silent on stem,
immovable; just as all still things
grow animate like bow-stirred violin strings.

The power in men and leaves and all
things changeable is not within themselves
but in their million counterparts—the full
accumulation. These the world resolves
into men moving, becoming revolution
surely as blown seed takes root, flowers in sun.

2

These men are millions and their numbers   *workers*
grow in milltowns, flow from coastlines,
buzz with the saws in lumber forests, rise
in cities, fields, to set the signal blaze.

Boys fresh from classrooms, their professors,   *students*
bid farewell to books read well and loved,
join the hard climb, pick up friends on the way
to a rarer earth attuned to a newer day.

And soldiers down rifles as workingmen gather   *soldiers*
in cities, on squares, at the most dismal corners:
no mourners, but grim with the task of the hour,
the conquest of industry, Soviet power!

Come brother—millhand—miner—friend—
we're off! and we'll see the thing through to the end.
Nothing can stop us, not cannon not dungeon
nor blustering bosses, their foremen and gunmen.

We will return to our books some day,
to sweetheart and friend, new kinship and love,
to our tools, to the lathe and tractor and plow
when the battle is over—but there's fighting on now!

3

The tidal wave flowed first against the coast,
swept the Pacific, burst on Louisiana's gulf
bordering Mexico, and workmen's hearts glowed
with the fire of the fight.

The news spread eastward, dinned in Minnesota:
men wanted bread who strode across wheat fields.
Hands left the steering wheel, vehicle stalled
before filled granaries.

And southward: dusk-skinned men in Alabama
paralyzed plantation, joined with white brother,
emptied the mine shaft, silenced the clang
of pickaxe probing for ore.

Montana miners remembering Dunne
struck Anaconda, Rockefeller, copper;
and Foster's spirit in Pittsburgh, Gary, Youngstown,
swooped over steel mill.

Soon there will be no line on any map
nor color to mark possession, mean "Mine, stay off."
Brother, friend—and you, boss!—the tidal wave
sweeps coast to awakened coast.

4

You who would move, live freely among men,
regain lost grandeur, dignity and all
the varied riches of your worried toil:
observe America today: its fields
plowed under, trampled underfoot; its wide
avenues blistered by sun and poison gas,
its men grown reckless of bayonet and gun.
Regard the legion in your midst who hide,
hands twitching and empty, in hovels and see
their eyes grown dry, impotent of tears . . .

Charter the next airplane, cross the continent,
see under you the colors of the map changing
as rivers crack the earth and bleak hills bulge,
their shadows darkening unlovely barren fields.

Heavy dust hugs the dry exhausted pastures;
chimney smoke rising from factory bears
the agonized sweat of driven men, it carries
the poison gas, it grasps their coughed-up lungs.
Their blood is dust now borne into the air—
the huge dark menacing cloud above our land.

Circling the tall peaks I dreamed I saw
your face, beloved, turned on levelled plains.
Clouds burst about you, fresh rain streamed
down mountainside, fed parched earth, bore
strength to shrivelled root, food to burned tree,
swept drought of midsummer sun and autumn rot away.
Fields ripened to fragrance and the world's wealth
turned soil aside, gleamed in the new kernel
till kinder sun speared cloud and earth returned
to joy, florescence in the harvest-dawn.

The plane zoomed under dust-cloud and I knew
this was mere mirage, saw dream as dream

but in it prophecy. Turned toward the real:
men fallen on field and wharf, shot down
at mine gate, trodden under horse's hoof.
Bullet in back, betrayer, jowled misleader
dealt death and sorrow, mangled limbs and tears
at empty chairs at frugal empty tables;
in a hundred beds the warm comforting body
sweet at your side at midnight, gone . . .

O you who would live, revive the natural love
of man for fellow man for earth for toil:
commemorate these fallen men anonymous;
retrieve from rigid hands their strength, desire,
their vision from glazed eye, from dying brain their fire.
Mark the compass-toe—their last footprint—
and follow through! Precision now is needed
in limb, in sight, certainty in the heart.
Give meaning to these slain! Call no halt, sound
the siren for new striving, now clear, defined.

5

The line leaps forward on a hundred fields,
staggers—breaks—reforms—returns
like molten steel to momentary molds
throughout America. The multimass learns
how desperate and doomed the enemy is,
how sure its own ascendant growing power.
Clear-eyed, alert, the stalwart legion grows
to recognize the imminent bright hour,
inevitable now. And time can but delay—
never impede—the winning of the world
by men for mankind. See approach the day
when millions merge and banner is unfurled!

Now the army moves, marks time, gives blow
for blow, sustains slain, shivers in retreat;
advances, counters thrust—and now moves . . . slow . . .
with lives, encounters lost. But never defeat.

TO MY CONTEMPORARIES

Room with Revolutionists

FOR J.F. (Joseph Freeman)

based on a conversation
between Freeman + the
Mexican painter David
Alfaro Siqueiros

Look at this man in the room before you:
he is young, his skin is dark, his hair
curly and black, his eyes are strangely blue,
he comes from a warmer land under the sun.
He hears a North American speak calmly
of a beautiful and faithless mistress
and is amazed. This man's a revolutionist,
painter of huge areas, editor
of fiery and terrifying words, leader
of the poor who plant, the poor who burrow
under the earth in field and mine.
His life's an always upward-delving battle in
an old torn sweater, the pockets always empty.

And this his companion across the room:
younger than he: the smooth deep forehead
sheathing a subtle and redoubtable brain;
his hair dark, eyes upward-slanting at the corners,
lips clean-etched and full. This man,
nurtured in a northern city,
is a poet, master of strong sensuous words,
artist in his own right. His oratory
before many listeners is like the sudden
startling completeness of summer rain:
warm, clear and clean, soaking into
the very heart of you, the sun just beyond.
This man is my brother, Communist, friend,
counsellor of my youth and manhood. He has crossed
the seething continent a hundred times,
leaving behind him his words
and the sound of them and their meaning.

The heavy drowsy wine of a tropic land
and the sharp bouquet of the northland intermingle
here in this room: these two are held
umbilical to a greater source and destiny,

TO MY CONTEMPORARIES

welded each to each more firmly
than each to his native land.
                        Their vision
parallels their warmth, transcends all frontiers.

Look at them here at ease
relaxed in this pleasant room:
you will not see them again
together for many years.
Tomorrow each will go
his separate way on the maps of the globe
across great distances, talking, painting,
composing poems, organizing,
welding together South- and North-men,
destroying boundaries.

                                    1934

TO MY CONTEMPORARIES

Three Who Died

Scan the heavens of our future, comrades
—visibility unlimited!—
you who have discarded yesterday's paper
have read how three young scientists sealed
the door of their gondola leaving Soviet earth,
soared into unknown sky. Ascended
higher than man has ever flown before
and stared on the greatest Pacific, suspended
thirteen miles above earth. Their radio
clicked in Moscow
flashed to every hamlet on the globe:
Our greetings to our leader—leaders themselves—
the seventeenth congress of the Party of Revolution!

Was it yesterday or last week that you read this?
        Crushed in the fog's embrace
        they crashed to earth.

And we who grieve, who mourn their death,
enshrine their memories as deathless;
those who break our class-foes' lines
forever live within the heart's vast kremlin.

The three who died, the many who live on,
the millions—comrades of the fallen three,
all—they are flesh of our living flesh,
their bone and sinew, bone and sinew of October.
O huge generation of men who returned
from war to face a newer and older foe—
humanity's ageless and classless battle with
the swift stream's power and the heaven's thunder.

Look at these men in the world before you,
witness the huge film of the burial of our dead:
try to understand, you whose brains are leashed
to a boss's payroll. Try to see,
O you who grow sightless as your world expires.

We who have eyes can see through the bourgeois blindness
where even the living are blanketed in fog.

Our eyes survey the world from the heights
the deathless three attained.

1934

Witness at Leipzig

Under torture in a Nazi concentration camp, three
Communists renounced their views and signed a
statement implicating the Communist Party in the
Reichstag fire. They were brought to the trial by
the Nazis as witnesses for the prosecution. On the
witness stand, however, knowing that their tes-
timony would mean life or death for them, they
declared they had been tortured into signing the
statement and, reaffirming their positions as Com-
munists, they turned their testimony into a valiant
and crushing attack upon the Nazi prosecution.

I am glad I am here: I have said
what my heart not my mouth has uttered
always, in dungeon under lash and where
to mutter under the breath meant death.

I have come through forested distances
over bloody highways where the dead
have trod; have killed words in me, shouted
unheard in sound-barred rooms—and all

my blood which flows too fast remembers
cries, mad laughter of wracked friends,
comrades lost to the living, wedded
to God! the swastika stitched on.

Yet I am proud I have come, have spoken here:
this stand before you, justice, is my guillotine
surely as truth is on my lips today,
withheld these months in tortured secrecy.

Dimitroff speaks this truth: his sentences
resound beyond the rafters of this room.
Hear Nazi judge, at you! and you, brown prosecutor,
his words like doom are aimed.

I tell this too—this court's condemned
before dawn rises on my severed head—
to you, gentlemen: these close walls
have ears and tentacles that reach

beyond all prisons and above all time
that you conceive. I say our Party
knew nothing of the fire but foretold your death
who now claim mine. I know this stand's

my last, this room the final room
where I shall walk alive and talk
to enemy or friend. Yet I am strangely
proudly glad that this is so.

TO MY CONTEMPORARIES

Poem for May First

Not Christmas nor the new year white with snow
and cold with dying names emasculate
marks for our lives the *new* year. Only spring
arrived at its fulfillment, at the peak
of verdurous blossoming
connotes the quick
deep breath of hope
again—the sharp release
of man grown tense with winter, now set free
to soar again (this day when our grasp,
grown powerful, foretells
its final fusion with our scope), to surge
in multitude toward greatness.

                    On this day
the small deeds of the year, infinitesimal,
unnoticed in the smoke of skirmish, cleave
fiercely together. The edifice grows huge,
becomes unvanquishable mass: the voice
and eyes and ears of us who have grown strong
on bitter bread, dry root—our nourishment.

And now we march!
             The brain will not deny
the days that come with verdure nor the eye
ignore the splendor of the changing year
invested with surprise: bells clanging in the ear
with sound that drowns the singing of the birds
and voices rich with prophecy—the words
fraught with great deeds.

                Down countless avenues
the senses feel impending change: the clues
that guide our burdened hearts, heavy with pain,
awakening class-memories—
                they burn again!

O comrades of my dawns and days and nights
O you who live with me
you at my side in battle
and at midnight talk
after the fruitful day
learning to meet the challenge of tomorrow's foe—
welcome this spring!
this burning first of May
this ever-recurring day pregnant with history
born in this land which witnessed our birth—
this land will be our own!
                            Remember now—
delve backward through the years' accumulated dust:
Haymarket—Spies, George Engel, Albert Parsons—
the noose drawn tightly—gasping "I have nothing,
nothing, not even now, that I regret . . ."
Fischer and *Lingg,* their shadows on a wall
magnified a millionfold, cast by a setting sun
westward to California, east to Hatteras
where embattled workers sought an added hour of day.

Mark their names well: their death
                          and now recall
the spring that came the next year and years that followed
and the wars that bled us and the war that bore
shining through the mud and mangled limbs the dawn,
life for the men of Russia
                     and for us
victory in sight, a star grown clear in the skies.

Mark their names well: now feel the memory
that coursed in action through your father's veins,
given to you at birth, to a million others:
the dereliction of our youth, the sordid
childhood ripening to bitterness,
the aimless wandering from place to place
seeking—what? You did not know, nor I.
But scattered images remained, grew sharp

and deep, indelible: Wisconsin farmhouse,
barn wall sagging inward into emptiness,
Chicago midnights on the lakeshore, beauty
trampled on by hunger, no rest, no rest—
icy roads across the Alleghenies,
the clear bright brittle air of winter
and at night we hugged the walls of public buildings
but could not sleep.

        Back to New York again:
there was warmth there was food there was time to think,
to merge the broken images, to synthesize
Mendota's midnight beauty and New York by day—
Haymarket and Union Square in 1933 . . .

Nothing has been lost. The photographic plates
grow clear in the solution—the worlds at war—
unforgettable—
        the image looms and casts
a huger image on the growing screen,
projection of our lives and struggles.

           Comrades
here is my hand! Here's all of me, my friends,
brothers in arms and fellow builders! We
together through the long transition marching
will notch the trees along the way.
        This May
has deeper meaning now than ever.
          Close your ranks,
touch shoulders—ready?
        There's our signal—
           March!

Unit Assignment

Now the beginning: the block divided,
I choose my tenement,
press bells that do not ring, ascend
by feeling stairs where no lamps shed
light to guide a stranger and am led
by banisters toward a door.

Again a futile bell. I knock,
hear scuffling through the wood, a voice
gruff and questioning. I explain.
Enter. Am home.

"This is my block," I say. It is.
"Just four doors down." "And this," he says,
"is my wife, and this my son, my daughter.
Here is the living room."

He clears the best chair for me,
momentary host, curious, proletarian;
the family—my son, my daughter—gather
around me, listen to the familiar word
Communist falling from unfamiliar lips.
Strange, too, they must have mused,
its sound is good when he says it,
and what he says it means is good.

The evening passes quickly: tea is drunk
from glasses, cups, an old cheese jar.
My host, John Winter, fifty-four,
asks questions, listens, deep in thought.
I tell him what I know, I cite
stories in The Daily, demonstrate
items killed, never to appear
elsewhere. "What is this?" he asks—
the word *unity* is in his brain.

My son, my daughter listen too.
They who were most suspicious now

join us, and all I say
enters them in images of food,
of jobs, the wanted weekly pay.
They too see what I mean is good.

The skyscraper bells ring out eleven.
I leave a copy of The Daily. Am asked
again to spend an evening with them. Rise.

John Winter walks me to the door, holds
my hand in his a moment, saying goodnight.
"These things you were saying—
They're good."
He fumbles for words.

"I shall return," I say.

Unit Meeting

Coming together at night, in rented halls, in bedrooms,
talking and smoking till dawn seeps through drawn curtains,
each word we speak cuts through smoke leaving our lips;
like battle cries our program recorded indelibly.
Here, now, tonight—twelve of us gathered:
three others missing: we know where they are, what doing.
No speeches. What's said is simply uttered, understood,
clarified by others for all speed to action.

Here, or another room will be our meeting place
next week and the week after, next year, next decade.
No heroics, no orations, no false eyes at glory
(glory is completed deed, no dream-designation)
but carefully planning, after day's work's over,
we pledge our days and nights, our years to communism.

Season of Death

This is the sixth winter:
this is the season of death
when lungs contract and the breath of homeless men
freezes on restaurant window panes—men seeking
the sight of rare food
before the head is lowered into the upturned collar
and the shoulders hunched and the shuffling feet
move away slowly, slowly disappear
into a darkened street.

This is the season when rents go up:
men die, and their dying is casual.
I walk along a street, returning
at midnight from my unit. Meet a man
leaning against an illumined wall
and ask him for a light.
                            His open eyes
stay fixed on mine. And cold rain falling
trickles down his nose, his chin.
"Buddy," I begin . . . and look more closely—
and flee in horror from the corpse's grin.

The eyes pursue you even in sleep and
when you awake they stare at you from the ceiling;
you see the dead face peering from your shoes;
the eggs at Thompson's are the dead man's eyes.
Work dims them for eight hours, but then—
the machines silent—they appear again.

Along the docks, in the terminals, in the subway, on the street,
in restaurants—the eyes
are focused from the river
among the floating garbage
that other men fish for,
their hands around poles
almost in prayer—
wanting to live,
wanting to live! who also soon
will stand propped by death against a stone-cold wall.

TO MY CONTEMPORARIES

Definition

Knowing this man, who calls himself comrade,
mean, underhanded, lacking all attributes
real men desire, that replenish all worlds
men strive for; knowing that charlatan, fool too,
masquerading always in our colors, must also
be addressed as comrade—knowing these
and others to be false, deficient in knowledge
and love for fellow men that motivates our kind,

nevertheless I answer the salutation proudly,
equally sure that no one can defile it,
feeling deeper than the word the love it bears,
the world it builds. And no man, lying,
talking behind back, betraying trustful friend,
is worth enough to soil this word or mar this world.

1934

based on experience of being slandered at the Daily Worker in 1934 + fired as a result

* Brunner puts this phrase in the "atavistic vocabulary of the times"

sonnet form — 8 + 6

To My Contemporaries

1

Jazz notes and Brahms intermittently
fleck the dusk-silence. Through the silhouettes
of sombre trees a lustrous blue
colors the heavens. The note still lingers
of the last thrush; its whistling rings
as if just uttered in the quiet air.
Now there is peace, and sounds are only
heard from afar: the distant train
winding its way along the river shore
bound for the city of tumult; the faint
night-blurred music of a gramophone
from a distant farmhouse; the occasional
noise of the insects
                    and in this lighted room
shadows of moths on the walls, beating against the bulbs.

Now more than ever seems it rich to live,
to pluck the ripened fruit, to plant the seeds
whose growth and blossoming our heirs shall know
in years to come upon a richer earth . . .

But we have lived in furore all our lives.
This quiet stuns us like a fist's impact
against the jaw; and nothing as idyllic
as rural peace can now replace
the accustomed clamor of our daily lives—
the hurried visits, the spasmodic talks,
the too-few interludes that we have known,
the midnight meetings in smoke-filled rooms
and noise of numberless voices arguing.

And so we sit in separate rooms, you
intimidated by the silence, vaguely
feeling all's not well, too tired to read,
too restless to lie still, too stirred
to trace this strangeness to its source.

                                    And I
before this page write stray, fugitive thoughts:
things of half-meaning, impressions cut
far less than whole by this silence and its tension.
Here I am not surrendered to my poem
nor master of its words and images;
too great's the doubt in me to synthesize
fragmentary feelings, thought-lines that balk,
grow twisted, fade before they reach their ends.
I sit here only because the typewriter
is my oldest friend in this strange wilderness.
Sitting here thus I feel I've made
some last-straw contact with a friendlier world,
and clutch at it, refuse to let it go
lest I too sink to meaninglessness.

I invoke friends and fellow-Communists,
poets, sharers of my life and thought,
ponder the meaning of our words and deeds,
put questions that are answerless.

                        2
You, Funaroff—where's the victory?
We've been composing poems,
each in our separate rooms, for many years.
The scraping of your pen, furious on paper,
quickens the blood of the world, and mine.
A stone in the days of my strength
could crash the window of your tenement
all the distance from Eleventh to Fourteenth.

But where's the victory? I read
in the Daily Worker the other day:
the Chinese peasants seizing arms and bread,
in Mexico they fashion dolls of clay,
chimneys spout red leaflets in Berlin,
Italian flyers bomb the land with calls

of *Avanti popolo!* and in
England a poet quits ancestral halls
to call for the knife, *the major operation.*

The Indians are dying on their reservations,
black men are lynched, the jobless legions creep
from day to hungry day, driven from railway stations.
We have no place to sleep.

But in the subway on a winter morning,
travelling from the Bronx to Union Square,
the *Times* folded at the want-ad page,
we blink from slumber at each station-stop.
The girl across the aisle—her eyes are blue—
reading the *Mirror.* Open your eyes, it's you
she's smiling at. Don't close your eyes again.
Don't surrender to the ache in your limbs,
the heaviness in your head. Look at her!

I look. I see the oval face,
but when the dusty light-bars strike her,
the cheekbones and the hollows; and her eyes
removed from the paper, are blue and wise.
She smiles again.
                I could arise, I say,
mumbling to myself. I could arise
and go to where she sits and say
nothing that anyone could hear
but take her arm and face the door
and walk away with her,
guiding her to the platform in the rear
and look at her, into her eyes, deep
into her thoughts, and feel that the crowd
had disappeared and that no one was near
except the girl. I could say everything
without a word that any rider'd understand
and she would understand!

Look, Funaroff. Look up from the book!
You're a poet and companion. You can understand
the memories of faces seen on long-ago subway rides,
the persons whom you've known and tried to kill, but can't.
They grow the while you compromise with newer faces,
less clean-cut, blurred and blunted.
                                    You recall
our fathers' admonition: Covet not, my son,
but take what's yours by right.

It is hard to let go, it is pain to surrender
the fugitive fragments of an earlier self.
But the break must be made, the artery severed
and sewed again, the useless nerve numbed.

3

The country quiet baffles me again.
This silence is deceptive, the flowers a fraud,
the streams polluted. To live here is a lie.
Escape from chaos is impossible;
the world's too muddled, the skies thunder
with guns, projectiles dealing death
but also, remember, the terrible cleansing storm!

To live in villages today a man must also
create a village-suburb in the brain:
partition the skull, decree which part
shall live, observe, feel joy and pain,
and which vast area grow dulled,
the senses, all awareness, killed.

You, Funaroff, and Hayes, and the others:
enter with me the farthest regions
of space and time, the body moving
across huge continents, the brain surveying
the contours of the land, destroying
the cancerous trees and men, restoring
the spark to bodies overwhelmed

by drudgery and dross and dust.
Blueprint the hills and rivers, mark
the meadows and the factories.
Harness the hordes of middlemen,
bankers and bosses, fiddle players
to generals, kings and presidents;
sweep them together and tie their hands
with their servile strings and ticker tape,
and lead the parasite pulp with you
to moldy manors and somnolent suburbs,
into the dead lands, beyond the outposts
of workingmen marching. Then lock the doors
and destroy the keys. Leave them to die.

Return with me to cities where the wind
finds chasms between skyscrapers, where men
reveal their thoughts in action, where mills
and factories are continual testament
to the war that only villages can hide.

Rejoin with greater vigor, rejoice
in new days, new companionships.
Revive the rural landscape, the girl
smiling across the subway aisle,
the oppressive silence, the news that flashes
from China to New York
                              and synthesize
these memories within the single self
attendant on the mass of men
who march with us today, who blaze the way
from village to city, from city to the world
our minds foresee, our poems celebrate.

Uncollected and Unpublished Poems, 1933–37

To Those Who Fear
to Join Us

What we have, comrades—
surety and strength,
this strange serenity,
the calendar marked—
no enemy can claim;
they who are sunk in
uncertainty and madness
suffer more surely
now that their universe
weakens, decays.

We who have knowledge
of ends and of ways
know they can trace
only beginnings—
blueprints their sole
records of living.
Our goal is their end,
our star their last cinder
who wonder at decay,
shudder at loss.

What we have, comrades,
garbed in worn rags,
surpasses the silk
our enemies flaunt.
They will be worm-gnawed,
their gowns reflecting
last midnight's lamplight
in sunless chambers;
while we, companions,
boldly are robed—

the flesh, spirit laughing
possessing tomorrow!

Homecoming (August 7, 1934)

Atlanta sped him on his journey north
no send-off at the station
          but in a million shacks
in Georgia Alabama Carolina
hearts beat more strongly for his freedom
          —whites, blacks
whispered: now he's safe
          in safe arms for a moment
with brothers, comrades. Speed the time
when prison, chain gang, landlord, court
forever are left behind!

The train gained speed
          red engine streaming north
left Fulton Tower, crossed Mason-Dixon line
pulsed power on the rails
          leaped distance miles
soared to sudden freedom, roared
through cabin backyards, struggling gardens, saw
gleaming mansion towers in the distance rising
above the green horizon—said goodbye
and in Angelo Herndon's heart
certainty of strength, return to victory.

See hands raised in your honor, boy, fighter,
pioneer of our advance in perilous country:
heads massed in greeting as you pass
the nation's capital—city of William Penn—
Jersey towns still fresh with memory
          for us of 1776;
ecstatic tears in eyes of old mothers
(no others weep but old men and women;
leave them to their joy—give them this relief).

Girl, boy—young comrades everywhere—
man, woman: this is a day for joy!
We knew him from his words
          flame-flung in a southern court

until this day—this day we know
his presence at our side:
             the smile of joy at nearness
to comrade, friend—and proletarian pride
that these hands, heads
             (this great dauntless heart)
upraised, black and white
             think, feel for him
are clenched for him
             protect him with their might!
                                    1934

*August 21 issue of
New Masses*

*Welcoming Angelo Herndon, a black communist unconstitutionally
charged w/ "attempting to incite insurrection" for helping to
organize a Georgia hunger march, to NY after his release on
bail*

Something Still Lives

You have seen faces of dead men uncovered
for a few hours before their burial:
the cheeks hugging the hidden teeth, the skin
horrible in colors that make the skies matchless,
the hair, the long wavy hair (you sunken,
suddenly foolish knowing it still lives—
ironic longevity!) surviving the heart, the eyes
that saw, the mouth, the brain and the intricate
machinery of the guts . . .

In a silken bed I never saw
Valentino died; in an airplane crash
the Great King Knute; and during an after-dinner speech
the Mayor of Merryville choked on a sturgeon bone—
all accidental, too much gravy, or a weak heart.

But in their coffins for a day, I know
(or coffinless mostly) those who die
with lead-peas in their bowels—the shock
of sudden satiety!

        No accident here,
no coroner's verdict—but as in life
the corpse must make a sudden getaway
to foil the unctuous vultures and to feed
the hungry, infinitely preferable worms . . .

Let us carry him away (like Johnnie) now
and let him sleep; the inevitable worms
will be kind to him, the grass drenched every morning
and the black, obliterating soil.

Look at him once before the earth clumps over him,
glance at his dented face before we carry him away
with no sobs, no lamentation—we who know
that something besides the growing hair still lives.

Communists

And if our coming will demand
the coming of countless others? if our call
purifies the call of countless multitudes

who can but cry, not hearing, and
who can but touch, not feeling, and
who cannot see—who can only be seen?

We must make resonant our voices with
a newer resonance, one that will pierce
the eardrums of the deaf and dead, and rouse
the slumbering clamorous multitude, shouting
skyward—each his own voice only hearing.

We must in our coming spike
the hill we climbed to reach the gates
now open for us; dig deep grooves
in the mountainside: steps and rails
to lead the hands and hearts, upward
with us, of countless multitudes.

Nuthin but Brass

FOR CAB CALLOWAY

"Please, Mr. Orchestra, play us another tune."

Let the old broken hag die on the street:
the D.S.C. will haul the hulk away,
clean up the mess. Let the dinkey rattle
under the El all night all day:
nobody'll notice. The sky will go
purple or red or cloudy over us—
My St. Louis Woman and *Minnie the Moocher*
will sprinkle the star dust and cover us.

*   *   *

The last magenta light is dimmed in the dome,
the Academy heaven goes black as any night
save for the spotlight tinkling the glass
of the imitation crystal chandelier.

Music floats up from the pit, or maybe
the pipes in the wall are grinding through the hall.
The pink-and-gold curtain rises like an angel,
the balcony lights an enormous cigaret

an there aint nuthin left in the hall but brass:
three saxophones, three cornets, a huge bass drum,
a lone bass viol—and cigaret smoke
weaving metallic patterns in the spotlight.

He is a reed walking out on the stage
with a thinner reed in his hand. Each body
strains forward in its seat, each body sways
before his body answers to the low moan swoon

swooping down through him from the balcony,
from Harlem round the corner, from 14th Street,
from Soho and gaslit left bank rooms,
from bodies sensed in beds in a million rooms . . .

O the brass is alive, his voice is brass!
his voice is a drum and a flute and a low
silvery saxophone zooming in the night,
his body a cushion for all love and lust.

A million Minnies dreaming of the King of Sweden,
(wishing you were dead, you bastard, YOU!)
counting a million dollars in nickels and dimes
a million, billion, quadrillion times!

Baby, the world grows smaller than a rose
(smaller than a room, a single bed
where two warm bodies with space to spare
are attenuated reeds of reciprocal play).

Baby, the world aint a thing to us now
and we doan need no gin an no cigarets
an no spot on a dancefloor smaller than a dime
to congeal you and me in the bumps, baby.

All of it is true. No promissory note
is needed to insure the reality of dreaming,
the wail and the moaning, the break in the voice:
"Will you take this man?" "I do, I do!"
The song is wilder now, his voice is drowned
in waves of muscatel wine from the mouths
of the muted cornets and the derbied saxophones
and the pianist jigging on the keyboard.

They all suddenly rise and discard the derbies.
Awake, you little dreaming fools in the dome!
This is no wine. It's synthetic gin,
it's rasping tobacco, it's fragmentary love

and lust; and the voice you surrendered to
is now but a grinning mouth, and the cool
clean million is spent, you profligates!
and there aint nuthin left in the hall but brass.

Curtain. He's still grinning, but the smile
sags at the corners, at its soft beginning.
Put on your coats. The Academy splurges
a last time in light before it goes to sleep.

June 1932

Not Men Alone

What, you have never seen a lifeless thing flower,
revive, a new adrenaline in its veins?
Come, I shall show you: not men alone
nor women, but cities also are reborn;
not without labor, not before the hour
when flesh feels lacerated, mangled, torn.

Not only men are resurrected. I have seen
dull cities bloom, grow meaningful
overnight. Wherever class war comes
awareness is its courier, a newer life,
new depths in shallow, parallel streets
which may revert to commonplace, but never
relinquish scenes that have occurred on them.

Toledo's such a city. I remember
its dullness, how I always skirted
its edges on long trips west. Returning east,
I chose roads miles to the north or south
to escape its barrenness; the mind went dead,
the muscles flagged, in passing it.

Then the strike flared: the workers met
and merged at factories. The unions called
Down tools! and the militiamen
sped to the scene of combat. When the smoke
rose with the wind, a hundred men were maimed
but thousands more, the first time in their lives
were conscious of their needs, their role, their destiny.

I passed through Toledo yesterday.
The usual quiet prevailed, but from the eyes
of men and houses a newer spirit flamed.
The deadness I had felt before remained
but it was make-up only, mere disguise
for men aroused, a city awakened,
awaiting the propitious, inevitable day.

The Nine

Who will be masters of our land tomorrow?
These boys, playing baseball on the wide lawn
surrounding the Washington obelisk, run fleetly
from base to base. Far from the white home plate
the monument's shadow cuts the field in two
before the falling sun. No rebels, they know merely
the sure clear flight of the batted ball,
the gasping chase, the thud in the leather
when the ball's caught, the enemy team retired.
Umpires are enemies too: the caller of strikes
is careful: the scorn of children is deadly as gunfire.

Every day, at sun-summit, the two teams toss
the bat from hand to hand, choosing sides.
Nine spread out, dotting the field; nine others
huddle on sidelines and the game begins.
Inning by inning it is played, replayed;
disputes interrupt but never end it;
teams change, the power shifts, bats split
like hewn logs with the grain, but the game continues.

Not far away, their fathers and grandfathers,
ex-batters and fielders of baseballs, quarrel
in a white-domed building. Sides change.
Age erodes their brain cells. Men die, many
leave to return. Others stay to summon
quorums of quarrelers: whenever the quorum gathers
it sleeps; and a team of nine aged great-grandfathers
wakens them, scolds whether scolding's in order or not,
spares not the ignorant rod—these umpires appointed
by god in fat jowls and goldpiece for stickpin—
like the caller of strikes on the ball grounds.

Winter's Ghost Plagues Them

It is summer, it is warm in the city square:
Lafayette's sword glints in the rich sunlight.
Below him, at the pedestal, men sit smoking,
collars open at neck, discussing winter.

They sprawl, sleeves rolled back, on the hot stone,
they wander, from time to time, to the fountain.
A can of beer is passed from hand to hand
and they swallow deep: the foam frames their faces.

But always their movements sag with the heat:
always they reach for the hip-pocket kerchief,
dabbing wet foreheads, wiping the sweat from
face and throat, thick-veined, heavily breathing.

Beyond them, where grass creeps to dropping tulips
and midget trees rise from soil, dry and leafless,
a lone bird sings; his notes are like scales on
a long-untuned violin, the bow never rosined.

But the men at the statue's base discuss winter,
more real, more threatening than any season,
and winter's hunger and nights spent in doorways
pillowed in paper, seeking of cold stone warmth.

The men move slowly, they scowl at the lightning,
suck long and deep at their pipes. Deep in them
they offer thanks, praying for more warm weather
but winter's ghost plagues them and they fear the fall.

Rolfe's one long narrative poem

Cheliuskin

The current murmured northward, warmth
invading the far Arctic ice,
a stream within an ocean, flowing
into white distances, unknown.
Into the islands, home only
of fur-framed Eskimoes, their living food—
the caribou, the seal, the polar bear—
the gulf stream entered, curled between the floes,
and somewhere, between the ice peaks and the islands,
north of all routes mapped by man,
lost itself . . .
        . . . emerged again
a continent away, recontacting
its tropic source, its energy, its deep
cradle-mother of bird of paradise,
luxuriant grasses, volcanic peaks,
the lava which covers in successive strata
the multiformed cultures of man's history,
progression of his self-wracked destiny.

Into the islands of the north, among
the treacherous currents, jaws of ice
ready to ram all human vessels, rode
the Arctic ship *Cheliuskin*.

Among indefinite projections, blurred
by day and night-time—weird light heavy
on their unaccustomed eyes—they moved
slowly, slowly ahead, plowed surely
into the looming ice-heaps:
the fields of perpetual, legendary winter,
where flowers ceased under deceptive sun;
light but no warmth, no sight of green,
no feel or smell of soil:
        the soil
Columbus left behind to seek
the western passage: they who rode
beyond the edges of the charted world

into oblivion: miraculously
returned to venture forth again

and Hendrick Hudson, his fingers fast
frozen to the wheel: winds gone,
sails, mast, compass useless: only
the X-ray cold, ice entering the heart

and Peary, dreaming of Nicaraguan jungle,
the tangled blossoms curling in his brain—
warmth of the Carib sea remembered—
left Cape Columbia far behind
to plant a flag at the world's crown, symbol
of human striving, heroism. Returned
hailed as victor, but in his heart
knew he had not conquered, merely glimpsed.

These, first to venture, left their bones
frozen in ice, bitten by the snow,
but signposts none: the flag of no
nation survived the unvarying winter

till planes soared humming over Leningrad,
propellers sang over the northern seas,
the *Krassin* broke the Kara ice, shifting
its course, prompted by messages from home,
to greet the cargo ship—the name?
remember it: *Cheliuskin*.

> *We bade Leningrad farewell on July 12, 1933,*
> *warmly sent off by the people . . .*
> —Professor Schmidt,
> Commander of the Expedition.

At midnight, under the Norwegian cliffs,
the small ship tossed, crossed Barents Sea,
meeting no ice. Then through the straits

Matochkin Shar, emerged in Kara waters.
First easy going, but the boat rocked
sharply under wind's lash, sea's swell;
made fast our cargo, fortified our will—
and felt the fury of the Arctic, saw
our stem cracked, our plates crushed in,
but pushed ahead.
                        Sighted through fog and snow
the *Krassin*'s silhouette: waved hands in air,
hoisted the ship's flag higher and our crew's
voices rang across the white plains, bellowed
skyward above the foghorn, cutting the frost.

Strange entry in the log: "August 31st,
a female child born to the Vassilievs:
in honor of the sea was named Karina."

Continued through the ice. The voyage half over:
we watched the stars like luminous ice-chips
visible alike to us and our comrades,
the garrison at Wrangel Isle, our goal.

Remembering Red Square: home thoughts from abroad.

What shall I say? shall I remember Moscow?
transport myself in space-time to the winding river?
wonder who walks across the Kremlin Square
conversing with the guards at Lenin's tomb?
What are they doing? What are the comrades saying?
are they diving from floats in the Park of Culture and Rest?
are they picnicking under trees? playing in the sun?
boating on the river never stiffened with cold?
watching the children? feeding the little shaved-heads?
applauding the discus-throwing Comsomol?
and my wife? and my children? what doing? There
where winter's also cold but the city filled
with comrades, brothers, friends.

> Not here
where beyond the vessel's line lies death.

But we—we must, advancing, conquer it: defy
the javelin-pointed ice, the ground-glass snow,
vanquish the remaining miles to Wrangel Station,
bring food to the frozen, warmth to winter faces,
provisions to our outpost, symbol of socialist
will to restore man's dignity on earth.

> *But never rest, no swerving from our charted course.*

Onward toward Bering, mouth of the Pacific,
into the Chukchi Sea, the small ship groaning
in the tense grip of ice, the horizon alive,
landscape moving on the water: floating islands
tossing toward head-on collision, floes covering
nine-tenths of the great sea's surface, until
our ship lost power, floes joined together,
air survey promised clear sea soon ahead
and we pushed on: each face tightened,
fearing delay, and more than delay, death;
fighting to reach clear waters, knowing
fifteen knots only barred us from our goal.
Engines hissed steam and the ship bulged
against the ice, grinding!
ripped! and fell back trembling.

Useless now to force passage seaward.
Our only course now eastward with the drifting mass.

> *February 13, 1934: last of the Cheliuskin.*

The packed ice groaned against the hull, the wall
of mounting floes advanced until the vessel,
clutched in a death-vise, shivered, cracked.

And water spurted at the flaming boilers,
exploded steam in air. Careful, careful,
our comrades relayed food from deck,
provisions, tents, great furs from the dying vessel.
The women and little Karina we covered
with warm hides, tented them against the snow.
In Arctic night we staggered, transferring tools and cargo
from ship to ice-field.
                    Then the *Cheliuskin* growled
like a great, hurt dog, and slipped; its massive bows
sank rapidly. The last command rang out:
"All on the ice! All comrades leave the ship!"
The gangway twisted, fell; bridge crashed; a great
black cloud of soot belched from the tilted funnel.
Ripped at by wind, the black smoke covered
our faces, bitter, watching the ship's last seconds.
The ground gale lashed us as the stern rose
flourishing screw and rudder.
Then the waters closed over her . . .

For two months we lived in fur,
encamped on ice, eyes to the sky.

Everything calm today: yesterday's dream
of passage and clear sea has given way
to prayer: keep our ice field solid under us

we live in tents: at night in sleeping bags
we hear the gale winds blowing over us
we have enough warm clothing: also food

we shall get along: men of our kind always
find in adversity new stimuli: besides
with wireless rigged nothing's to be feared

Moscow knows what's happened: they'll send men
and sleds and planes enough to carry us back:
our people will not forget their pioneers

we sleep in layers: legs on top of legs
lying fanwise: feet to center: each like
primitive man furred from head to foot

13 below zero: hammer and sickle already
wave from newly-reared flagpole: radio rods
rise above beams left from our boat: we

remember the sunken ship with gratitude:
in the evening the gigantic northern lights
glow in a half-circle to the north: we eat

kasha and biscuit: settle in tent to sight
the first plane flying our way: visibility poor
but we strain for the motor's sound in the sky

104 of us—if only an airship were here
to lift us from the ice!—today a five-ball wind
33 degrees of cold: oh-ho! how cold!

News from Moscow! the *Smolensk* is on its way
from Vladivostok, three large planes on deck!
The *Stalingrad* too has sailed and a dirigible's coming!

Then the roar of an engine rouses us. We look.
Like a grasshopper in the deep sky, Levanevski's plane!
We're found! We're saved! They're flying here, they're coming!
First to arrive in two months from the great land!

> *On February 13 I telegraphed Moscow that*
> *I was ready to fly to the Cheliuskin's*
> *assistance. My wife cried and my children*
> *set up a wail but I managed to soothe them.*
> —Pilot Levanevski

Sweet to the ear the sound,
to the body the feel of the motor
humming ahead: in the hands
the controls steady.

We flew to Berlin, to London,
ten days in New York, then orders:
Proceed to Vankarem. We tried
the plane, prepared to fly.

Then American planes, repainted
with USSR on the wings:
started the engine, tested it:
all O.K. The crowds

squeezed through to shake hands—
goodbye!—and I opened
throttle to the full:
she raced ahead and we soared.

Then hours toward Nome: course westward,
range open: we circled and climbed,
gained altitude in cloud:
mountains fled below us.

Through snow we zigzagged, guided
by black specks, telegraph poles:
landed at Nome: the airmen
received me, gave me a badge.

Then clear through to Wellen
under bright moonlight: sighted
the last northeastern outpost
of the Soviet frontier:

left sun behind us, plunged
into dense cloud: a storm
hit the plane like a fist:
then bad bumps. The machine

bucked: I felt her go heavy:
ice gripped wings, filmed windows:
I watched and waited, strained.
Trembling we dove toward darkness:

hit the ice with a crack-up
barely averted: saw blood
drip from my tunic: poured
iodine over the wound.

Housed in a Chukchi *yaranga,*
that night delirious: then,
healed by the cold, I cabled Moscow
"Feel fit to work and am ready."

Then others came: lone plane gave way to squadron
startling the northern silence, seeking the icebound crew.
Through blinding storm and cloud, over peaked mountain ranges,
wings sagging, encased in ice, the Soviet airmen flew:

Lyapidevski from Matthew Island, Galyshev from Khabarovsk,
from Nome, Levanevski and Slepnyov, Kamanin from the *Smolensk:*
hundreds of others in motion: commanders, compass in hand,
guiding the ice-crashing vessels, stokers heaving coal.

In threes, in fours, the marooned boarded the fragile planes,
roared through the air to home, laughed at the sight of land,
cheered at the landings by countrymen, warmly taken back
to the bosom of friends, of earth: hand clasped in warm
                    rough hand,

till the last of the frozen exiles thawed out at the banquet table;
then returned to work, to map the way for future, greater Cheliuskins.

FIRST LOVE
and other poems

DRAWINGS BY LIA NICKSON

FOR MARY

1

Entry

speaks as a plural subject

Running from the shadow-coach,
silent on the darkling plain,
we whispered: be careful.

Arnold

Recalled the always-dimmed headlights, the full halt,
the silence, the unspoken word.
All yesterdays blurred
while scouts advanced a mile,
returned, reported: All's well.
And in the deep dusk we relaxed, whispered,
thinking: now, now the beginning;
hastily passed the loaves of bread around,
tinned sardines, *Gauloises,* chocolate, cheese,
stuffed them in pockets; filled a few canteens
with wine; drew the stiff curtains down
and, choking, smoked—all fifty of us—
a final cigarette.

Then, two at a time, leaped the wide ditch,
ran cross-meadow, carefully climbed
the flank of a sharp ridge,
knowing already
what the word *enemy* means.

We counted heads in a hidden gully: all here.
The driver said *Salud* and disappeared,
whisper-humming the *Marseillaise*. Our guide
greeted us: *Salud!* Gave us instructions in Catalan
which somebody translated into French, others
to English, German, Finnish, Italian.
None but a few understood the original words.
But all understood.

Slowly the long single file advanced
silent through sleeping country, leaping ditches,
treading the worn earth, avoiding pits and twigs
ready to snap, betray us.
But we set the dogs to barking:
wherever we went, there was the sharp alarm

of the watchdogs yelping, howling, barking,
bursting the drowsy silence, giving alarm
to cowled sleepers of the countryside.
We could see them, almost: uneasy, turning
heavily, punchdrunk with sleep, raising
the hundred-ton head of night from the magnet pillow,
trying to listen—and failing,
falling again, eyes easily closed while
the sound of the dogs merged with their heavy dreams,
fused with the peaceful dark and, in the sky,
seen through the peacetime window, the lone visible star.

Then, in the huge darkness, out of forbidding sky,
the Pyrenees loomed, frightful, gigantic,
wonderfully to welcome us.

And the word ran down the line like a snake's
body, coiling, undulating:
Stop now. Rest.
We halted, gathered in a small, warm gully
again. *Feet higher,* the whispers said,
Gets the blood out of them, eases them for climbing.

Going toward what we hated, feeling no hatred,
only the *now, now* pounding
before it's too late in the brain,
we paused, nibbled at bread, cheese, chocolate,
cupped our cigarettes' glow in careful palms,
stooped to drink at a spring, then stretched
bodies full on the thick grass,
resting waiting listening
searching the uncharted skies
where border patrols flashed rainbow beams
of light into the darkness; straining
eyes for distance, seeing much,
foreseeing more; wondering:

Will we make it? Will we make it?
No question of daring. The deed, begun, was done.
Now only the mountains faced us, the moon rising,
and only a shallow river in its dry summer bed.

Moving, the man ahead always in sight, thinking:
   this Spain we go to, this is no land of
   postcard ruins, though we have seen them. This is
   not what remains of half-remembered lectures:
   bull fights, the matador suave in silk,
   his mastodon enemy, buffalo-shouldered,
   facing him. No land of *flamenco*
   or Rabbi Israel's son courting the phobic maid
   under a moonlit balcony near Zaragossa.
   No land of oranges, or olive groves,
   or vines heavy with grapes in geometric vineyards,
   nor steel that sings and bends like a slim girl dancing,
   nor *gitanos* and *guitarristas*. No,
   none of these tourist dreams alone is Spain.

Spain is yesterday's Russia, tomorrow's China,
yes, and the thirteen seaboard states.
Spain is all lands and all times when clash
the hopes and the wills of the men in them;
the kindliest, seeking only life,
and the cruellest, in love with death.

We were right: how right we never discovered
there in the midnight fields of slumbering France.

                                        1937
                                        Madrid

FIRST LOVE AND OTHER POEMS

City of Anguish

FOR MILTON WOLFF

At midnight they roused us. In the distance we heard
verberations of thunder. "To the cellar," they ordered.
"It's safest under the stairway." Pointing,
a veteran led us. The children, whimpering,
followed the silent women who would never
sing again strolling in the *Paseo* on Sunday evenings.
In the candle-light their faces were granite.

"Artillery," muttered Enrico, cursing.
Together we turned at the lowest stair.
"Come on," he said. "It's better on the rooftop.
More fireworks, better view." Slowly we ascended
past the stalled lift, felt through the roof door,
squinted in moonless darkness.

We counted the flashes, divided the horizon,
90 degrees for Enrico, 90 for me.
"Four?" "No, five!" We spotted the big guns when
the sounds came crashing, split-seconds after light.
Felt the slight earthquake tremor when shells fell
square on the Gran Via; heard high above our heads
the masculine shriek of the shell descending—
the single sharp rifle-crack, the inevitable dogs
barking, angry, roused from midsummer sleep.
The lulls grew fewer: soon talking subsided
as the cannonade quickened. Each flash in darkness
created horizon, outlined huge buildings.
Off a few blocks to the north, the *Telefónica*
reared its massive shoulders, its great symbol profile
in dignity, like the statue of Moses pointing,
agèd but ageless, to the Promised Land.

2

Deafening now, the sky is aflame with
unnatural lightning. The ear—

like the scout's on patrol—gauges each explosion.
The mind—neither ear nor eye is aware of it—
calculates destruction, paints the dark pictures
of beams fallen, ribs crushed beneath them; beds
blown with their innocent sleepers to agonized
death.
          And the great gaping craters in streets
yawn, hypnotic to the terrified madman,
sane a mere hour ago.
                    The headless body
stands strangely, totters for a second, falls.
The girl speeds screaming through wreckage; her
          hair is
wilder than torture.
                    The solitary foot,
deep-arched, is perfect on the cobbles, naked,
strong, ridged with strong veins, upright, complete . . .

The city weeps. The city shudders, weeping.

The city weeps: for the moment is silent—
the pause in the idiot's symphony, prolonged
beyond the awaited crashing of cymbals, but
the hands are in mid-air, the instruments gleaming:
the swastika'd baton falls! and the clatter of
thunder begins again.
                    Enrico beckons me.
Fires there. Where? Toward the *Casa de Campo*.
And closer. There. The *Puerta del Sol* exudes   often considered
submarine glow in the darkness, alive with   the heart of Madrid
strange twisting shapes, skyfish of stars,
fireworks of death, mangled lives, silent lips.
In thousands of beds now the muscles of men are
aroused, flexed for springing, quivering, tense,
that moments ago were relaxed, asleep.

3

It is too late for sleep now.
Few hours are left before dawn. We wait for
the sun's coming . . . And it rises, sulphurous
through smoke. It is too late for sleep.

The city weeps. The city wakens, weeping.

And the Madrileños rise from wreckage, emerge
from shattered doorways . . .
                       But always the wanderer,
the old woman searching, digging among debris.
In the morning light her crazed face is granite.

And the beggar sings among the ruins:

  All night, all night
  flared in my city the bright
  cruel explosion of bombs.
  All night, all night,
  there, where the soil and stone
  spilled like brains from the sandbag's head,
  the bodiless head lay staring;
  while the anti-aircraft barked,
  barked at the droning plane,
  and the dogs of war, awakened,
  howled at the hidden moon.
  And a star fell, omen of ill,
  and a man fell, lifeless,
  and my wife fell, childless,
  and, friendless, my friend.
  And I stumbled away from them, crying
  from eyeless lids, blinded.
  Trees became torches
  lighting the avenues
  where lovers huddled in terror
  who would be lovers no longer.

All night, all night
flared in my city the bright
cruel explosion of hope—
all night
all night . . .

4

#4, 5 first published as "Madrid" in a collection of poems published in Madrid in 1937

Come for a joyride in Madrid: the August morning
is cleared of smoke and cloud now; the journalists
dip their hard bread in the *Florida* coffee,
no longer distasteful after sour waking.
Listen to Ryan, fresh from the lines, talking
    (Behind you the memory of bombs beats
    the blood in the brain's vessels—the dream broken,
    sleep pounded to bits by the unending roar of
    shells in air, the silvery bombs descending,
    rabid spit of machine guns and the carnival flare
    of fire in the sky):

Frank Ryan—member of IRA since 1918, leader of the Irish Volunteers

                "Why is it, why?
when I'm here in the trenches, half-sunk in mud,
blanket drenched, hungry, I dream of Dublin,
of home, of the girls? But give me a safe spot,
clean linen, bed and all, sleep becomes nightmare
of shrapnel hurtling, bombs falling, the screaming of bullets,
their thud on the brain's parapet. Why? Why?"

Exit the hotel. The morning constitutional.
Stroll down the avenues. Did Alfonso's car
detour past barricades? Did broken mains splatter him?
Here's the bellyless building; four walls, no guts.
But the biggest disaster's the wrecking of power:
thirty-six hours and no power: electric
sources are severed. The printer is frantic:
how print the leaflet, the poster, or set
the type for the bulletin?
                After his food
a soldier needs cigarettes, something to read,
something to think about: words to pull

the war-weary brain back to life from forgetfulness:
spirited words, the gestures of Dolores,
majestic Pasionaria speaking—
mother to men, mother of revolutions,
winner of battles, comforter of defenders;
her figure magnificent as any monument
constructed for heroes; her voice a symphony,
consoling, urging, declaiming in prophecy,
her forehead the wide plateaus of her country,
her eyes constant witness of her words' truth.

Republican activist Dolores Ibárruri, la Pasionaria — role in the defense of Madrid

5

Needless to catalogue heroes. No man
weighted with rifle, digging with nails in earth,
quickens at the name. Hero's a word for
peacetime. Battle
knows only three realities: enemy, rifle, life.

No man knows war or its meaning who has not
stumbled from tree to tree, desperate for cover,
or dug his face deep in earth, felt the ground pulse with
the ear-breaking fall of death. No man knows war
who never has crouched in his foxhole, hearing
the bullets an inch from his head, nor the zoom of
planes like a Ferris wheel strafing the trenches . . .

last stanzas published in the New Republic in 1939 as a rebuke — as the cause is lost as Europe gears up for a broader war

War is your comrade struck dead beside you,
his shared cigarette still alive in your lips.

1937
Madrid

Death by Water

On May 30 1937 the small Spanish coastal steam-
ship *Ciudad de Barcelona* was torpedoed and sunk
off the coast of Malgrat by a submarine which the
Non-Intervention Committee preferred to desig-
nate as "of unknown nationality." More than a
hundred volunteers, twelve of them Americans,
perished.

Nearing land, we heard the cry of gulls and
saw their shadows in sunlight on the topmost deck,
or coasting unconcerned on each wavecrest, they rested
after their scavenging, scudding the ship's length.

And we thought of the albatross—an old man going crazy,
his world an immenseness of water, none of it to drink;
and the vultures descending on an Ethiopian plain:
all of us were the living corpse, powerless, bleeding.

And suddenly the shock. We felt the boat shiver.
I turned to Oliver, saw his eyes widen,
stare past the high rails, waiting, waiting . . .
Others stumbled past us. And suddenly the explosion.

Men in twenty languages cried out to comrades
as the blast tore the ship, and the water, like lava,
plunged through the hull, crushing metal and flesh before it,
splintering cabins, the sleepers caught unconscious.

Belted, we searched for companions but lost them
in turmoil of faces; swept toward the lifeboats
and saw it was useless. Too many were crowding them.
Oliver dived. I followed him, praying.

In the water the sea-swell hid for a moment
Oliver swimming, strongly, away from me.
Then his voice, calmly: "Here, keep his head above."
We helped save a drowning man, kept him afloat until

dories approached. Looking backward, we saw
the prow high in air, and Carlos, unconcerned,
throwing fresh belts to the tiring swimmers.
Steam, flame crept toward him, but he remained absorbed . . .

2

On shore, later, a hundred of us gone,
we are too weak to weep for them, to listen to
consoling words. We are too tired
to return the grave smiles of the rescuing people.
Too drained. Sorrow can never be the word.

But beyond the numbness the vivid faces
of comrades burn in our brains: their songs
in quiet French villages, their American laughter
tug at responding muscles in our lips,
shout against ears that have heard their voices living.

Fingers, convulsive, form fists. Teeth
grate now, audibly. We stifle curses,
thought but unuttered. While many grieve,
their hands reach outward, fingers extended—
the image automatic—ready for rifles

until night brings us sleep, and dreams
of violent death by drowning, dreams
of journey, slow advances through vineyards,
seeking cover in wheatfields, finding always
the fascist face behind the olive tree.

August 1937
Madrid

Catalogue

Futile, now, in our days of grief,
are tears and unaimed anger. No more
than the simple enumeration of losses
is needed—the skeleton facts:

of Rosa who in her hospital bed
turns unbelieving eyes from her amputated leg
yet sings in her grave contralto to the soldiers
gathered around her;

of Roger, face paler than pillow,
smiling at reporters, patiently explaining,
pointing to the mutilated arm, telling them
"This we feared and expected."

Or Janssen, coughing his lungs away, sleepless,
awaiting the inevitable permanent darkness,
but fiercely, night after night, filling pages
with wisdom, his reasons for living.

Or sightless, unmoving, Robert Raven,
hungry for learning, body tense,
his ears straining, eager for the voice of
the patient invisible reader.

Now, in our days of sorrow, we gather
the armaments of deadly undying anger:
our purpose builds the million rifles, ready
for use, invincible.

Our pity perfect as comradeship seeks
the tiring solution. Brain and strong spirit
stalk it through streets alive with shrapnel,
impassable with barricades.

And our compassion rises in us like rivers
at floodtime, endows us with lightning speed and vigor,
power needed for healing, love for survival,
the passion for new creation.

Yes, tears are futile in our days of grief,
and unreined anger. Nothing more
than the simple enumeration of horrors
is needed—the undying fact.

FIRST LOVE AND OTHER POEMS

Eyes of a Blind Man

FOR COMMANDANTE FORT OF THE FRANCO-BELGE
BATTALION OF THE FOURTEENTH (INTERNATIONAL)
BRIGADE, WHO STARED AT A WOMAN IN THE CASA
DE REPOSA DE GENERAL LUCASZ, IN MADRID,
IN THE LATE AUTUMN OF 1937.

Her voice is a magnet into which flows
all I remember. It is her voice I see.
Not her mythical eyes alive with reflections
nor her moon-lucent throat nor the way her head's poised
proudly above it; nor the luxuriant hair
flowing backward from temples like grass from a lake's shore;
no, nor the nose and its breathing nostrils.
Neither mouth nor lips nor the vivid teeth
do I see, nor her finely-lobed ears.
Her voice is all that's visible to me.

By her voice I note her coming and her going,
engrave her movements as a beach records
continual change of tides. All that remains now
is the memory of sight, like a special statue
seen in a childhood museum. The rest
is sorrow to sense, strong wine to smell,
anguish to possess, even in the mind's eye.

But her voice remains, palpable, lucid, real.
Her voice is now what her eyes and the curve of her lips are
to all other men.

September 7, 1937
Madrid

Casualty

It seemed
the sky was a harbor, into which rode
black iron cruisers, silently, their guns
poised like tiger-heads on turret-haunches.

It seemed the sky was an olive grove, ghostly
in moonlight, and Very-light, with deadly crossfire
splitting it, proving a new theorem with rifles,
unknown in any recalled geometry.

And then he woke, choking. Saw sky as sky
in purest moonlight; and the searchlight beams paled
against it, and he heard Tibidábo's guns
burst against space. Then one bomb, shrieking,

found the thin axis of his whirling fears,
the exact center.

March 17, 1938
Barcelona

FIRST LOVE AND OTHER POEMS

Epitaph

FOR ARNOLD REID
D. JULY 27, 1938
AT VILLALBA DE LOS ARCOS

Deep in this earth,
deeper than grave was dug
ever, or body of man ever lowered,
runs my friend's blood,
spilled here. We buried him
here where he fell,
here where the sniper's eye
pinned him, and everything
in a simple moment's
quick explosion of pain was over.

Seven feet by three
measured the trench we dug,
ample for body of man ever murdered.
Now in this earth his blood
spreads through far crevices,
limitless, nourishing vineyards for miles around,
olive groves slanted on hillocks, trees
green with young almonds, purple with ripe figs,
and fields no enemy's boots
can ever desecrate.

This is no grave,
no, nor a resting place.
This is the plot where the self-growing seed
sends its fresh fingers to turn soil aside,
over and under earth ceaselessly growing,
over and under earth endlessly growing.

July 30, 1938
Villalba de los Arcos

[Handwritten annotations:]
published New Masses 1939 as "For Arnold Reid"
Reid was a political commissar in Barcelona + did not have to leave + go to battle
— they met in 1939 at U.W. Madison

3 days into the last great campaign of the civil war

written on the spot where Reid died

1st published in 1938 in Volunteer for Liberty
reprinted later in 1938 in New Republic
reprinted in 1939 in the Daily Worker

Elegy for Our Dead

There is a place where, wisdom won, right recorded,
men move beautifully, striding across fields
whose wheat, wind-marshalled, wanders unguarded
in unprotected places; where earth, revived, folds
all growing things closely to itself: the groves
of bursting olives, the vineyards ripe and heavy with
glowing grapes, the oranges like million suns; and graves
where lie, nurturing all these fields, my friends in death.

With them, deep in coolness, are memories of France and
the exact fields of Belgium, midnight marches in snows—
the single-file caravan high in the Pyrenees: the land
of Spain unfolded before them, dazzling the young Balboas.
This earth is enriched with Atlantic salt, spraying
the live, squinting eyelids, even now, of companions—
with towns of America, towers and mills, sun playing
always, in stone streets, wide fields—all men's dominions.

Honor for them in this lies: that theirs is no special
strange plot of alien earth. Men of all lands here
lie side by side, at peace now after the crucial
torture of combat, bullet and bayonet gone, fear
conquered forever. Yes, knowing it well, they were willing
despite it to clothe their vision with flesh. And their rewards,
not sought for self, live in new faces, smiling,
remembering what they did here. Deeds were their last words.

September 20, 1937
Madrid

The Guerrillas

Suffering through the winter months, with food
and warmth of fire denied them, they remained
lost in their labyrinth forests, chained to blood
of comrades, dead and dying there. It rained
afterward, when the spring came. They survived
by shooting flying creatures and by songs
they improvised at evening. But they moved
like senile men with bodies scarred by thongs . . .

Slowly, with only flecks of sky to show
the stars to them at night, the sun by day,
they won the right to penetrate, to know
the wreckage of hope may be redeemed, the way
to openness, and sea-winds, and the earth
that sun can reach and rouse to luminous birth.

Polonius -b Hamlet - "This above all, to thine own self be true."

To Thine Own Self

If this uncertain living, these days that mount
directionless as terror, haunt us too deeply,
help us to find solutions, to count deeds
well-done which otherwise might fall behind
meaningless as steel tracks speeding in sunlight
unchangingly away in train-momentum's vision.

⌐ cf "Definition"

No words men speak are really, finally, true.
No friend can know nor understand completely.
No woman means everything. No one pursuit
captures the spirit to exclude all others.
And no single star is ever always faithful;
the mariner must lean on compass more than sky. ⌡

So freely disavow the proved uncertainties
and seek from self. Perfect an artless guide
to steer unswervingly through seas and woods
and city nightmares. Set the firepoint north
or south: the wind that comes to blow to cool
your captive vision will revive and free it.

poems in this section generally lyrics, some written before Rolfe
left for Spain + others after his return
Spain + the war generally absent
attempt to retreat from the revolutionary poems of the early + mid.'30s into
a poetic stance more personal and oblique

2

After Wang Chi

And now, thirteen centuries later, the flower of man
still falls fuddled with drink: the petals shrink
under ferocious sun and drop to earth to rot
quickly away. Going to taverns we no longer sharpen
the mind's steel for thinking, nor hone the tongue's blade
for clean incisive speech. Too facile, a canoe
that skims unruffled waters, has the brain become,
        untrained for effort that breeds large utterance
(as a woman bears children) and great remembered deeds.
Yet, seeing most men weak and others behaving like drunkards,
we must together seek strength; hands joined, remain sober.

Pastoral

The lonely evening crouches, darkens as the hour
ages to dusk; waits in the cool shadows.
Last gold pigment gleams on gray shacks of the poor;
final sun retards the death of green in meadows.

No smoke rises, wraithlike or billowing,
from low silent houses. Herd and herd-keeper
alike drink the lengthening darkness, pillowed
luxuriously in coolness. It soothes the sleeper

fallen exhausted on field; it lulls the human
moaning of the crushed. Fallow, the deep red soil
flows upward to gray sky; and fireflies illumine
bark of scarred tree and hut's peeling wall.

The river flows like tallow, is yellow no longer.
The water is silent, except where dark branches
droop to dip foliage in the flow; and anger
of tired arms is cooled, bodies balanced on haunches.

The lonely evening crouches, poised; darkens, grows black.
Dusk deepens, mountain and field forfeit outline.
Faces merge softly; no white man draws back
when black approaches, singing, in the night-scene.

> August 1936
> Washington, D.C.

Pastoral (2)

Now, on this bluest of mornings, we wake
to watch the winter receding before sun,
the light like lava down a shaken crater's
slanting side compelling conquest: oblivion

to snow preserved in last hidden corners,
water pooled in earth's deep crevices, bored
by beast for winter sleep. Death is no longer
in the air we breathe, nor frost in the fruit's core.

Now singing we rise to watch the infant deer
rocketing down wood lane, timid suspicious eye
hypnotized with green, counting as a faun does,
calculating growth-time before ripening.

Sharp beaks of sparrows stab the swollen soil,
still heavy with moisture where the last snow fell,
seeking fresh sustenance for flight; and all
living things follow them, bright with new hunger.

This is true season's end, true quest's beginning:
man discards artifice of ice, becomes artist
of natural summer, mature, eyes set on winning
the warm world entirely, to the farthest horizons.

Night World

She is asleep: one breast, uncovered,
records her breathing. Under the lamp
I remain wakeful, mind divided,
from breast to book the eye wandering—
soon to close the pages lest the rustling
disturb her senses slumbering.

And I rise from bed: midnights like these,
with mind alert after love, surely
guide the full spirit toward discovery,
clear-eyed wisdom reviewing the day,
the month, the seasons; recalling the events,
the full-flowered blossoming of all my years.

Lids closed, the eyes are watchful; the brain
carefully stalks the thought like a tiger
following the accurately-scented prey
through tangled jungle foliage.

                              The way
to certainty is charted now,
the sensitive ears alive to sound,
antennae poised for touch, and in the head
all tissue quivering like violin strings.

Before the hour demands surrender,
before the body tires, I see all friends
wonderfully perfect, and the earth changed
to match the works, desires of my days;
loving all men and mankind, and the world
unblemished as her rising falling breast.

The Ship

We shall watch its final plunge from afar,
keeping sinews strong and our minds free
of its sea-soaked rot. We shall be everywhere
when faces turn, fresh-eyed, to the wind:
not here, where decay is constant, but on shores
that beckon as this antique vessel dies.

I do not mean we will desert,
but no ship, sinking, is worth salvaging
in seas where masts are numerous and men are
enough to board them, steer them to port.
We shall be here only to save the living cargo,
carry it untouched to greener shores

while the old vessel, having served its lords,
transporting human vassals and rich plunder,
sinks upon the water, empty, with only
rats running, panic-driven, on its decks;
finally surrenders to the cleansing sea,
weighted with age and its rusty slave chains.

1936

Prophecy in Stone

FOR PAUL STRAND

Enter the ruined hacienda: see Christ
in fifty different tortured poses,
varnished, carved to semblance of life, endowed
with breath almost: here where the camera eye
restores the initial spirit, reveals
the permanence surviving death. Ferret out
a race's history in a finger's curve,
see sun-washed walls flaking to dust,
the dust to powder won by the wind;
deep gashes, rust of rain and sun,
stones fallen, and the black deep grooves
where peons crucified conquistadors,
nailed them to walls, whips clutched
in paralyzed hands tense in agony.

See too the solitary mare
grazing in the barbed enclosure surrounding
the dead mansion of glory: and the mountains
rising beyond, and the pendant clouds
hung in the skies, identical with
horizons Coronado never conquered.

Marks of boot and fingerprint remain
on the rainless scene: nails jut from walls
long cleaned by wind and bird of flesh and bone.
See here, a continent away, the evidence
of grandeur ground to death by time and man,
and the lonely spirit, sun on the anguished eyes
of the carved Christ; and the deep patience
men of another century engraved
on these stone walls and images—lines like words
shouting: "We are enslaved!"
                              lines in prophetic
thunder: "We shall rise,
                              conquer our conquerors."

1936

The Arctic Remembered

Have you gone skiing down hill through snow
still soft on the earth? felt it fold away,
harden under you? and caught the particles
of ice still in air on your cheeks and chin?

Or pointed your skates southward on brittle ice
with the wind behind you from the north, blowing,
bulging your jacket, ballooning trousers,
fiercely, you a mile each move careening?

Or loosed the sail of your iceboat in midwinter?
seen the wind fill it, carry you away,
the sharp steel runners singing on the ice,
while you held tightly, shifting body's weight,
tempting the rough spill but the heart certain
that life is strongest when the danger's fiercest?

And you felt like shouting and you laughed, and tears
the cold bit out of you ran down your cheeks
and you filled your lungs with the cold air,
sharp as spice, and laughed again and shouted.
But its sound made no dent in the wind's sound
and the sound of snow falling and runners ringing
and the air going by like a hurricane!

    Do you remember
the moment you plunged into the bank of snow
and sprawled, all warm inside? and rolled
and rose to your feet and felt your cheek
and sensed that your skin was changed and tougher,
your cheekbones harder and jawbone straighter?
Remember? Recall? Try to think, remember:

that's the way the Arctic altered us.

2

Knowing the ice in the air as the flower knows
sun, living daily in intimate closeness
to cold as a man lives always in touch with

the woman he loves, we never completely
found calm in the Arctic: never grew quiet:
daily changed as the petal in sunlight
opens, and blossoms, and blooms: always stirred
as the touch of the woman is always a fiery
touch, though expected, long known and loved.

Song

There is indeed now reason for rejoicing,
for risen is the sick child, red again his cheeks.
Look, he is heartier than his doctors: his eyes are
clearer, brow unwrinkled. Listen as he speaks
the language of small ones: tumbling are his words like
toy blocks, music-boxes, flowers falling, spilled
freely over the precious rug. Profusion of sound pours
from unformed lips but forming: his words cannot be spelled.

Take him up, hold him closely, high in air balance him.
Man, you live again! This is your youth's dreaming
clothed with life, careless, kicking, capable of great growth,
able to sustain you with a small smile, compensate
for million losses, million hopes unheard. Your son is
that moment which urged battle, fierce, before you surrendered.

Song (2)

Keep the dream alive and growing always.
You will have far to go to find
substitute visions for the one you hold
living, newly-born, warm in your cupped hand.
Infant, it needs protection: warmth against cold,
the finger-barrier to ward off wind,
the closed palm against rain and snow,
the eye to see and the nourishing will.

This is your vision: keep it glowing
like the furnace door open in the shadowed mill,
the solitary cap-lamp in the mine,
the lonely eye at midnight. Whether at toil,
or study, or love, these things—like dreams,
like imaged worlds and creatures—need nurturing always.

Essay on Dreiser (1871–1945)

Death underlines our loss. The man who moved
mountains of men is dead on a mountain peak.
And those he hated, those whom he always loved
are quiet now: we will not hear him speak,
flushed, impulsive, angry again. He never
truly achieved old age despite his years;
never evaded combat, rarely ran for cover;
in his eighth decade undertook new chores,
left jumbled notes to plague the stunned survivor.

Whether we care or not, we are his heirs
and ours the busybody task is: to decipher
the massive marginalia of his plodding years,
the words piled high on words, the flowing river
of novels, polemics, poems, apologies.
No matter where we turn, we will be bogged
deep in a brooding delta of discrepancies,
in work diffused too widely to be catalogued,
a life too intricate for neat obituaries.

And questions still confound us: why,
more than ten years ago, in the illiterate south,
caught in the compulsive human act, did he deny
the very power that gave his novels worth—
his own virility? And he, who profoundly knew
what casts the malignant mote in mankind's eye,
why did he gibe the English, bait the Jew?
To say he typified the world's protracted youth
is true but does not tell the essential truth.

His foibles were not his alone. Voltaire
in another century and to a like degree
debased his precious coinage in the fire
of similar falsehoods; and even in our day
men who lead nations through blood, sweat, tears,
adding immortal moments to our history,
at other moments mouth the ugly lie
that quickens hatreds and prolongs for years
the myths that send men brutally to kill, to die.

But now he is home, he is safe. No more
will he dig in the lower depths of our despair
nor engage in public boxing matches nor
praise motherhood, damn poverty and laissez faire.
His death embarrassed us: in the city where he died
no liberal journal dared identify the spade,
to call him what he was, a communist.
To do so would have pricked the provincial pride
which now will label him our foremost novelist.

His death still leaves the major question-mark
unanswered: how a man of vast confusions,
of usual failings, reflecting all the dark
complexities of our ignorance and passions,
can yet create a life in life, illumine
those crevices we others shrink from, and explore
the tortuous highways of the soul, the human
heart and its tempestuous truths—the core
of our most devious motives in eternal war.

But speculation serves no purpose. Dreiser
was what he was. No judgment is complete.
Much as we wish he had been surer, wiser,
we cannot change the fact. The man was great
in a way Americans uniquely understand
who know the uneven contours of their land,
its storms, its droughts, its huge and turbulent
Mississippi, where his youth was spent,
whose floods entomb its truest sons in the ocean's sand.

December 29, 1945

3

barbed wire

Postscript to a War

FOR MICHAEL GORDON

We must remember cleanly why we fought,
clearly why we left these inadequate shores
and turned our eyes, hearts, Spainward. We must never
lie to ourselves again, deceive ourselves with dreams
that make sleep sluggish. Our world
is new now, clean and clear: our eyes can see
the perfect bone and tissue now, remembering
the flesh cut open, the gangrened limbs, the rot
that almost, almost . . . but did not reach the heart.

And if we find all known things changed
now, after two years amid fabulous truth;
if we find dulled the once sharp edges
of trivial loves; even if we find
our truest loves indifferent, even false—
we must remember cleanly why we went,
clearly why we fought; and returning, see
with truth's unfilmed eye what remains constant,
the loyalties which endure, the loves that grow,
the certainties men need, live for, die to build,
the certainties that make all living tolerable.

February 24, 1939

Biography

It is so hard to be victorious,
to seek, find
         and in the search remember
each groove the mind cut, each ponderous
weight of hard lumber
            before the plane glided
hand and eye behind it
peeling the bark, revealing the luminous grain.

Name: John Makepeace. This is my history:
born in Sauk City, saw first
in my tenth year a rigid bird in the sky.
At fifteen left school. Print blurred before me,
became cloud in my mind
          the mind that hummed with motors
singing the bird's song.
           No nightingale
with wings at rest against the bosom feathers
but wings of deep-grained metal, planed
to smoothest nudity, unstained, unpainted,
wings held to body like a cross, unbending,
song not from furred throat but from the heart beating:
the heart of steel: the valves in perfect motion
forcing the oil like blood through the veins,
the gas like air through the lungs, singing
from deep in the unbending body its song
of thunder in the sky.

          Print blurred before me.

Then the war came. I breathed the air of the bird,
felt blood's flood in my ears.
This is my history.

Look at me today: my friends are cordial:
they shout to me in the street, gripping my hand, my arm,
guiding me through traffic, eluding autos
singing as the plane sings—but the key is minor.
My mind dodges as they swerve but legs and arms

grow rigid, trapped. My friends are kind.
My whole body is a rebel horde
in arms against its general, the brain.

Often I sit at home, alone, at night:
I, John Makepeace, thinking about tomorrow,
all my tomorrows
      thinking: Have I the guts
      to do it now, to die
      now, while death's knowable,
      now to cease living by
      will of self, in dignity?
      Or must I wait till death
      comes drooling over me,
      face distorted, eyes turned
      inward, and the mouth
      mumbling I'm Napoleon . . .

I rise with difficulty from my chair.
The curtain, blown against me, is a vulture, waiting.
I jerk away in fear, enter the other room,
turn on the light, stare at the traitorous mirror:
the eyes regarding me are not my eyes.
The pupils are too wide, the whites too bloodshot.

Returning, I sink into my chair. The breath
spurts heavily from my lungs. My blood's no longer
blood of my youth. Each time my heart beats
I hear the soaring bird singing, see it frozen
flowing through sky. The pictures on the walls
are blurred and far away, like clouds, vast stretches
of gray and blue before me.

I wonder when the fuel will burn into my brain.

I think about tomorrow.
Have I the strength?
It is too hard.
This is my history.

About Eyes

The terror of the serene plane is in their eyes:
look deeply, see the wings dip, and the revolving nose

split sky and cloud, ten thousand feet above
the remembered city of women with violent hearts,

incredibly aged children, dark-eyed, who recall
the propeller's sound and the panic
from the days of the womb's darkness.

The eyes contain, reflect more than the image photographed
in the almanacs, the newspapers, the albums airmen are fond of.

The joy of the plunge through mist into sun is unknown to
the wide anonymous eyes of the dwellers in bombed cities.

The eyes reveal everything: the inhuman grace
of the silver flight, and the first melodic hum,
deceitful, cruel, of the synchronized guns and motors

and the arc-plummet fall of the bombs, the grotesque explosion,
the hysteria of the insane siren, the last deception.

Survival Is of the Essence

Survival is of the essence, but only after submergence
completely in chaos, in combat as clearest eyes see it.

Whether one lives to return is immaterial, is
an accident of time and space. Arnold is proof of this

and Roger, who sagged to earth under an olive branch, feeling the
circumscribed earthquake under him, erupting with the roots of the tree

or Muriel, bewildered in Barcelona, learning in
a few explosive days the meaning of love and of history

and the man, light-footed, blue-eyed, who turned in the other direction,
away from the harbor, facing Madrid, thinking: *Die Heimat ist weit.*

These saw and understood. These dipped for an ageless moment in
deepest experience their eyes, their hands, hearts, lives.

They who even in libraries are with those who breathe under death
are worthy of honor, fit to be cited, eulogized, remembered.

But not those meddling tourists who spend a day with the troops,
returning with excellent photos, the torso above the trench,

who boast they slept with both sides and dined with the commanders
and peered through high-powered glasses and dimly perceived the lines

far in the distance; and return well-fed, unhurt, prepared to forget—
because they have never really known him—who the real enemy is.

I will remember the man who faced the Mediterranean
where peace was for the moment, the girl at his side,

but saw beyond the blue moment, beyond his own death even,
and turned south, singing: *Unsere Heimat ist heute Madrid.*

Marching Song of the Children of Darkness

Whether we fight with rifles or carry knives
for self-protection, whether we hide in towns
or caves or hillsides, or masquerade as clowns
or senseless mutes in faceless city dives,
all of us suffer in common the selfsame fears,
identical terrors, torments, nightmare dreams
that sicken our wakeful moments too; it seems
our only escape is blindness. Not love, not tears.

Yet the will to survive persists, even in time of peace,
and its twin, the desire to triumph, hobbles along,
not uniformed, nor in step, nor even with a song
to set our cadence, or give our hearts release;
yes, all of us are guerrillas: each, as his life unfolds,
must fight man's inhumanity—the monstrous synthesis
arrayed against him, in chaos, in malice, in this
most cruelly impossible of all possible worlds.

Song (3)

Through all the cowering world, crouching, shrinking
before the hypnotic eyes of an invisible Torquemada,
we seek the multiple magical isle whose boundaries are

    north, the eagle view from Montserrat
    west, the winding street behind the Tarragona cathedral
    south, the green peace of a never-discovered ocean
    east, the wisdom and strength of a world-visioned mind.

Through all the hysteria, the insanity of sirens and
the fear in the wrinkled foreheads of seven-year-olds
and the horror in their quick eyes which have seen more horror
than the military strategist dares to imagine,
we seek the unique and magical island:

    call it Capo Verde, where the transatlantic clipper
    glides slowly to sea for refuelling. Call it Hangman's Bay
    where the solitary illiterate dreams of his pirate grandsire
    and, lonely, wanders in greenest fields, his footsteps uncertain and heavy.

Through all the imaginings of innocent people
seeking simply peace; through all the anxiety
of the boy in stiff khaki, wondering, watching
the machine-gun instructor fondling the death-giving barrel,
hypnotized, seeing the complex bolt and the chamber spread
in precisely-named parts on the earth as the mechanized death is assembled,
we seek the island: bounded on the
north by abundant music, the pipes full-bodied and sonorous
west by the villagers' festivals on Sunday evenings
south by the interlocked arms of boys and girls in the Plaza
east by the bodies in sunlight diving into the swift green river.

May 22nd 1939

When Toller died, the roses at his bier
put forth new thorns of sharpest anger,
warning the mourners with lean and bitter power,
pitying the unhungry valedictorians.
When Toller died, for a moment the world
was quiet, suddenly stilled: the bombs over Barcelona
hung for a shattering second motionless over wild
fearfully beating hearts and eyes fixed skyward.

The speechmakers could not see, beyond the closed lids,
the landscape of horror engraved on the tortured eyes:
the prison yard at Neuburg, the swallow against the bars,
the planes above the olive grove beyond the turning river,
the horizon of Nazi faces murdering Muehsam,
advancing to murder the world—when Toller died.

Erich Muehsam

Soledad

Nothing respects your solitude. The planes
like exhibitionists cavort all season long,
stabbing the sky, sky-writing as they dart
like insects on the surface of a summer pond.

Autos outside your window do not roll
in rhythm natural to man. The brakes
grate even against ears accustomed now to noise
of plane and engine and the bombs of war.

Silence is something lost, something forgotten,
known only as things are known in memory.
Silence and solitude, the two wings of the bird
of contemplation, flap on the turning spit

while the man with the slobbering lips looks on
and grins, and eyes them with an idiot's stare.

Sentry

Asleep, breathing like an enormous child,
wounded, but soothed by the cool salve of night,
the army lies exhausted on its stony bed,
its lonely eyes clear on the outpost, envying the sleepers,
dreaming the special waking dream of solitary sentries,
but tense, fearing the naked knife in each blurred shadow.

Whether in Guinea or the Apennine hills,
during or after battle, or in manouever,
each sleeping man is obsessed, weighted with anger,
uneasy at midnight against the mysterious mass,
asleep on the next ridge or beyond the ocean,
whose voice and touch are death, he knows as enemy.

The dreams are dinosaurs and moths, various
as ways of wounds and mutilation in battle;
and nightmare imaginings agitate the night
with wild muted sound, while here and there a shriek
rises. But no one stirs except the outcast sentry
who envies the sleep that brings the dream and the shriek.

War Guilt

Men dying in battle speak after speech has failed.
Their last mute testaments are written in their eyes:
also their prophecies. These go unrecorded; are
alive only in other men, and die when they die.

I, who survive, remember the eyes of the dying:
their shout as the film closed over: *Traitor, traitor!*
the helpless words: *I accuse.* The rebuke: *You live on.*
Only the rarest times and men the pardon: *I forgive.*

Now with probing foot again we climb the uncertain hill,
each weighted with rifle, pack, biography—
last heaviest of all. Ahead, new explosions
create horizons more vivid than any day.

A man walks calmlier toward night
who carries many midnights in his heart.

Recruit

Knowing I leave tomorrow, I look
fondly, finally, around me and drink
all colors and contours deeply, like wine;
press perfect landscape to imperfect memory.

Leaving a well-loved place forever is
like rising a last time from loving or
like closing an unfinished book or seeing
for the last time a friend who is not of this world.

I wanted to leave a part of myself here,
a friend, a wife, a son to grow up among
these trees and valleys and hills I have loved.

But the summons was too sudden
and my time too brief
and my prophets false.

Spanish city - round arches, ruins, bullet holes
Woman - lyrical beauty + intensity won through suffering

4

FIRST LOVE AND OTHER POEMS

The Melancholy Comus

*Rolfe + Chaplin were
friends who met after
Rolfe moved from NY to
LA in 1943*

FOR CHARLES CHAPLIN

1

Look closely: from nowhere he leaps into the screen
and fills it with light and with luminous joy
and shadow of authentic mystery.
He smiles, but the eyes are haunted. Or the eyes
glimmer with laughter, but the lips tremble.
He moves, and we see a man move. Look again:
it's a woman walking with the grace of women.
And still another time: a child smiles from the screen.
Yet nothing clashes; man, woman, child are one,
natural variant aspects of the selfsame image.
Grace is there, and the generous sex, and strong
decisive gestures, and hurt, and the helpless exposed
face of the child, desiring love, a smile,
eager for approbation, quick to perceive the frown,
the hidden annoyance, the unsaid words "I don't want you."

But over all, as we watch from the darkened hall,
we feel the toughness, we know the tenderness,
we sense the great love and the mastery.
In him, blended perfectly, are man, woman, child:
that synthesis so few attain,
that delights us, pleasures us to come upon
but would in our own selves, indeed, embarrass us.

2

Mimic of the small dry crumbs of our joy
and the inedible shoestrings of our indignation
and the hurled pie of outrage and of hurt
and the sudden soul-washing sight of the lovely girl,
he mirrors the true motions of our regimented lives,
our nerve-ends, our goose-stepping muscles. And he sings
our unwavering happiness and unchanging sorrows
and our loneliness from which there is no escape.

3

Because he is what we would be
we love him. Since we cannot love ourselves,
knowing too well the blemishes that mar
our lives, our loves,

our rich, inhibited love
encompasses his image on the screen:
our brains think his thoughts,
our hands feel what he feels,
our own feet ache in his comic shoes.

4

The brain has arrows,
the mouth has swords,
but the body, fluid and flowing, is all music.

Even in prison,
exposed, alone,
he builds the vaulting towers of the inner castle.

The eyes have malice,
the ears have chains,
but the hands are winged like the fingers of a pianist.

Surrounded, held at bay
by policmen of the mind,
his faith is tethered subtly to tomorrow's sunrise.

The heart has miracles.

The soul has wings.

5

Slowly the walls of the world's room press inward
as in a penny-dreadful or a Kafka dream,
and the naked whimpering Soul and Ego, unprotected,
shrink and clutch each other in a bleak embrace,

loveless, awaiting extinction, pleading "Faster, faster!"
but the walls move slowly in their mechanical grooves,
gently, unhurried; and the terrified, fleshless lovers
watch them, the maniac's shriek locked in their frozen throats.

And I look: my body, with all its frailties and fears,
inhabits the skin and bones of both; my body
recoils from the doom that looms closer as mountains of ice
closed down, long ago, on a green and younger earth.
But I turn my eyes away, thinking "I do not see it,
and what I do not see does not exist,"
and I conjure pleasanter visions in which the world
is not converging wall but ever-expanding heaven.

But sometimes my imagination fails me.
Sometimes I cannot help but see what is real
and menacing and hateful as any chamber of horrors
glimpsed by a child on a Sunday museum-tour.
Sometimes I despair: I feel as the suicide feels
the moment before he pulls the innocent trigger or tests
the chair he stands on before he kicks it away or lets
the razor's edge leap toward the vibrant vein.

And in anger I cry to those who will listen:
What kind of world is this where he who speaks of man,
and man's sorrows, and man's deep longings,
and man's unmitigated loneliness,
is looked on as a leper? And he who speaks of love
is laughed at, reviled, showered with steel and filth?
While those whom we are taught to listen and look up to
say *peace* as if it were a foul word.

Song for a Birth Day
in Exile

Let the oboe and the flute
sound triumphant, joyful, sweet.
On this harvest day, a child
enters our bewildered world,
delicate, developing,
and capable of everything
in human life and growth. Today
Elena, daughter of José
and Evita, comes to prove
the deathlessness of human love.

Amid the torments of our night,
nostalgia of our exile, flight
from the edge of Europe where
barest survival fights despair,
she comes to mimic and delight.

May the genii that bestow
gifts on babies give her these:
strength and loveliness and peace,
the will to see, the eye to know,
the ear for song and poetry,
the tongue to speak, the voice to sing,
fingers of fine dexterity
to caress each living thing.
Give her more: the power to choose,
in this choice-starved life, what's fine
and worth her choosing, plus the luck
to find the living growth, the clean.

May she never know the lack
of any human sustenance,
impulse to dance, the true response
of the warm perceptive heart.
May she never live apart
from the life her people live
in their passion to survive,

FIRST LOVE AND OTHER POEMS

nor forget, through joy or grief,
the deep and tragic sense of life:
the words that Unamuno spoke
before his heart, confused with wisdom, broke;
the legends that have grown upon
the still-green grave of Valle-Inclán;
or the prodigious canvasses
of that other Spaniard who,
brush in hand, in Paris's
teeming streets still comes and goes,
illumining man's agonies
and joys for all with eyes to see.

[handwritten margin note: Unamuno died under house arrest after a speech]

[handwritten margin note: Picasso's Guernica]

In her blood Asturian
mountain freshets rush and flow,
sounding their springtime clarion.
From ancient, fertile Mexico
she inherits passion, grace
to face the world she'll have to face.
Brooding Galicia will provide
aura of mist and hills and sea
(music heard and visions seen
enfold her tightly, tenderly).
As she grows to womanhood
may her stars conspire that she
learn all the old subtleties of mood,
all the tonalities of green.

Dear friends, Evita and José,
cherish this new-born child, this day
of birth and rebirth. Keep her safe.
Teach her to love, as you love, life.
Teach her to be, as you are, free
in this half-prisoned century.

And may Elena's infant charms
bring you boundless joy and make
you happy with her smallest smile;

for you are surrounded by
love of friends as by a cloak,
kept warm by strong, embracing arms,
secure in insecurity.

Long life, true grace upon these three—
this living, human trinity.

September 8, 1949

The Cell

To find it, mold it, plant its density
in the imaginative field—this is his fantasy,
wish-dreamed, wish-remembered, wish-transformed
from wish to actuality like pain.

And now, a thousand wish-stones set in place,
mortared with his longing, aligned with his desire,
he feels the structure is complete, immutable.
And so it is. And so it truly is.

For now the stone is mortar, and the mortar
part of the actual stone; and their circumference
enfolds the dread field in which his fantasy
continuously finds it, molds it, plants . . .

And so it grows.
And so it monstrously grows.

FIRST LOVE AND OTHER POEMS

Lanes of Death and Birth

And in the evening, perilously swathed
in darkness, spirals of light, the warmth
of spring impending—sandalwood and sandals,
shoe to soil restored—we walked again,
as in *our* world's beginning, through a Silence:
buds still held umbilical to tree,
flowers to earth, stars to the magnet sky,
words to the cautious brain.

                    Observe this man
and woman, dabbler in the niceties
of why and how and whence: your quest
will be more fruitful and more comical,
more mirth-inspiring than the measured time
you spend among the numbered guinea-pigs
in a dismal cellar. See, they cry,
their muscles slightly twitch, they talk
or do not talk, they walk upon the earth
and disappear into their muddy holes.

And all the time I wanted to see the Circus.

Pebbles, dislodged, pattered the stream surface
below us—mile or meter? In my hand
her hand the leaning of a child, the tug
of momentary terror, but her eyes
were in me, lending vision to my own.
Low branches, roots across the path, and words
unsaid—we hurtled past them into peace:

peace and the flow of endless waters, peace
and the surety of stone, peace and the glow
of life from the distant city in the heavens,
peace and your image, grown real, grown true.

What you will understand of what I said
or left unsaid, some day, will surely be
not what was in the words or of the words

but in and of the voice and in the mingling
of our voices with the water-voice:
singing—old serfs and peons—

Stenka Razin
dancing around the sombrero of Zapatá—
Christ in Harlem—Old Black Joe in Gaul—
Caesar upon the Mount of Olives—

You
in sunlight on the sand along the gulf-stream
flowing as water flows in the northland, here,
at midnight, past this solid rock, alone.

The water's clean and cold. There are no sharks.
1932

More than Flesh to Fathom

The three gypsies, her skirt, and the tint,
before glow beginning, of her throat's hollow
moved to florescence suddenly, the pulse
passively resounding. And you, did you know
the spectrum ever to forsake us here,
among these darkenings that I shall know,
perhaps, never? For the certainty
eludes me knowingly: nudes on the stair,
the air yellow, the snow unknown, the scythe
complementing plow and sickle, yellow grain
turned black in silhouette against the day.
These and some other things my homage claim
beyond the homage due them.

                    And the rain,
uncorked, suddenly, flowed into my veins,
and I along my skin, parched, dry,
silently cursed the uncontrollable cry,
feeling my body, grown column for the heavens,
strain, and bend, fall silently to sleep:

    Upon the speckled wall there grew
    flowers I could not pluck and grass
    stabbing to touch and limitless
    landscape I could not penetrate.
    Only the sobbing brook, the muddy
    flow of the turgent stream I knew,
    and blindly clutching a twig, I heard
    the thunder curse, the lightning strike
    and cloudbreasts yielding gall and roar
    of animals uncaged.

              Samson,
flabby after too many days of love,
    tugged fiercely at the pillars of his world.

Whose was the warmth and coolness? whose the hand
my fingers clutched amid the treachery

of earth that would not hold me, ground that sagged
and voices that I could not understand?

    Item: the warrior poised, the deck
    trembling upon the waves, the body
    caught for a moment in mid-air. Then
    seaweed. The shark teeth. Peace.

I know, in retrospect, chronology toward oblivion.
But reawaking is pain, is slow.

originally published as "Three Sonnets" in Saturday Review of Literature 1946

At the Moment of Victory

1

At the moment of victory he examines his own heart.
The gun-barrel's cool but the fires still leap
upward from the conquered field, and from his brain
the heat flares in circles and he cannot sleep.
Turbulent and tamed, he remembers those other
countries which are neither victors nor defeated:
those countries of maps and molecules, withered
under neutral sun. Bemedalled and fêted,
he returns to his land-locked starting-point, conscious
he has been well used, like a finely trained stallion.
Now that he's free to graze again, he munches
his cud of applause; but he knows for every million
creatures and men now liberated, other
millions remain under fieldstones, white and smothered.

2

He remembers the fevers, the symptoms of disease.
The electrocardiographic chart records
the preordained murders, the handsome mercenaries
of the corrupt madman and his shrieking words.
And if he is fortunate he will store away
like winter clothes in mothballs the expedient devices:
how to kill with the heel of the hand, and how
to twist the bayonet and throttle dangerous voices.
Devoutly, with all his soul, he hopes—
echoing the diplomats—for a modus vivendi
wherein paths lead peaceward and living shapes
all deeds and words, not only sermons on Sunday.
But the poker chips of profit and of loss,
piled high on the pulpit, hide the preacher's face.

3

He knows, at last, good will is not enough,
complacency a fraud, and that the Golden Rule,
given without measure, can split the deceptive staff
the shepherd leans on, and make of man a tool
in any scoundrel's hand and brain, so finally

he can be shaped to murder or to war:
with all the goodness in the world he soon may be
senseless, corrupted, malevolent as fire—
until the proud boast *Les hommes de bonne volonté*
dies on his chattering lips as he recalls
how all the causes he espoused, existed by,
went singly to their deaths, leaving identical wills
and warnings: without strength and purest purpose they
ask only for betrayal: *Les hommes* sans *volonté*.

1945

FIRST LOVE AND OTHER POEMS

Elegia

written in Los Angeles in 1948 after the Hollywood blacklist was in effect

Madrid Madrid Madrid Madrid
I call your name endlessly, savor it like a lover.
Ten irretrievable years have exploded like bombs   *1938–1948*
since last I saw you, since last I slept
in your arms of tenderness and wounded granite.
Ten years since I touched your face in the sun,
ten years since the homeless Guadarrama winds   *mountains N of Madrid*
moaned like shivering orphans through your veins
and I moaned with them.
                 When I think of you, Madrid,
locked in the bordello of the Universal Pimp,
the blood that rushes to my heart and head
blinds me, and I could strangle your blood-bespattered jailors,
choke them with these two hands which once embraced you.
When I think of your breathing body of vibrancy and sun,
silently I weep, in my own native land
which I love no less because I love you more.
Yet I know, in the heart of my heart, that until your liberation
rings through the world of free men near and far
I must wander like an alien everywhere.

Madrid, in these days of our planet's anguish,
forged by the men whose mock morality
begins and ends with the tape of the stock exchanges,
I too sometimes despair. I weep with your dead young poet.
Like him I curse our age and cite the endless wars,
the exiles, dangers, fears, our weariness
of blood, and blind survival, when so many
homes, wives, even memories, are lost.

Yes, I weep with Garcilaso. I remember
your grave face and your subtle smile
and the heart-leaping beauty of your daughters and even
the tattered elegance of your poorest sons.
I remember the gaiety of your *milicianos*—   *largely untrained volunteer militias*
my comrades-in-arms. What other city
in history ever raised a battalion of barbers
or reared its own young shirt-sleeved generals?

Garcilaso de la Vega (1501–36): soldier-poet, wrote "First Elegy"

And I recall them all. If I ever forget you,
Madrid, Madrid, may my right hand lose its cunning.

I speak to you, Madrid, as lover, husband, son.
Accept this human trinity of passion.
I love you, therefore I am faithful to you
and because to forget you would be to forget
everything I love and value in the world.
Who is not true to you is false to every man
and he to whom your name means nothing never loved
and they who would use your flesh and blood again
as a whore for their wars and their wise investments,
may they be doubly damned! the double murderers
of you and their professed but fictional honor,
of everything untarnished in our time.

Wandering, bitter, in this bitter age,
I dream of your broad avenues like brooks in summer
with your loveliest children alive in them like trout.
In my memory I walk the Calle de Velasquez
to the green Retiro and its green gardens.
Sometimes when I pace the streets of my own city
I am transported to the flowing Alcalá
and my footsteps quicken, I hasten to the spot
where all your living streams meet the Gateway to the Sun.
Sometimes I brood in the shadowed Plaza Mayor
with the ghosts of old Kings and Inquisitors
agitating the balconies with their idiot stares
(which Goya later knew) and under whose stone arches,
those somber rooms beneath the colonnades,
the old watchmaker dreams of tiny, intricate minutes,
the old woman sells pencils and gaudy amber combs,
dreaming of the days when her own body was young,
and the rheumatic peasant with fingers gnarled as grapevines
eagerly displays his muscat raisins;
and the intense boys of ten, with smouldering aged eyes,
kneel, and gravely, quixotically,
polish the rawhide boots of the soldiers in for an hour

from the mined trenches of the Casa de Campo,
from their posts, buzzing with death, within the skeleton
of University City.
                        And the girls stroll by,
the young ones, conscious of their womanhood,
and I hear in my undying heart called Madrid
the soldiers boldly calling to them: Oye, guapa, oye!

I remember your bookshops, the windows always crowded
with new editions of the Gypsy Ballads,
with *Poetas en la España Leal*
and *Romanceros de los Soldados en las Trincheras*.
There was never enough food, but always poetry.
Ah the flood of song that gushed with your blood
into the world during your three years of glory!

And I think: it is a fine thing to be a man
only when man has dignity and manhood.
It is a fine thing to be proud and fearless
only when pride and courage have direction, meaning.
And in our world no prouder words were spoken
in those three agonized years than *I am from Madrid*.

Now ten years have passed with small explosions of hope,
yet you remain, Madrid, the conscience of our lives.
So long as you endure, in chains, in sorrow,
I am not free, no one of us is free.
Any man in the world who does not love Madrid
as he loves a woman, as he values his sex,
that man is less than a man and dangerous,
and so long as he directs the affairs of our world
I must be his undying enemy.

Madrid   Madrid   Madrid   Madrid
Waking and sleeping, your name sings in my heart
and your need fills all my thoughts and acts
(which are gentle but have also been intimate with rifles).
Forgive me, I cannot love you properly from afar—

no distant thing is ever truly loved—
but this, in the wrathful impotence of distance,
I promise: Madrid, if I ever forget you,
may my right hand lose its human cunning,
may my arms and legs wither in their sockets,
may my body be drained of its juices and my brain
go soft and senseless as an imbecile's.
And if I die before I can return to you,
or you, in fullest freedom, are restored to us,
my sons will love you as their father did
Madrid   Madrid   Madrid   [   ]

November 6, 1948

field
flowers
faces

composed in Camp Walters
in Texas in 1943

First Love

battle

Again I am summoned to the eternal field
green with the blood still fresh at the roots of flowers,
green through the dust-rimmed memory of faces
that moved among the trees there for the last time
before the final shock, the glazed eye, the hasty mound.

But why are my thoughts in another country?
Why do I always return to the sunken road through corroded hills,
with the Moorish castle's shadow casting ruins over my shoulder
and the black-smocked girl approaching, her hands laden with grapes?

Spain personified
poetry

I am eager to enter it, eager to end it.
Perhaps this one will be the last one.
And men afterward will study our arms in museums
and nod their heads, and frown, and name the inadequate dates
and stumble with infant tongues over the strange place-names.

But my heart is forever captive of that other war
that taught me first the meaning of peace and of comradeship

Vincent
Sheean

and always I think of my friend who amid the apparition of bombs
saw on the lyric lake the single perfect swan.

1943

special justice of
the Spanish cause ;
moral specificity of a
historical event

Iambic hexameter
Yeats' "Wild Swans at Coole"
"Among School Children"
"Leda and the Swan"

Rolfe drafted in 1943 + sent to Texas to train in an anti-tank battalion

deploys the resources of the medium against the oppressive force of
history (Thurston) —
∴ political poetics

Uncollected and Unpublished Poems, 1937–43

Eyes of a Boy

FOR HILARIO, who stared like this at his divisional com-
mander, Valentín González, before he was killed at the age
of fifteen on a hill near Venta de Campesinos in Septem-
ber 1938.

There is greatness in you, greater than your shoulders
sturdier than a grown tree. There is warmth which my father,
my own father, never had. I like to look at your eyes,
brown, warm, sometimes soft as a woman's,
soft as my mother's, or your heavy-lobed ears
catching each sound in air, whether of rearguard traitor
or enemy boast, whether of plane flying
or bullet whistling or shell shuddering by.

And your beard, your black beard, Barbas! Your face
now arrogant, now soft, now laughing with
a special laughter. There is always a joke being
whispered in your ear, which you never keep to yourself;
the whole world must hear it and share in your mirth.
And your teeth, small and even, now sharp and clean with
the last lusty meal; and your wide mouth moving,
the heavy lips humorous, smiling at your men,
your two young commanders, Merino and Policarpo—
whom you call *My sons*—talking with companions.

It is painful, sometimes, to be young, small, a boy.
I am impatient to grow, to become a man,
big enough to lug the rifle of your faith,
old enough to march alongside you, Campesino,
to be with you in battle. Yet even now, I think,
I'm old enough.

August 25, 1937
Aláládes Henares

1ˢᵗ called "Voice of Spain"

Radio Madrid—1937

Day after day, night on bombarded night,
we walk down Alcalá under the enemy moon,
past the great park, the silent Ministries,
alive within. Day after shell-wracked day,
under the friendly sun that betrays the enemy plane in the sky,
down the wide Alcalá. Under our arms
the precious manuscript, the words that, spoken, are
as million life-giving guns, reaching the world's lost corners;
then into the padded underground room, silent, awaiting the gong,
the recorded flamenco, the sweet guitar: then speech.

Do you, brothers in my own land, listen
at million receivers in a thousand cities?
Do you, friends of my own town, hear
and understand? These words are for you.
For you the description of battles, for you the exhortations
to work, to help us, to understand. Do you,
loved ones, closest of comrades, listen as we speak?
and you, my brother, my dearest friend, my wife?
What do you hear? Four thousand miles is
a distance for giants. Yet we, human,
speak across seas and continents
to you, whose radio anger must
respond, whose airplane answer bring
immediate strength to the weary,
warmth to the chilled bodies
of men huddled in trenches;
to you whose million voices
are flame to the *dinamiteros,*
bullets for our rifles,
truth for our battle's spirit,
death to the beast-face.

And if you listen to our words and answer,
victory is certain, and the bullet of fascists
bewitched. There is a special magic on it
that misses the essential us. But in ours

a magic that finds,
a magic that penetrates
and, penetrating, brings
life with the death it carries.

August 18, 1937
Madrid

Not Hatred

One does not feel hatred,
loading the rifle, firing, reloading,
hearing the empty cartridge shell clatter on stone.
One does not hate
the single visible enemy face two-hundred meters away,
soon to be dead by my bullet.
One feels, not hatred,
only a terrible calm.

One hates
not those men sighting, getting their bead on you.
We might have been, perhaps are, brothers.
One hates
only the single beast-face of fascism.

It is a new feeling, never before known,
to shoot men, taking careful aim,
but not to see them,
only the shadow behind them:
the brute-face, the swastika
that guides their malevolence,
that makes them intolerable,
less than human,
that makes them enemies.

>   August 10, 1937
>   Madrid
>   revised Dec., 1938–Jan., 1939
>   Paris—New York

Paris—Christmas 1938

You will remember, when the bombs
invade your softest midnight dream,
when terror flowing through your limbs
brings madness to your vulnerable room;

you will remember, when you stare at walls
familiar, patterned in a memorized
design, and watch the plaster as it falls,
abrupt, concussive—and you shrink back dazed

and all your body, that a moment past
was quiet, relaxed upon the comforting bed,
will stiffen, flex in fear; a host
of insane images will bring the dead

of many cities back to life again:
the dead you pleasantly ignored, and hid
from self and others; you will clutch the lone
solace of men who soon too will be dead

and count your sins, and know that they were crimes,
and curse your quiet, and respect, at last, these dead;
yes, you will remember—when the initial bombs
insanely fall into *your* life—Madrid.

Dec., 1938–July, 1939
Paris—New York

1st draft written immediately on leaving Spain

context – principled defense of a cause under assault

Brigadas Internacionales

To say *We were right* is not boastful,
nor *We saw, when all others were blind*
nor *We acted, while others ignored or uselessly wept.*

We have the right to say this
because in purest truth it is also recorded:
We died, while others in cowardice looked on.

Just as the man is false who never says *I*
nor asserts his own deeds in pride, or disclaims his wrongs,
so too would we be less than truly what we are

if we did not now, to all the embattled world,
proclaim in pride: *We saw. We acted. Fought.*
We died, while others in cowardice lived on.

November 1939

Munich

Who is unhappiest, the villain or
the coward or the ineffectual saint?

The dreams of Europe's statesmen are befogged but transparent
they float like gray clouds above the neatly-stacked rifles
in a thousand armed forts, over the agonized heads and
tormented eyes in a thousand refugee camps.

Hitler, we know, stares at his eyes in the mirror
nightly; holds out his hands to test their steadiness;
is haunted and spurred by his dreams
wherein a million spectral faces
accuse him; fears to slip in their blood or stumble
over his own spiked words.

The name of Mussolini will be remembered as long as
the barbarous use of a violent cathartic—
his great gift to mankind—is mentioned among men.
He is the perfect bravo, haloed and naked to the waist in snow,
the hair on his chest and arms still black in his sixth decade
as in the most youthful days of his renowned sadism,
as his heart with fear and the intimations of death.

And the gentle, bleeding, suffering soul of Léon Blum
was, and is, their contemporary, but will have nothing to do with them,
abhors them, in fact: his orations defy them.
He deplores and applauds, or condemns and condones.
His life's a testimonial to the manner our century
enshrines and remunerates the simple virtue of impotence.
I clearly remember the day (it was Paris, the climate was pure)
when the tears rolled down from Monsieur Blum's eyes as he spoke to the
    Spanish delegates
in the voice of a grieved, just man:
Gentlemen, I cannot he said. *My hands are tied.*
And with the most elegant gallic gesture of his hands
the word *non-intervention* was given to Spain and to history.

In London, Chamberlain, an old man with the gout
but with body still lean and keen young prep-school eyes,
won heavenly peace for Albion for a few years by emptying
the available wells of Chinese blood, and African, and Spanish,
by strangling the Viennese voices and the laughing streets of Prague.

These are the men our history books will record as
pre-eminent in our own immediate past; who gave
the fourth and fifth decades of our century their unique
character, their unusual object-lesson value.
But there are others who will not be forgotten.
Their faces are still fresh in the newspaper-eye despite
their complete submergence, their several eclipses:
Schuschnigg, who withheld the sign from the underground defenders
beyond the decisive hour, then walked into the lash of
the sealed room across the border. And that other one, whose people
stood armed, ready to fight and die if they must, like the people
of Spain, still holding the Ebro,
but could not utter the simple, single word.
And the cause was lost.
And his people went down, betrayed.

While those others, the minor connivers,
statesmen, envoys, secretive messengers,
blind men, cowards, movers behind the scenes, and saints,
hovered like shadows and stand-ins in the wings:
Runciman   Daladier   Halifax   Bonnet . . .

Repeat the names softly, snivelling,
like the witches wailing, stirring
the vile concoction in the muddy pot:
sotto voce:
Runciman   Daladier   Halifax   Bonnet . . .

Whether the meal settles firmly or not,
whether the wine sends sun or fog
purling through their veins, their sleep
is fitful, broken, eccentric,
full of the stuff of nightmares.

We should not envy them their dreams.
May-August 1939

finished May 1939 but redated to extend
its effective historical testimony

May 1939 - Hitler + Mussolini met
to plan the conquest of Europe

August 22, 1939 - Nazi-Soviet pact

In the Time of Hesitation

What's in the wind? There is no wind.
What's in the air? Dust.
The dust hangs yellow in the stagnant air,
oppressive on the treeless drill-worn fields
where eager boys with ancient eyes
master their manual-of-arms, till soon
instead of group, they call themselves platoon.

Here, under smouldering Texas sun,
summer beginning and training ending,
daily we read the morning headlines,
nightly we turn the dial, listening
for the words that do not come, the deeds
that hang, suspended like dust in air,
over festering *Festung Europa:*
the deeds, millionfold as there are men among us,
but simplest and singular in definition:
some say *invasion,* others *second front.*

And I, one among many, remember
other clouds upon other horizons,
the urgencies of other years and other deeds
which now, so soon, are dust upon the air,
dust wherein the million half-remembered faces
and million haunted eyes accuse without voices,
repeating the agonized question: When? When?

Man's memory is brief, but somewhere, always,
hearts quicken when the word Madrid is spoken
and minds recall its lonely betrayed splendor,
the lost war but the undefeated men
whose hungry flesh became a barricade—
strong, and weak, as steel is strong and weak;
whom treason could not conquer nor hunger weaken
nor bomb nor shell destroy. And now,
imprisoned in the ruins of their immortal city,
their whispers like a huge pulsating wave

beat against the shores of America,
asking: *How soon? How soon?*

Here, on these Texas plains, we simulate
all the innumerable movements of invasion:
down ropes into a hypothetic barge,
from barge to sandy beach, then uphill past
barbed tanglements we cut to let the others by;
then on to the attack. Only combat missing:
actual shell, flesh-mangling bomb, bullet with million eyes.

And I, who have known the muddy embrace of war,
who have lain upon her body of sharpest stone
and trembled with the vast commotion of her passion,
regard these men, my comrades-in-arms, as children
too young to look into her eyes of furious fire,
too innocent to lie in her corrosive arms—
but know how wrong I am when I remember
one hour with her makes men or corpses of us all.
Yes, men or corpses. But Europe cannot wait.
The world cannot wait. And even the Texas plain
will be fertile or scorched, as the war is lost or won.

May 1943

PERMIT

ME

REFUGE

Thomas McGrath

In a time like ours all true poems have to be laments or manifestoes. There have been other such times; but perhaps it is only in ours that the poem has to be both things at once.

Edwin Rolfe grew up in the city, became a radical, was a maker of manifestoes. Later, although he loved the variety of urban life, toward the last he made some poems about its ugliness, its cruelty, the terrible anonymity of its people.

He was not just a writer: he fought for his belief in the Spanish war against Franco and fascism, against real bullet-shooting guns that could kill. He believed that the word must become flesh, that saying and doing must become one.

I think it is one of the finest things about Rolfe that after initial popular successes he moved on to explore more difficult country. This last group of poems shows us bench-marks of that long survey.

I want to bear down on this, because it is an almost impossible thing to overhaul a style, a method of making, after having had some measure of success in it. Yet he refused to repeat the easy successes of an earlier time and fought stubbornly for the way to name the new thing that a degenerate age had created. This brought a new wryness and toughness into some of his poems. He had crossed the cold summit, the height-of-land, had found the best way for his speech.

These poems are the first things in the beginning of his best period. In that sense they are first poems rather than last, though it would be hard to surpass such earlier things as his "Definition," "Elegy for Our Dead," or "First Love."

Rolfe had a gentleness that was shocking. Just the same, there was a lot of iron in him. He was capable of fury and rage. But no malice. He was very good with young writers, although they, lacking a knowledge of the ground of his experiences, usually found it easier to love than to understand him.

He was a *serious* poet—that is to say, he did not believe that one could create a whole corpus of work out of little moral or mock-moral allegories concerning birds and animals, or out of the eccentric learning of pedantic uncles. He was always smelling the real sweat of the terrible Now, the terrible Always. Probably all really good poems have that smell.

So, at the last, you could say that he suffered and he acted. The acting was more than the suffering because he was a revolutionary and, simultaneously, a poet. How hard this is to be, true poets and true revolutionaries may know. At the end he was trying to write that not-quite-yet-written poem which is both lament and triumph. A hard work, and as good a signature as any.

A Dedication

Here, then, the equivocal catch of a long voyage,
part land-, part sea-won; half accident, half choice:

the colors of your fireside spectrum, but arranged,
blended in bolder pattern, sign of their slow sea-change.

And if, all my Penelopes, there's little you recognize,
blame Time, not me; nor strain your sceptic eyes.

It's the world that's altered. Look, and you shall find
my singular faith and all my old companions at my side.

The catch is curious, I grant, but the turbulent seas
of my long and wavering wanderings shaped every heresy.

Outlandish, fragile gifts; but the spirit's more robust
than had I sailed in calmer seas where the tame fish cluster.

Accept them, then, cleansed now of the salt-exiling sea,
proofs of the homeward journey through all those perilous years.

Many an Outcast

Many an outcast calls me friend
   and with that word compels
my pity to embrace his loneliness,
my meagre share of goodness to expand
till friendship and intense
    compassion warm us both.

Many a weakling thinks me strong
   and with his thought endows
my weakness with an unsuspected power,
unearths within my heart a fire
and in my mind an iron
    that was not there before.

Many a fool has called me wise
   and, doing so, has forced
the little sense I had to rise
up from its deep morass of ignorance
clear to the surface, there to solve
    his problems and my own.

And loveless girls have called me *love*.
   These do I most enshrine
because their simple longing builds
love amid lovelessness, and gilds
even the tarnished feelings till they shine—
    yes, theirs and mine.

Bequest

Be proud, young rejoicers, jesters, poets,
of the rich lore of your art, of your sure way
of seeing the heart beating when all others
describe the deceptive skin and the hypocrite eyes.

Tell of the wars but do not forget the dawn's
light on the first squad of sentries: how they see
with wonder the new day's birth and how its light
is meaningful beyond their power to explain.

Neither ignore the seasons, nor their clothes
upon our earth: men remember the grass
and sun and the snow of winters: these remain
always with them, beyond words, even in dream.

Yes, these are the things that live in men longest,
that glow in their sacred moments, that spring to the brain
as seed leaps toward the earth, to grow, to flower
in darkness, to kindle life, always to be reborn.

This is our art, O brother, comrade, friend:
speak of these things always or others will forget them.
The wisest father's best bequest to his son
is his own unwritten work, the words of the poets.

Catalogue of I

When I write I am no longer I alone
but more, much more. Male? American? Yes.
Solely and purely of this century? True,
but insufficient, inexact. I am the arm too
tearing from Paris street the paving stone,
the voice, two centuries old, shouting *Aux barricades!*
the Alicante orphan, the widow in Madrid,
the stunned revived survivor of Stalingrad,
the cotton-clad exile in the caves of loess,
the pueblo-dweller in dry and dying Taos.
And more: I am the pilgrim of every race,
of every age, landing on every shore:
he of the slant eyes, blond hair, black face,
and the galley-slave who fainted on his oar,
and those who die in fields, mines, factories,
more numerous than those who fall in war.
Yet I am he as well: the soldier, the recruit,
he who fights, falls, runs, wins, dies,
and fights again. Not he who causes war
or welcomes, profits by it. I am the everywhere
everyman of the thousand tongues and eyes
and billion always dying deathless brothers.

Who fears inclusion in this catalogue of I
is useless, valueless, deserves to die.
Yet he, my doomed and unloved brother,
is also I, is also I.

November 24, 1948

What Does the Novice Soldier Think

What does the novice soldier think,
 dreaming upon his rifle,
virgin in use as he in war,
 in the time of official peace?
Do his thoughts encompass battles, wounds,
 deaths received and inflicted?
Or is it all a fastidious play
 with the exits and entrances planned?

No, there are no violent breaks in lives,
 not till the final violence
which itself is frequently gentle, too—
 a passing from dream to dream,
subtle, scarcely noticed, if ever;
 remembered only in fragile
fragment—if you are the lucky one,
 ordained to awake in the morning.

Poem

Consciousness, said Don Miguel, *is a disease,*
thus with one huge untruth demolishing
the thousand wisdoms of a jewelled life;
belied his precious broodings, all his
poems of love and loss. Foretold, forefelt
by twenty years the coming of that evil
no-man with his humanless mystique

Consciousness is a disease. The philosophic
cart pulls the nag, destroys the moving beast,
brings death where life was. It is as if
the stranger, lost in the gaunt hills
of a gray uncharted country, heard a wild
amplified shriek upon the air, and then himself
in pain cried out, the echo evoking the cry.

Vincent

The Borinage receded, at last, like a bad dream
although he strained to retain it in his vision.
Like sodden sand, dark and weighted like leaden
reluctance, he watched it slip through the sieve of his hand
and memory; until at length all that remained
was the somber cottage in the somber region,
the room illumined darkly, and the workmen,
with faces smudged by the cold stuff of fire,
eating their sodden roots at the end of a bleak day.

Later, much later, the damp still deep in him,
eating away at the arteries of his burdened brain,
he saw, for the first time, sunlight. And was dazed,
then dazzled out of his darkness. Child of the cold fog,
he fell in love with light, saw how it foamed
in specks and dots and whorls and hurricanes
of brilliant hysteria; and his burning brush
cut fiercely through the cold traditional palette,
exploding into pigment more radiant than sun.

Then, toward the end, mixed madness and self-murder,
killed cold, and coddled forms, killed ways of seeing
object as object. Turned wheatfields into seas,
flowers to forests, faces into fields
of constant, bitter combat; and a small room
into a history more true than any book.

Finally, defeated as all are finally defeated,
severed and sent off the famous ear, preparing
a small symbolic grave prophetic of the last one.

Called, weaker every moment, for help, help!
But no one heard except a penniless brother.
And no help came. What could he do but die
who saw the blazing truth denied, the lie
of coldness wooed, praised in salons, enshrined?

Went down at last. And those—how few—who mourned,
mourned a mad and victorious man,
an undefeated eye.

Now the Fog

Now the fog falls on the land.
Imagination's eyes go blind.
And the smoke, sole residue of written wisdom,
bears poet and prophet to their doom,
their grave, their wavering edgeless tomb.

Knaves masqued like sovereigns decree
what we shall say, listen to, see.
The habit of slavery, long discarded,
becomes our normal comfortable suit.
Soon we will savor the spoiled fruit
as taste-buds wither on nerveless tongues.
The belly will defeat the brain
in combat perfunctory and painless,
and the gutted brain not find it hard
to crawl inside the colorless Pale
of a stamped official registration card.

And this was the land that Ponce found
seeking his lost youth; the land
young mariners, following old stars, set free . . .

The fog falls, settles, seeps into the land
among the despairing, the despised, the blind;
and only rare and blest oases of courage
mark the blurred landscape, lest even the iron
rust—in all of us, agèd and young—
of the English tongue.

1950

Night World

The lovers tremble in the lost night,
their eyes blurred with torment, their lips
glazed with the moon and kisses. They sleep
unquietly, their senses seared with memory.

Outside their bridal catacomb the moon
rides the cloud-stallions, angry, bucking
the vindictive heavens. The moon remembers too
his own treason to the trusting world;

knows that numberless children, still alive,
will deem him enemy, remembering
his guidance of the plummeting plane, and his
betrayal of their slumbers, mothers, dreams.

The lovers shudder among thorns: their eyes
glisten in the dark, till sleep again
bombards their bodies—and a lone dream-misted eye
rides its own beam to the most distant star.

The Glory Set

On receiving the full official set of postage stamps
issued by Greece in 1937. Called "The Glory Set,"
since it memorializes ancient Greece, the stamps
draw upon Hellas' proudest legends.

Dear friend, although the stamps are oddly beautiful,
their irony is even more remarkable.
Their origin in a disordered land
kindles my doubt. I cannot understand
the self-destroying wars my long-loved Greece
persists in, not alone since Pericles
but also (a time I still can tune my lyre on)
the age—it's only yesterday!—of Byron.
No matter. Thank you for the gift and, far above it
by peaks of feeling, the affection of it,
knowing affection oftentimes transcends
the fabulous births, the sad and absurd ends
of noblest nations and of dearest friends.

Between these engravings and the Golden Age,
between the artist and his diminutive page,
a Stygian river rages, its tide afoam
with night, and blood, and unrepentant Time:
two long millennia, unrecoverable
in men's imaginings, or art, or will.
These miniatures, that bear the simplest speech
of simple men to points beyond their reach,
confuse us with their beauty, as a gun's
bullet, though small, cuts off all whirling suns
from a soldier's dying vision. Too late
these tributes flower from a desert state
that once was green in man's first blossoming,
when Æschylus and his chorus mimed and sang
the tragic ways of man, his flesh and bone,
and Phidias unlocked the secret of all stone.

Now, though this copied beauty still amazes,
it's coined by politicians, not by muses
who long ago abandoned this rocky, arid
peninsula for pleasanter lands, and married
peoples less obsessed with ancient Greats,
who challenge the living, not the moribund Fates,
to carve from harsher elements the contours
of breathing beasts, not legendary centaurs;
who break the dead-hand grip of fabled glory
and, pulses passionate, create a hardier story
wherein our own tangential visions can
turn all dead gods to living, acting men.

Mystery

The corpse is in the central square, in the spring sun.
The hilts of two jewelled daggers tremble on her breasts.
The blood is cold, corked, on her black and rigid nipples.
Her face in death is beautiful. She has obviously been raped.

Around her walk the busy men, their heads filled with figures.
The women go by with their empty baskets, obsessed with menus,
with many mouths, with the ancient alchemy of mothers
transmuting lead to gold and coppers into bread.

Only the pigeons and the anarchic children hover around her,
the doves bemoaning the death and the child-eyes grave
on the casual brutal bier. All others hurry past.
The sight is familiar as dust in the city air.

Somewhere, it is assumed, an invisible detective
broods darkly in a dark room, his black shoes on the desk,
assuring and reassuring no one in particular
with slow words and fumbling words, in the ritual of despair:

"Sooner or later, mark my word, we'll identify the woman,
and from that to finding the killer is just a small step . . ."
Only the children stand silent, and stare, stare
at the broken body, the lifeless face, the living opulent hair.

All Ghouls' Night

Goaded by outraged Soul,
   Conscience conspired
to kill the two-faced Ghoul
   both of them feared.

Compounded of deceit
   and avarice and horror,
shrieking *I am the state,*
   Ghoul unleashed his terror,

destroyed all loveliness.
   Instead seals agony
on Soul's astonished face
   and anguished body.

Now, as the girl expires,
   Repeat after me, Ghoul
prompts, *and walk through fire*
   to save yourself, damned Soul.

And stricken Soul, complying,
   turned to Truth and said:
Though my actual beauty dies,
   this sacrificial deed

love always, for my death,
   though cruel, is pure,
and my expiring breath
   kindles a cleaner fire

in which some day all Ghouls
   themselves will turn
on sulphurous spits and foul,
   and only Lies will burn.

July 26, 1951

Mystery II

Unlike the neat dénouement in the popular novel,
the mystery is never adequately explained:
why the lad with the brilliant I.Q. ended up in a hovel;
why, when the lovers set out on their picnic, it suddenly, brutally rained.

And the sold-out innocent can never understand
how the Fates, that conspired against him, that turned him into a sot,
were simply the normal doing of his best, his truest friend
who, promising all things faithfully, quite naturally forgot.

The final chapter, as usual, long-looked-forward-to,
is strangely, predictably ripped from the overweight book—
so what can we, dear frustrated readers, think or do
who invariably find the richest prize in the hands of the crook,

the lovely virgin with the dazzling hair won by the diseased roué,
and all our golden Tomorrows wrecked on the boneyard of Today?

PERMIT ME REFUGE *1ˢᵗ published in 1954 in the California Quarterly*

In Praise Of

To understand the strength of those dark forces *a*
phalanxed against him would have spelled surrender: *b*
the spiked fist, the assassin's knife, the horses' *a*
eyeless hooves above as he fell under. *b*
To understand the sum of all this terror *c*
would *a priori* have meant defeat, disaster. *d*
Born of cold panic, error would pile on error, *c*
heart and mind fall apart like fragile plaster. *d*

Therefore I honor him, this simple man *e*
who never clearly saw the threatening shapes, yet fought *f*
his complex enemies, the whole sadistic clan, *e*
persistently, although unschooled. Untaught, *f*
he taught us, who could talk so glibly, what *g*
the world's true shape should be like, and what not. *f*

menace of postwar anti-Communist paranoia + the only strategy left to fight it: stubborn unreflective resistance in May 1952, Rolfe turned on the radio + learned that his friend the playwright Clifford Odets had just betrayed himself + his friends by testifying before HUAC   224

PERMIT ME REFUGE

1st called "Ballad of the Lost friend"

Ballad of the Noble Intentions

What will you do, my brother, my friend,
    when they summon you to their inquisition?
I'll fire from the heart of my fortress, my brain,
    my proudest possession.

And what will you say, my brother, my friend,
    when they threaten your family's food instead?
Like Christ, I'll be silent. Man does not live
    only by work or by bread.

I will think of the poets who fashioned my mind,
    of the singing strokes of my vivid Old Masters,
of the meaning of my own works. These outweigh
    all minor disasters.

And what if your treasures are trampled by swine?
    What if they foul your art and your science?
I'll answer with anger, go down, if I must,
    hurling pearls of defiance.

I will answer with anger, speak up with passion,
    defy them again with my famed indignation.
But what if they babble of danger, and cite
    the imperilled nation?

For it's *they* who imperil our country, my friend,
    they are the worms at the core of the matter.
How will you answer their glib accusations,
    their hypocrite chatter?

I've only contempt for these cloven-tongued men,
    these pack-rats that roam our land in committees
with their claques and their clatter, spreading their lies
    through our sleeping cities.

I will stand like an oak in maturity, like
    a craft of fine timber against the sea's fury.
But what if these little men posture and act
    as both judge and jury?

I'll read them bold pages from Areopagitica,
  quote Milton and Marvell to rout and abuse them.
The best words of men of all ages will rise
  to my tongue to confuse them!

* * *

And what did you do, dear brother, dear friend,
  when you stood at last in the pygmies' forum?
I spoke with good sense, old friend, I talked with
  restraint and decorum.

I decided that boasting like Milton were vain,
  or refusing, like Marvell, their guineas with anger.
I patterned myself after Waller, who lived
  more richly—certainly longer.

I engaged them in skilful debate, since I felt
  that mere youthful defiance was unrealistic.
I told what I knew, or I thought, to be true;
  it was harmless, anachronistic.

And what did you say, dear brother, old friend?
  What were the truths you hastened to utter?
Not words—just a disinterred corpse from a grave,
  on a neutral platter.

And there were some living men too that I named.
  What harm could it do them, after two decades?
Besides, as I've reason to know, it was all—
  after all—in the records.

Just look at the transcript, dear brother, dear friend.
  Is there anything in it to make a man shudder?
Is there anything there to make anyone think
  that I've lost my rudder?

judgment

No, nothing at all, dear stranger, lost friend,
    nothing to move me to grief or to mourning.
It's yourself you betrayed, it's yourself who lives on
    as a living warning.

Your act of survival betrayed *not* your friends,
    but yourself most of all—no need now to cavil.
Live on, as you must, but be happy with Waller,
    not Milton, or Marvell.

For you've toppled the bridges you had with your youth,
    your promising present and excellent future.
No masterpiece ever can heal such a wound, nor
    a surgeon's suture.

You killed your own scope, sad stranger, lost friend.
    My affection is dead; it's too frayed now, and grieving.
And *that* was your crime; in the noon of your life
    you resigned from the living.

                                                    1952

Idiot Joe Prays in Pershing Square and Gets Hauled in for Vagrancy

Let us praise,
while time to praise remains,
the simple bullet,
the antique ambuscade
and the fanatic justice-crazed assassin—
we who have made
and used napalm
and casually—
alone among all men—
dropped on Man
the only atom bomb.

On Rico LeBrun's Crucifixion

Caged in the carnal canvas like a sea
enclosed in gunboats by the metalled man,
it writhes, groans, pivots on its axis
like Christ, His formal cakewalk up to Calvary.

And all the false-faced followers, who cry
"Save our Saviour!" spin on their webbed feet,
mimicking cries of mercy, but their eyes,
blinded with clarity, are hard, are dry.

The flaming arms grope skyward, and the sky
plummets to lowest mankind, asking What?
Be true? Be lizard? Be like Pavlov's rat
beating your brains against the iron door?

Or like ennobled man, defile, betray
your inmost image.
           And befoul
the rare jewels that millennia bear up.
                    1951

After Tu Fu (A.D. 713–770)

The innocents were condemned to death in the Hall of Justice.
In the Hall of Peace, the war was declared.
In the name of Mercy, the bomb was dropped on the two cities.
O my maimed brothers, beloved stricken brothers,
dig deep again in the great caves of the East:
again our wise men talk in the Hall of Peace.

Kill the Umpire!

He's the infallible man:
calm, caller of balls and strikes,
hits and errors, fair and foul.
He tells us when we're safe or out.

Each of us desires his favor.
Each has his enemy, his chosen side.
We need not only the big battalions
of bats, but also the aid of God.

And he *is* God. We worship him when
his word delights our partisan eyes.
But when his justice moves the other way
we rage, we fume, we shout for his blood.
We would follow him home, if we could, through swarming
streets, through alleys, suburbs, country lanes,
creep up on him from behind and kill him—bang!—
with a pop-bottle. We always kill God.

But since we cannot reach him, we're content
to murder him in our thoughts, to shout
Unfair, unfair! Buy him a pair of glasses!
He's blind as a bat!
                    But the game goes on
according to its rules, which he upholds
by eye, by arm, by his called decision.

Each game has its own peculiar laws
and each its own direction, history;
and he who calls the critical turns
is a lonely man, a man without a country,
a prophet without honor in his own land.

We who sit in the grandstand, watching
the home team lose the heart-breaking close ones,
revile him, damn him—the solitary man—
stare at him, dressed in black like a judge,
his face encased in the steel-wired mask,
the eyes behind it steady, wise;

fearing, knowing the outcome, yet
powerless to prevent the sure defeat.

We sit and watch in outraged silence.
We hate him because whatever he says is true.

And If You Don't See What You Want, Ask for It

What is he saying? What is the Madman saying
whose voice cuts through the night of stars and cells?
I hear the words but I do not understand.
I do not, can not, will not ever understand.

Back where you come from! the Sane Man says.
All right, I'm going, says the Hurt Man.
Enraged, the Sane Man locked him in a cell.
And I, the invisible listener, the Bystander, go mad.

We hold these truths, the Sane Man says.
His meaning's simple, obvious. But no,
to hold is not enough, these truths must be locked
in the same small cell with Him Who Comes From.

If you don't like it here go back where you came from!
The voice was vicious, the tongue was fury.
I tried. But I failed. The border was closed.
Only my father had entry there
with his dual eternal citizenship. Not I.

PERMIT ME REFUGE

Political Prisoner 123456789

Serial accumulation of victims
obliteration of individual differences
interchangeability of their suffering

I heard this man called traitor, I saw him shamed
before his friends, forsaken by companions;
his wealth and worth destroyed, his picture in the papers,
the caption cautioning "Beware, this man's an enemy."
His age, description given, his children named, his wife
mentioned profanely, his private habits exposed;
the walls of his few rooms torn wide for all to see,
the walls of his life's efforts crumbling, broken—

—yet knew the deed was a lie, the accusations false,
the men whose mouths uttered them not fit to tread
the same earth he walked, nor able to oppose him
by other means than falsehood. They lied to save themselves.
This man is still my friend. And thousands more,
in their truest thoughts and acts, daily do him honor.

Nelson told that Rolfe had in mind the Hollywood Ten
one of them [#10], the screenwriter Edward Dmytryk,
recanted + cooperated w/ HUAC

A Poem to Delight My Friends
Who Laugh at Science-Fiction

That was the year
the small birds in their frail and delicate battalions
committed suicide against the Empire State,
having, in some never-explained manner,
lost their aerial radar, or ignored it.

That was the year
men and women everywhere stopped dying natural deaths.
The agèd, facing sleep, took poison;
the infant, facing life, died with the mother in childbirth;
and the whole wild remainder of the population,
despairing but deliberate, crashed in auto accidents
on roads as clear and uncluttered as ponds.

That was the year every ship on every ocean,
every lake, harbor, river, vanished without trace;
and even ships docked at quays
turned over like harpooned whales, or wounded Normandies.

Yes, and the civilian transcontinental planes
found, like the war-planes, the sky-lanes crowded
and, praising Icarus, plunged to earth in flames.

Many, mild stay-at-homes, slipped in bath tubs,
others, congenital indoors-men, descending stairs,
and some, irrepressible roisterers, playing musical chairs.
Tots fell from scooter cars and tricycles
and casual passersby were stabbed by falling icicles.

Ah, what carnage! It was reported
that even bicarb and aspirin turned fatal,
and seconal too, to those with mild headaches,
whose stomachs were slightly acid, or who found they could not sleep.
All lovers died in bed, as all seafarers on the deep.

Till finally the only people left alive
were the soldiers sullenly spread on battlefields

among the shell-pocked hills and the charred trees.
Thus, even the indispensable wars died of ennui.

But not the expendable conscripts: they remained as always.
However, since no transport was available anywhere,
and home, in any case, was dead, and bare,
the soldiers wandered eternally
in their dazed, early-Chirico landscapes,
like drunken stars in their shrinking orbits
round and round and round and round

and (since I too died in the world-wide suicide)
they may still, for all I know, be there.
Like forsaken chessmen abandoned by paralyzed players.
they may still be there,
may still be there.

A Hunter Went Killing: A Fable

The small birds flew from tree to tree
  at the shore of the blue lake far below.
Cold was the day; and singing, free,
the swallows darted from tree to tree.

Small, insignificant creatures, they
  played in the green leaves carelessly,
swift as all life is. Cold was the day,
perfect for song and flight and play.

A hunter strode to the lake's shore,
  sighted his gun toward the sky, and fired.
Some birds fled crying, and many more
lay bleeding on the blue lake's shore.

The hunter stood at the edge of the water
  and fired and reloaded ceaselessly.
Tears fell from his eyes beside the water—
from the smoke? the cold? the small birds' slaughter?

Said one bird to another: "Look! He cries
  as he fires his firearm endlessly.
The tears run streaming from his eyes
each time a wingèd brother dies."

The other replied to his merciful friend:
  "Never mind his eyes, nor his flowing tears.
Think of sky, not the earth where the hunter stands.
Don't pity his weeping. Watch his hands."

January 13, 1953

Bal Masqué

Look: between life and death hovers
the singular rose with wavering petals.
And the manic eyes—twin tarnished mirrors
where all our raving wishes are betrayed—
glare like a beast's upon our garden.
Then, then only, the brass gong sends
its fearsome invitation to the world,
vibrating, its sound sonorous and tomblike,
its decorous siren sedately clamorous,
demanding the pleasure of all our presences—
from womb to grave—at the Gala Event.

And we line up like living puppets
carved in a crazed alchemist's dungeon
and colored with his mad imaginings;
line up like children awaiting the terror
of the giant stranger's question, or those
small dwellers in the morbid glen.
Invisible strings tug at our fingers,
pull at our feet, demanding Home,
but the eyes of the palace wink and glitter,
the eyes of the palace drop tears of smoke;
and, rooted, we stand; protesting, are drawn in.

A thousand chambers welcome us,
divest us of our odd superfluities:
the heart that finds its beat inside a kiss,
the flesh where major minor clash,
the bone, the muscle and the cartilage
that shape the weeds and flowers of the brain,
the brooding brain itself; till we are left
like exquisite toy dolls whose eyes
blink open and shut, whose manufactured mouths
seek the stone nipple, whose supple fingers
grasp—but inside is sawdust emptiness.

Fabulously gowned now, all of us
advance in broken rhythm to the ballroom

from whose huge dome the candelabra aim
small suns of light upon our formal heads;
whose corners gleam like lighted continents
where privacy is publicly outlawed,
where to think secret thoughts is to outrage
the big Band Leader on the tallest stage;
where even an innocent unguarded eye
means sudden expulsion, the culprit sent,
clutching his emptiness, to banishment.

Nothing is casual here. We stand
in preordained spots like artificial flowers
whose petals fear no winds, whose bloom
is death disguised in the colors of life.
The spotless tables groan with fruit,
waxen and vivid, with hollow centers.
Scattered among them, cleverly concealed,
the true and living apples gleam;
but no sign warns the color-dazzled eye
or the thirsty tongue that the Old Witch
has poisoned them all with a subtle venom.

Yet even the drop of poison must await
its proper, precisely-calculated moment.
Meanwhile, the stately music starts
with oboe, horn, a flight of flutes
like infant birds toward the chandelier
whose lights like a million dervishes
spin on their crystal axes, whirl
reflection of the flute-like birds
like shining bullets through the crowded hall
until they pierce, all uncontrolled at last,
each gowned, elaborate and empty breast.

The wound is the magic signal to begin.
Thus tapped, each rigid dancer moves
her tapering limbs, his trembling fingers.
The heart would beat, if there were a heart,
and breathing, if there were breath, sigh out

with pleasure if it knew what pleasure was.
But since this ballroom is unique,
heart and breath and pleasure hang
on the silent music, the motionless baton,
the rigid poise of the dancers, whose eyes
are drained of sight, whose ears of sound.

Now, between life and death, between
the petals of the singular rose,
the dancers cross and intermingle, move
at last in a parody of passion.
The formal minuet separates
the formal sexes, and they stir like leaves
bent suppliant by a formal wind.
And then the intoxicated strings
stagger, break in upon the gentle reeds;
the minuet disintegrates
to waltz as the drunken violin sings.

Soon, violently—though nothing really moves
except the poisoned crystal darts—
the brass invades the reeds and strings,
the waltz gives way to jazz, to bop,
to palsied shimmy, to the lindy hop,
then slides, with skirts askew and eyes
vacant and glazed, into the Big Apple.
The palace hall becomes a jumping joint,
the eyes of the palace weep tears of smoke,
and nobody, no, not even the nameless dancers,
nobody gives his right name, no!

But the big Band Leader knows us all,
sees through the subtle masquerade
the lie of each elaborate disguise.
His penetrating eye uncovers
the curled claw in the lover's stroking hand,
the larcenous mote in the honest man's eye,
the hero's heart, where fear and panic lie
below the sleep-filmed surface of his dream,

and all the self-seeking calculations,
the intricate add-subtract machinery
behind all gifts, all human charity.

Knows more: knows where the small bones lie
of buried error, and the infancy
of all our polished, self-deluding lusts;
knows where desire is habit, habit chore,
chore monstrous, and where hidden infamous
wishes ride their uncoiled worms
to the foul nest and center of decay;
knows where the small arterial wall
thickens, a river bank choked with silt
and slimy twigs and rotting weeds—
the throttling fingers round our pulsing needs.

The eye, all seeing, disregards
the medals, honors, all the bright awards
bestowed by coward on his fellow-coward,
by butcher on his fellow-slaughterer
in the world's vast and bleeding abbatoir;
seeks out the sounds and feelings of our lives,
casts the true eye of understanding on
all words, all symbols and all notes of music
and recognizes all who live by them:
those to whom they are pure delight
and those who use them consciously to frighten.

Yet over us all a private angel hovers,
a Persian amulet, a talisman of love,
a lucky horseshoe, a treasured silver dollar
we will not spend although we starve.
But the dollar is often lost, the talisman
misplaced like an urgent self-reminder note;
and the amulet can betray its wearer
to the enemy eye, the enemy dagger.
In the same way, the private angel
plays tricks, plays false, at last betrays us,
plays Iago to our agonized Othello.

Conscript's Song

On this cold mercenary hill
my heart is numb, my brain is shrill,

cursing the cause that brought me here
to manic war, to panic fear.

Companions to my left and right
dig in, but have no will to fight.

Like white worms on the frozen ground
Our minds churn in a sad-go-round.

We dream of childhood longingly
who never shall know posterity

but strangle, strung upon the last
link to our own most savage past.

Words Found on a Cave's Wall

The time came, at last, when only two things had meaning:
friendship, for compassion; consolation, for love;
the time when only harshest animal warmth
kept us, and our hope, alive in the dark caves
of the soul's winter.

For they, who had the strength
to kill all thought, all spirit, with their savage scalpels,
went mad with their own power's impotence
against our fragile flowering granite. And how better
kill an idea than crush the inseparable flesh
which is its womb, its cradle, and its soil?

Nevertheless we endured in the long darkness,
sharing our warmth and our desperate hopes
in the mole-tunnels of our catacombs;
yet never, quite, amid despair,
never quite lost the fertilizing hope
nor surrendered the clear and kindling idea
that shone serene as candle-light in the gathering gloom,
that some day all false idols would be shattered,
all repressions lifted, all
the cudgel-wielders fall under the double weight
of our steadfastness and their savagery.

The year, dear never-to-be-known stranger,
is not, alas, the year that you read this.
It is three centuries and a decade
since the death of Him Whom they will not acknowledge.
The place is Rome. The Emperor's Constantine.
The catacombs we live in, and die in, are real.
And these farewell words, unborn reader, friend perhaps,
are both our epitaph and prophecy.

September 20, 1950

Still Must I Love You

Still must I love you, though you have grown remote.
Through leagues of unseen barriers I must feel
always your body near my own and steal
the fugitive solace of your face, your throat
trembling with your breathing, your gleaming hair
imprisoning the sun at morning and your eyes
opening brightly to meet the kindling skies,
alive to the day, expectant, keen, aware . . .
and many times, for moments, have I found you again:
in every girl whose body I have taken
on nights of solitude, in festivals
when your image—only—comes to life. Even then
invariably I wake to hear the immediate bells
ringing like mad in a mad world, cracked and shaken.

Manuela

Lovelier than the river in the spring
Manuela walks, her body flowing by . . .

Ageless she is, and cageless: she is only
music and sky, flowers and wine, the deep
feel of dark shimmering water at my thigh.

Her face at midnight is all life; at dawn
the sunlight makes a prison of her hair,
her brow, her throat, and all that's hidden; then
I enter her, an eager prisoner.

The convict of the night returns to her.

I could lie still in wonder at her side
but her breathing and the wind that stirs her hair
make my hands jealous, restless, and my body
loses its calm, and I must waken her.

After the storm Manuela sleeps again.
Her body is a haven and a fire,
lovely as autumn on the nearby hills.

I have no need of her now: she is only
music and bread, flowers and earth, the dark
feel of deep murmuring water at my thigh.

Lovelier than the river in the fall
Manuela walks, her body flowing by . . .

Undersea Poem

A word unearths the hidden dream,
draws its essence up from the morass
where it lies gleaming like a drowned jewel
for the living hand, man's lyric touch.

A chance gesture fills all the emptiness
around the jewelled but unfound idea:
a dim sound, a chime of sudden music,
or the fancied glint in a girl's eye.

A stray shadow on the chamber wall
before sleep-misted eyes, or a casual
light in the street or, in the sky,
a passing, unknowable brilliancy.

And all, all, like the touch of the vivid hand,
retrieve the stray fugitive, plumb the well
where the drowned child lies lost, its words
unspoken, in its unsuspected hell.

August 15, 1949

Dawn Song

The dusk of dawn, the prophet called it:
that birth-hush of gray when from the eastern sky
the colors spill and spread as from a careless
primitive's palette; and overhead
the trees whose invisible branches moaned the whole night long
leap suddenly to green;
and greenest, purest song
bursts forth from the frail throats
of delicate birds. Alas, too soon, too late
the dawn comes on
and wakes the sleeping world
and breaks on me.

But I, its sole insomniac, in a drugged trance,
having reversed the old inheritance
of prehistoric ancestors, cry out
with pallid joy;
and find myself, a modern mariner,
becalmed in the clamorous morning.
Unlike those savages
who dragged themselves to darkest holes to die,
I long to die in daylight. And to this desire
all night in travail I fight the windmill pain
of breathing, living, of my treasonous heart
that pounds the blood like lacerating drums
through the dark deltas of my arteries
and brain. At last it comes,
too late, too soon, the dawn:
and wakes all life and calms me into sleep.

At my small window
the violet glows, and the invading gold
startles my room with coldest sun. Outside,
across the avenue as narrow as a shroud,
the memorized landscape wakes anew.
A lone sparrow sings a raucous madrigal
from his red podium; then, flying, soars
the sudden sky of day, graceful, aflight,

a stone's throw distant, but with no thought of stone,
no consciousness of anything but dawn,
a bird's dawn, wherein no human thought
or pain or joy or waking plays a part,
nor of this heart that, with its world
of friends and loves and acts and memories,
pounds on toward certain doom.

The dawn comes with its birds and forebodings,
wakes all the sleeping world in a fever of trembling.
I rise from bed, force the granite from my chest.
We argue, body and myself, for mastery,
and I know we are all on the brink of a smiling, delicate disaster.
Nevertheless I bathe, I dress, I smile at my wife,
do all the expected things, in the early dawn,
as I hear the beating wings swoop down
on all the world; and take my vitamin pill
and pretend I see no ends, only beginnings,
and that all is undoubtedly right,
all's magically well.

Bon Voyage

Permit me refuge in a region of your brain:
carry and resurrect me, whatever path you take,
as a ship creates its own unending wake
or as rails define direction in a train.

Permit my memory refuge: but not the recent years
when grains of dross obscured the bars of truth.
Delve deeper back in years to your first youth,
passionate, clean, untarnished by small fears.

And if your conscience truly bears my memory,
rekindle if you can the dying candle-light:
let the wake not lose its contour, nor the bright
reflected sun waver as the rails glide by.

My wake and rail attend you, welded and wed,
through the blind tunnels of the years ahead.

Uncollected and
Unpublished Poems,
1947–54

Exodus 1947

Midnight, moonlight, most ancient of all seas:
In the heavens, the turbulence of Greco's dreams,
Below, the hull groans, strains, and plows ahead,
The soothing water slaps the steel in innocence.
Imagine the scene: an old ship in an old night
riding the waves of an ancient sea,
carrying an ancient people to an ancient land.

Deep in the vessel's heart, the engines throb
and the hearts of the living cargo throb in sleep,
The night is full of sounds: sounds of breathing,
of dreams of death, of nightmare; all the muted sounds
of a city at midnight. But this city is afloat,
men, women, children, old grandfathers; and all,
all, even the babes in arms, are ancient mariners.

And no light anywhere, for this is an enemy sea.

Blues

Got a two-handed woman, she loves me night and day
got a two-handed woman, loves me all the way
If she ever up and left me, don't know what I'd do or say.

Got a two-breasted woman, tastes as sweet as bread,
got a real hilly woman, sweet as fresh made bread,
If she ever up and left me, I'd feel that I'd gone dead.

Got a two-legged woman, god those legs are sweet.
got a two-legged woman, live and long and neat,
She breathes from her hips to her knees right down to her feet.

Got a two hipped woman, big as the wide earth,
got a two hipped woman, big as the wide earth,
When I hold them in my hands, I feel it's my own true birth.

She's only got one trouble, know it when we go to bed,
Yes, just only one trouble, bothers me when we're in bed,
She's got two of everything, she's also got two heads.

Yes, my two-headed woman, watches me fore and aft,
my big two-headed woman, watches me fore and aft,
If it wasn't for the rest of her, I'd sure go daft.

My friends say she's a monster, call her mighty queer,
they call her a monster, call her mighty queer,
but they never bedded with her, my own true woman and dear.

So my own advice to lovers, here and everywhere,
my true advice to lovers, here and everywhere,
Is make a virtue of misfortune, always call your own love fair.

The Poisoned Air Befouled
the Whole Decade

The poisoned air befouled the whole decade,
corrupting even those whose childhood vision
contained no hint of bomb or nuclear fission,
backed them against walls, cowering, afraid.

Even the purest in heart were daily bombarded
with the subtlest lies and slanders, so that at last
the grip of their fingers slipped from the main mast
of their lives' integrity; and, shoddily rewarded
with glasses to squint through, sticks to lean upon,
soiled coins to buy their bogus luxuries,
they tottered, well-fed hirelings, to the grave.

Knowing this, I choose fondly to remember one
who, victim like the others, nevertheless gave
no quarter to the blackguards and their infamies;
held up his wounded face, looked through his pierced eyes,
saying, Truth is everywhere truth, lies always lies.

September 30, 1949

Are You Now or
Have You Ever Been

I admit it: there was a moment of pity
a vulnerable second of sympathy
my defenses were down
and I signed the letter asking clemency
for the six Negroes the letter
hereinafter known as Exhibit A

I signed the letter yes
the signature is indubitably mine
and later this at another time
I wrote a small check yes small
since my income is small
perhaps ten dollars not more
for the fund these people were collecting
to keep the refugees alive

and then again in a moment of weakness
I promised and kept my promise
to join the demonstration at the city hall
protesting the raising of rents
no you needn't show me the photograph
I was there I admit I was there

but please   believe me
everything I did was done through weakness if you will
but it's strange how weakness of this kind snowballs
multiplies
before they approached me with that innocent petition
I was may it please the court exactly
like you like every other man
I lived my own life solely suffered
only my own sorrows and enjoyed my own triumphs
small ones I grant you
asked nothing from
gave nothing to
any man
except myself my wife my children

so there you have it
it is all true
Exhibits A and B and C
and the witnesses don't lie
I wanted to help those six men stay alive
I thought them innocent
I honestly believed the rents were too high
(no, I own no tenements)
and the anguish of the refugees starving far from home
moved me I admit more than it should have
perhaps because I still retain
a fleeting childhood picture of my great grandfather's face
he too was a refugee

Letter

Dear wife after less than half an hour
of simple questions and answers
the grand jury indicted me
they even had photostats of my cancelled checks
photostats of my signatures
photographs of me among others
in that demonstration at the city hall.
So now I suppose I shall have to stand trial
what the outcome will be I cannot say.
To say I am bewildered by what has happened
is to understate it. Nevertheless
my confusion is less now than when the hearing started.
Now, before I return
there are a few things I would like you to do:
first, cancel our checking account
(from now on when I give I'll give in cash
and the bank can not, I see now, be trusted).
Second, send the children up to Jim's
in the country until this blows over;
I don't want them to face the cruelty
of their classmates, possibly even their teachers.
And third—and this is most important—
find out who those people were—
the people who asked me to sign that letter,
who asked me for that small contribution,
who prompted me to join the demonstration.
By the time I return
I want to know them better
I have lots of questions to ask
many things to find out
and they're the ones I have a hunch
who can tell me everything I want to know.

Poem

The girl lashed to the stake
and the figures around the pyramid
of faggots and horror are weirdly alike
in the seething glow of the fire.
The one on the stake writhes in agony of pain,
the others in agony of obscene pleasure.
One burns in her flesh,
the others in flesh-lust.
One loses, horribly, her life;
the others   everything except their lives.

"Witch! Witch! Witch!" shouts the circle of frenzied faces
at the burning woman on the stake,
past loneliness, past agony, past everything.
The repeated word is a roll call of those present,
naming not her on the stake
(nor Him on the Cross)
but themselves.

Malibu
August 29, 1949

A Letter to the Denouncers

Dear sir: the summum bonum is
Solvency, which sufficiently defined most simply means
Spuds in sufficient quantities,
an untapped phone, and daily pork and beans.

Sir, as you start for work each morning, please
check your clothes-closet for skeletons,
your dreams for inconsistencies,
the radio in your car for microphones.

This too remember: old man, tired man, fool,
after their final sessions with their analysts,
shape all their Methods to one glowing Goal—
Safety. And so they draw up lists.

And *what* lists! One, born of maliciousness,
another of envy, a third of gratitude—
name first the friend who straightened out their mess,
then him who found them work, and self-respect, and bread.

Naturally they're honest; they've merely changed their views.
They flinch before the paradox of Means and Ends.
So, hating dubious Means, each casually betrays
his benefactors, boon-companions, friends.

A crazy crowd applauds these eager choristers
who sing as wingless birds have never sung before.
But you, dear friendless friends, dear lonely sirs,
recall whom *you*'ve befriended, and beware, beware.

1949 (After Reading a News Item)

His first official act was to bless
The planes that bombed their Barcelona home.
Ten years have passed. Today his Holiness
Welcomes the Catalan orphans into Rome.

June 19, 1953

This court, supreme in blindness and in hate,
supremely flaunts its lickspittle estate;
kills Jews today, as twenty-five years ago,
it killed Italians.

Pastoral—1954

Who used to lie with his love
    In the glade, far from the battle-sector,
    Now lies embraced by a lie-detector
And can not, dare not, move.

Ballad

What are we having for dinner tonight?
Whom are we having for dinner tonight?
    Raw nerve ends on toast
    Pickled cops' feet
    Suckling pig with a gag in its mouth
    And no talk—its ears are wired for sound.

Little Ballad for Americans—1954

Brother, brother, best avoid your workmate—
Words planted in affection can spout a field of hate.

Housewife, housewife, never trust your neighbor—
A chance remark may boomerang to five years at hard labor.

Student, student, keep mouth shut and brain spry—
Your best friend Dick Merriwell's employed by the F.B.I.

Lady, lady, make your phone calls frugal—
The chief of all Inquisitors has ruled the wire-tap legal.

Daughter, daughter, learn soon your heart to harden—
They've planted stoolies everywhere; why not in kindergarten?

Lovers, lovers, be careful when you're wed—
The wire-tap grows in living-room, in auto, and in bed.

Give full allegiance only to circuses and bread;
No person's really trustworthy until he's dead.

Early Poems

Where Buildings Congregate

In winter you have
forms   shapeless   draped
on radiators   flesh melting
sweating grease

Others   in bulk
roast on kitchen stoves

I know one form
stripped to white bone
who has known these
yet will survive all winters.

May Day Song

We have slept too long. 'Tis time now to awaken.
   Let us rouse ourselves and shed no futile tears.
We have slept too long; by now we must have shaken
   Free from our minds the lethargy of years.

We have been weak. Now we must gather courage,
   Courage to shatter the false democracies,
Courage to shout our song to greet the new age,
   Courage to bury the old, dead centuries.

Let us rise boldly, fresh with right and power,
   Hot with the strength that knowledge of truth brings.
Raise the red banner, for quickly comes the hour
   That means the end of financiers and kings.

We must be tough steel, so strong that none can bend it.
   We must be hard rock, that none can penetrate.
We must shout our song, that none may ever end it.
   We must ring the death knell of the system that we hate.

Let us shake to earth the leeches that oppress us,
   Those who toil not, yet gather the earth's sweets.
Old justice dies; let a new one caress us:
   Only he who works shall be the one who eats!

May 1928

Any Slave

And now, having torn the giant rock from the wall,
black, gleaming dully in the dim minelight,
split its tonbulk into a thousand ebony chunks
and seen the last car go screeching down the rails
groaning with its burden, stop for a moment.
rest in a black dusty crevice
buried deep in a corner where no light shines.
Put out the light on your cap and crush
        the fire in your brain,
dream you have swallowed cool water
        from a mountain stream,
dream that the painsharp coal dust
        is a bed of crushed grass in summer,
that your face is spring wind-cooled and not coal-smeared.
Let your chin fall to your chest,
        your arms hang limp at your sides
and think. Hard.

        They have buried me here in the earth
who was born to live in sun. They have buried me
deep, deep in the earth where black dust squirms
        in my lungs,
where morning's a hellclang of bells
        and evening a whistle-scream—
Come now. It hurts. And a million others also
know the day only as mounting hours
        and not as pellucid light,
night for its aching limbs, not for its stars,
life only for pain!

        Now you have arisen!
You are out of the dust-filled crevice,
        savagely tearing at rock.
Break the coal, miner! Let it fall like autumn meteors
around you, at your feet, in the cars screeching to light.
Listen to the clang of the pickaxe,
        to the song of hammer on rock!
Then stop, return to your home.
        And again—think.

1928

Portrait of a Death

Gaunt tentacles in greedy disarray
betray the slowly-sinking octopus:
old anarch who discovers that the day
for him grows dark and that day dawns for us.
The ticker-bandage on his wrist connotes
arterio-sclerosis of his veins;
no longer can the wireless cry for votes
to speed false dawn when day already wanes

but slow, the jarring night looms in his brain,—
and sure, the death of sterile wisdom comes—
disintegration finds him and in vain
he blusters louder while his life succumbs
to poisons that his own great bulk gave birth.
His the swift death! and ours again the earth!

1931

Sunday Evening Revery

There is so little to remember
besides streets spiralling at dawn
and at dusk, when I go home;
and what remembered images I have
I have despite myself: the salve
of one or two eternal moments
clinging to the brain.
                                    When I
go nodding through the evening streets,
nodding to Phil, nodding to Bella,
nodding to Mr. Mendelbaum
just home from Stern's Hotel in the Catskill Mountains,
I swear I do not see
the faces that I see;
it is not I who smiles
but a disconnected muscle
no longer welded to my brain.

(and the men and the signs and the stores
gape vacantly, and everything I pass
is an always-clicking movie machine
using my eyes for a screen)

Always, I return home, white and empty.
(these things ricochét along the skin
leaving me undisturbed, unchanged within
so I may fill my empty bed
at night with equal emptiness)

Within me is the memory
of many unremembered things:
a face, a fragment of a dream,
a time-dimmed thigh that moves and clings
vaguely to my loins . . . Beyond these particles

I have no memory.
                                    February 1931

Barn in Wisconsin

There's still some life left in an old red barn
half-hidden behind a rolling swell of earth.
The walls don't bulge as when the barn was full
but hold on tightly to the earth and roof,
shielding the emptiness within. They sag
like empty faces in Milwaukee flops.
But sap still oozes from the painted wood,
through "Burma Shave," "Castoria for the Kids,"
and "Chicken Dinner" ads. The planks still fit
snugly in one another's grooves, and nails
are rusty only in the parts exposed;
they're clean and shining where the cleanness counts.

You ask Lloyd Jones about his farm sometime.
He'll tell you everything you want to know:
how many acres and how few of them
he still can call his own; how good the house
once looked and felt, before the mortgage days;
how soon he thinks the place'll go to ruin.
And then, if you have any time left, ask him
about the barn.

        "I'm saving it," he'll say,
"for corn to hang along the walls some day
in late September, and I'm saving it
for hay to stack up in the loft, and bags
of rutabagas when the yield's been high.
Everything else can go to hell," he'll say,
"but not the barn. The barn is me. I worked
for eighteen years in building it. No barn
was ever built in less time."

        Then you'll know
he means that walls and roof alone don't make
a barn so much as the smell of apples in it,
the feel of produce and its ageing in it.
You'll know his sweat is in the bins and shelves,
his bone is in the nails and planks of it,

his tissue is in the shingle-covered roof
and in the old red paint along the walls.

Then once before you go tell him you may
drop in on him again if ever you pass
that way again, and look once at the barn.
When his eyes follow yours across the ground
you'll see the life left in the old red barn
and then you'll feel the life in him: he'll say,
"I'm saving it." And then he'll add, "Some day . . ."
                                 1930
                                 Janesville, Wisconsin

APPENDIX 1

The Sixth Winter

FOR SOL FUNAROFF
1911–1942

There still is coal in many houses,
I know, watching the chimney-smoke
the bitter wind drives south. There is
much gayety, banquets told of in *The Times,*
parties thrown by Lady So-and-So
at her Florida estate, where prattle-
the shallow debutantes, the debonair and groomed
and empty young men who lounge around the pool,
their correctness reflected in the correctly-heated water.

Receptions, too, are a daily occurrence:
at the Waldorf, at the Plaza, at the City Hall,
for the lady novelist, for the visiting politician,
for the captain of industry and the general
        who beams good will, friendly understanding,
        closer ties between these two great nations,
his sword dangling at his side.

These things I read in the papers and
between the lines I reconstruct the scenes:
the tinkling of silver on translucent porcelain,
warm, buttered morsels of spiced food, poised
on forks, conveyed
to stomachs less delicate; the champagne
bubbling in fragile thin-stemmed crystal,
popping against sated lips, lips moist,
lips drooling, lips accustomed
to the curve of the silver spoon,
the afternoon teacup's edge,
the tilted wineglass.

          And from some unseen somewhere,
music; and soft, subdued, indirectly—lights;
and invisibly but always—warmth;

and cushions; and in the safe-deposit vault
the bankbooks, the jewels, the securities,
the cash, the gilt-edged bonds.

> And the other day
> my blood-brother Bill
> died frozen in Central Park
> asleep with *The Times*
> wrapped around his legs.

This is the sixth winter.
This is the season of death
when lungs contract and the breath of homeless men
freezes on restaurant window-panes, seeking
the sight of rare food
before the head is lowered into the upturned collar
and the shoulders hunched and the shuffling feet
move away slowly, slowly disappear
into a darkened street.

This is the season when rents go up.
Men die, and their dying is casual.
I walk along a street, returning
at midnight from my unit. Meet a man
leaning against an illumined wall
and ask him for a light.
His open eyes
stay fixed on mine. And cold rain falling
trickles down his nose, his chin.
"Buddy," I begin . . . and look more closely
and flee in horror from the corpse's grin.

The eyes pursue you even in sleep and
when you awake they stare at you from the ceiling;
you see the dead face peering from your shoes;
the eggs at Thompson's are the dead man's eyes.
Work dims them for eight hours. But then—
the machines silent—they appear again.

Along the docks, in the terminals, in the subway, on the street,
in restaurants—the eyes
are focused from the river,
among the floating garbage
that other men fish for,
their hands around poles
almost in prayer;
wanting to live,
wanting to live!
          who also soon
will stand propped by death against a stone-cold wall.

But there are other streets and other men.
I have seen them at work, I have heard their voices
cutting the winter air, the words
like knives through ice;
standing on boxes at street-corners, talking on the square,
halting the scorning men, gathering crowds
to listen to remember what they mean.

"The rifling of the city's treasury," one says,
"must end. We must have funds
to feed the foodless, rescue the rotting
men without roofs asleep along the rivershore
in summer; in winter lying frozen in doorways
in the snow in public parks at night . . .
Funds for children, for milk to replace
the dry, withered breast—beauty killed,
sought no longer in passion by lover's hands,
in hunger by hungry lips.
          WE DEMAND!"

And while he speaks, we listen in the square.
We are prepared for his words, we are stronger than to cry.
we are burdened with hunger but our eyes are dry.
We can see the blue-clad gunmen where
they stand, their hands on machine guns, mounted
on roofs surrounding the meeting place: police

like steel-blue vultures perched; and we brace
ourselves. They, not we,
are the hunted now and the haunted
by spectres not of want, but fear
festering in the brain.

In the committee room
committee men measure
the city's treasure,
determine for whom
this million; for what
that sop. They sign
the dotted line,
determine ways and means to rid
the city of vermin. Calculate
new budgets, minimum sums to sate
the hungry mouths, the populations
starved by the official rations
of previous administrations.
Will buy. Will sell. Large dividend
promised to hunger-contractor who will rid
the city of anger.

At last a bid!
Sold to the gentleman with the silk hat!
He is a former governor, a member of all
the uniformed fraternal orders. He agrees,
he sees the situation as we see it—
mayor, members of the board, the committee
of civic leaders and financiers.

For the stipulated millions he will feed
(he signs the papers) all the unemployed.

Whose hand is this which lifts the receiver,
dials the number? Whose the hand
tapping out signal? And whose voice

calls car and armored cycle to the scene?
We shiver on the square.
The north wind blows,
driving the snow
raging over roofs.
The wind like a sword
cuts to the bone.
We are ten thousands,
bottled on all sides.
But we are not alone:
In a hundred other cities
men gathered on stormy squares
shout also
        WE DEMAND!

Knowing our words are more than words,
knowing in our heart their truth,
feeling in our limbs the need to transform
word to action, oration to living deed
              knowing these
stirrings to be true, the seed imprisoned
straining to be free, to grow
to flower in freedom
           we do not mind
the guns at our massed bodies aimed, nor fear
the terror awaiting us at night
on empty streets, cold dark lanes,
who have nothing to lose but our chains.
Night thickens and the cops withdraw.
They—we—return to our homes,
I to mine.
        The dark streets again,
muffled with piled snow,
leading to black hallways: stairs
that creaking caution: Careful now, careful!
Stairs that bear the body's weight only
if you are careful!

                    just as carefully
as tenderly as governments keep men
precariously alive who groan for death.

Up five long flights (we who have homes)
with two companions, invisible but tugging
downward, dead weights on the skeleton:
Hunger the one, the Landlord the other,
his one hand clutched before my eyes;
his other like a leech at my lapel.

How many others climb the stairs to hell?
and fall upon the bed not to sleep
but lie awake to keep
the memory fresh until tomorrow
of ten thousand faces
                        legs, arms, brains,
enough to maintain
life for millions,
move mountains, create
where nothing was before;
ten thousand men
lying also on beds
those who are fortunate

trying not to sleep but to remember,
not to dream but make plans,
never to forget
tomorrow, always to remember
tomorrow, to set
the clock's alarm at the appointed hour before
we sink to restless slumber.

Primer amor

Otra vez soy llamado al campo eterno
verde con la sangre aún fresca en las raíces de las flores,
verde por el recuerdo difuminado de las caras
que se movían allí entre los árboles por última vez
antes del choque final, la mirada vidriosa, la fosa apresurada.

¿Pero por qué están mis pensamientos en otro país?
¿Por qué siempre regreso a la carretera hundida a través de las corroídas
    colinas,
con la sombra del castillo árabe que derramaba sus ruinas por mis hombros
y la muchacha vestida de negro que se acercaba con las manos cargadas
    de uvas?

Estoy ansioso por entrar en él, ansioso por acabar con él.
Quizás éste será el último.
Y los hombres después estudiarán nuestras armas en museos
y asentirán con la cabeza, y se enojarán, y nombrarán fechas inexactas
y tropezarán sus infantiles lenguas con los extraños topónimos.

Mas mi corazón estará eternamente cautivo de esa otra guerra
que me enseñó por encima de todo el sentido de la paz y el compañerismo
y siempre pienso en mi amigo, que entre la presencia de las bombas
vio sobre el lago lírico el singular cisne perfecto.

translated by José Manuel Cabezas Cabello

Elegia

Madrid, Madrid, Madrid, Madrid,
Invoco tu nombre de continuo, saboreándolo como un amante.
Diez irrecuperables años han estallado entre mis manos
desde que te ví la última vez, desde que por última vez dormí
en tus brazos de herido y tierno granito.
Diez años desde que toqué tu cara en el sol,
diez años desde que los vientos sin hogar del Guadarrama
gimieron cual ateridos huérfanos por tus venas
y yo gemí con ellos.

       Cuando pienso en tí, Madrid,
encerrado en el prostíbulo del Chulo Universal,
la sangre que se me precipita al corazón y la cabeza
me ciega, y podría estrangular a tus ensangrentados carceleros,
ahogarlos con estas dos manos que un día te acariciaron.
Cuando pienso en tu anhelante cuerpo de luz y temblores,
en silencio sollozo, desde mi propio país natal
al cual no quiero menos por quererte a tí más.
Sé, sin embargo, en mi raíz más íntima, que hasta que el clamor de tu
    liberación
no recorra el mundo de los hombres libres de cerca y de lejos
yo tendré que andar al azar extranjero en todas partes.

Madrid, en estos días de nuestra angustia en la tierra,
forjada por hombres cuya fingida moralidad
comienza y acaba en la cinta de la Bolsa de Cambios,
también yo a veces desespero. Sollozo con tu joven poeta muerto.
Como él maldigo de nuestra edad y enumero el exceso de guerras,
los destierros, los peligros, los temores, nuestra fatiga
de sangre, y esta ciega supervivencia, cuando tantos
hogares, esposas, incluso recuerdos, se han perdido.

Sí, sollozo con Garcilaso. Recuerdo
tu grave rostro y tu sutil sonrisa
y la cautivadora belleza de tus hijas e incluso
la harapienta elegancia de tus pobres más pobres.
Recuerdo la alegría de tus milicianos . . .
mis camaradas de armas. ¿Qué otra ciudad

en la historia reclutó nunca un batallón de barberos
o improvisó entre sus hijos respetados generales sin insignias?
Todos están en mi recuerdo. Si alguna vez te olvidare,
Madrid, Madrid, que mi mano derecha pierda su destreza.

Te hablo, Madrid, como amante, marido, hijo.
Acepta esta humana trinidad de pasiones.
Te amo, y por eso te soy fiel
y porque olvidarte sería olvidar
todo lo que amo y aprecio en el mundo.
El que no es sincero contigo es falso con todos
y aquel a quien tu nombre nada dice nunca ha amado
y aquellos que volverían a prostituir tu carne y tu sangre de nuevo
en guerras y cuidadas inversiones
¡sean doblemente malditos! Asesinos tuyos
y de su vanagloriado e inexistente honor,
de todo lo inmaculado de nuestra era.

Errando, amargado, en estos amargos tiempos,
sueño con tus anchas avenidas como arroyos en estío
con tus bellísimos niños agitándose en ellas como pececillos.
En mis recuerdos voy por la calle de Velázquez
hacia tu verde Retiro y sus verdes arboledas.
A veces cuando recorro las calles de mi propia ciudad
me siento transportado a tu fluyente Alcalá
y mis pasos se apresuran. Corro al lugar
donde todos tus vivos ríos afluyen a encontrarse con el sol.
A veces me pongo a cavilar en tu umbría Plaza Mayor
acompañado de los fantasmas de viejos Reyes e Inquisidores
que inquietan los balcones con sus idióticas miradas fijas
(que Goya conoció más tarde) y debajo de cuyas arcadas,
sombríos cuartos entre columnas,
el viejo relojero sueña con minúsculos, intrincados minutos,
la anciana vende lápices y chillones peines de ámbar,
rememorando los días en que su propio cuerpo fué joven,
y el reumático campesino con dedos nudosos como vides
ofrece anheloso sus pasas resecas;
y duros niños de diez años, con abrasados ojos maduros,

se arrodillan, y gravemente, quijotescamente,
pulen las bastas botas de los soldados con permiso de una hora
para volver a las trincheras de la Casa de Campo,
a sus puestos, entre zumbidos de muerte, en el esqueleto
de la Ciudad Universitaria.

                              Y las mujeres que pasean,
las jóvenes, conscientes de ser mujeres,
y oigo en aquella parte imperecedera de mi corazón donde tú estás, Madrid,
a los soldados gritando: *¡Oye, guapa, oye!*

Recuerdo tus librerías con las ventanas siempre llenas
de nuevas ediciones del "Romancero Gitano"
y de "Poetas en la España Leal"
y "Romancero de los Soldados en las Trincheras".
Nunca había comida bastante, pero sí poesía.
¡Qué corriente de versos empapados de sangre derramaste
sobre el mundo en tus tres años de gloria!

Y yo pienso: Gran cosa es ser hombre
sólo cuando el hombre tiene dignidad y hombría.
Gran cosa es sentirse orgulloso y sin miedo
sólo cuando el orgullo y el valor tienen significado, meta.
Y en nuestro mundo nada se dijo con más orgullo
en aquellos tres agonizantes años que "Yo vengo de Madrid".

Diez han pasado ya con pequeños estallidos de esperanza
y eres aún tú, Madrid, la conciencia de nuestras vidas.
Mientras tú sufras, encadenado, adolorido,
yo no seré libre, ninguno de nosotros lo será.
Si hay un hombre en la Tierra que no ame a Madrid
como se ama a una mujer, como se valúa el propio sexo,
ese hombre es menos que hombre y es peligroso,
y en tanto que dirija los asuntos de nuestro mundo
yo tendré que ser su implacable enemigo.

Madrid, Madrid, Madrid, Madrid.
Velando y durmiendo tu nombre canta en mi corazón

y tu tragedia embarga todos mis pensamientos y acciones
(apacibles siempre, aunque también he sabido coger el fusil).
Perdóname, ya que no consigo amarte como quisiera
—hay tanta distancia entre los dos—.
Pero una cosa te prometo, con la airada impotencia de la lejanía:
Madrid, si alguna vez te olvidare
que mi mano derecha pierda su destreza,
que mis brazos y piernas se hagan huesos sin carne,
que mi cuerpo se seque sin jugos
y que mi cerebro se resblandezca e insensibilice como el de un idiota.
Y si muriere antes de poder volver a tí,
o tú, con total libertad, volvieras a nosotros,
que mis hijos lleguen a amarte como su padre te amó
Madrid, Madrid, Madrid.

translated by José Rubia Barcia

Cary Nelson

To My Contemporaries

The book is dedicated to Leo T. Hurwitz. Hurwitz (1909–91) was Rolfe's closest friend in high school and a good friend thereafter. They shared an apartment in Manhattan after Rolfe returned from Wisconsin and Hurwitz returned from Harvard. Hurwitz went on to become an innovative filmmaker. He was active in the New York Film and Photo League early in the depression and a cofounder of Frontier Films. The 1976 *Oxford Companion to Film* credits him with having "pioneered left-wing documentary in the United States, beginning with *Hunger* (1932) and *Scottsboro* (1934)." With Paul Strand, he codirected *Heart of Spain* (1937) and *Native Land* (1937).

Although the table of contents for *To My Contemporaries* did not include any section divisions, three title pages were inserted into the book itself, "Credo," "Homage to Karl Marx," and "To My Contemporaries," each placed immediately before the poem of the same title. The effect was thus somewhat ambiguous, the titles serving partly as ways of highlighting those three poems and partly as understated section divisions. One of Rolfe's earlier versions of the table of contents included three explicit section divisions—"First Lesson," "Lanes of Death and Birth," and "To My Contemporaries." The back jacket of *To My Contemporaries* included the following comment by Horace Gregory: "Kenneth Fearing's *Poems,* Muriel Rukeyser's *Theory of Flight* and most recently this selection of poems by Edwin Rolfe is evidence of great variety within the latest phase of contemporary American poetry. It is significant, I believe, that all three poets share the same background of Marxian philosophy and urban environment, yet each of the three is distinctly individual; the philosophy, contrary to the hopes and fears of reactionary critics, has not hampered their growth, but has intensified their perception of those poetic realities which exist within our time.

"Edwin Rolfe's poetry seems as fresh, as casual as the spoken word and there can be no mistake about the content of what he has to say. The voice heard in these poems is assured and direct; the voice is didactic in the best sense of the word: it is both careful and sensitive and the discipline imposed upon it has its source in the very philosophy which proposes an actual design for living. That is why I believe such poems as 'Asbestos', 'To My Contemporaries', 'Homage to Karl Marx' and 'Definition' to be entirely successful. The world that Edwin Rolfe is building is a new world and he has found himself a place within it.

"To those who are interested in the best of contemporary poetry I recommend this first book by Edwin Rolfe, particularly that fine poem, 'Definition', a poem which I suspect transcends its immediate time and cause and should be remembered whenever men foregather in the difficult and bloody task of building a new society."

"Asbestos"

The poem was titled "The 100 Percenter" when first published in the *Daily Worker* in 1928. It was retitled "Asbestos" for its 1933 reprinting in *We Gather Strength*.

"Kentucky"

Rolfe dates this poem 1932. When it was published in the *Daily Worker* the following year Rolfe titled it "Kentucky—1932." It was no doubt inspired by—and certainly comments on—the conditions reported by a group of writers who were sent to Harlan County, Kentucky, to investigate the treatment of workers there. Under the auspices of the party-organized National Committee for the Defense of Political Prisoners, Theodore Dreiser, John Dos Passos, Samuel Ornitz, and others went there, as Daniel Aaron describes it in his *Writers on the Left* (1961), "to see for themselves whether the reports of intimidation, starvation, and bloodshed were true. The 'whole narrative of terror' was even more frightful than they had expected. Under the prodding of the operators, the authorities had dynamited soup kitchens, raided private homes, blacklisted 3,000 miners, jailed hundreds of others, and had deputized gun-toting hooligans" (178). Initial reports from the investigative trip appeared in the December 1931 issue of *New Masses*. When *Harlan Miners Speak*, the complete report, was published the following year, Rolfe reviewed it in *Contempo:* "They found a fascist array of terror against the striking miners, dictated over by the entire judicial system of the state, and controlled by the mine corporations. . . . The real meat of the book, it should be noted, is contained in the testimonies of the miners and their wives. Direct, outspoken, courageous in the face of beatings, hunger, assassination, their words dwarf the more expert expositions of the writers."

"Letter for One in Russia"

Carla: She is one of Rolfe's former girlfriends. She appears as well in two unpublished poems amongst his papers: "Day Left Behind—the Park" ("We will continue, Carla, our advance / through the deep grooves the night has carved for us") and "This Darkness in Ourselves."

"These Men Are Revolution"

Dunne: William Dunne (1887–1953) was a labor organizer from Montana. As vice-president of the Montana Federation of Labor he helped organize a 1917 strike against the Anaconda Copper Company. First a Socialist, he later joined the Communist party. In 1923 he was thrown out of the American Federation of Labor convention because of his party membership; it was the first time a delegate was taken off the floor. Through the rest of the twenties he held a number of important posts in the Communist party, serving, for example, as its representative to the Comintern from 1924 to 1925. He was a Comintern representative in Outer Mongolia in 1928 and joined the Politburo in 1929. Unpopular with party head Earl Browder, Dunne began to lose status in the party in the thirties. He was cut out of the national leadership in 1934 and returned to Montana, where he found himself unhappy with the less militant Popular Front policies instituted the following year. When Rolfe published the poem in *New Masses* in October 1934, he may have been consciously making a gesture toward a man who was in the process of falling out of favor. Certainly the reference to Dunne had that status when the poem was reprinted in *To My Contemporaries* in 1936. By the end of the decade, Dunne was a serious alcoholic; he was expelled from the party in 1946.

Foster: William Z. Foster (1881–1961). A Socialist party member at the turn of the century and an IWW member from 1909 to 1911, he then worked to radicalize midwestern labor organizations and during World War I led efforts to organize black and immigrant workers in meat-packing and steel. He was the Communist party's candidate for president of the United States in 1924, 1928, and 1932 and an effective party representative throughout that period. He chaired the party from 1945 to 1961.

"Room with Revolutionists"

This poem is based on a conversation between *New Masses* editor, poet, and Left journalist Joseph Freeman (1897–1965) and the Mexican painter David Alfaro Siqueros (1896–1974). Siqueros was a revolutionary Socialist who was politically active both in Mexico and abroad. Freeman went on to write novels and an autobiography. Since Rolfe's admiration for Freeman and Siqueros was based partly on their ability to function, respectively, as writer or artist and revolutionary, it may be useful to give some examples of this double life as each man lived it.

As a young man, beginning in 1914, Siqueros fought in the Mexican revolution. A period of art studies in Europe followed. He returned to Mexico in 1922 to complete such paintings as *Burial of a Worker,* but three years later abandoned painting to devote himself to union organizing and leading mine workers' strikes. In prison in 1930 he began painting again, producing works such as *Visit to an Imprisoned Peasant* and later *Proletarian Mother.* In 1932 he accepted exile in the United States, where he remained for two years. He returned to Mexico in 1934 to become president of the National League against Fascism and War. In 1936 he organized a painting workshop in New York and later that year journeyed to Spain to fight in support of the Spanish republic.

Freeman was born in the Ukraine and came to the United States as a young child. A Zionist in his youth, Freeman was a committed Socialist by the time he was fifteen. At Columbia University he became active in the antiwar movement during World War I. After graduation he spent two years in Europe as a correspondent, returning to New York to work for *The Liberator* in 1922. Three years later he published *Dollar Diplomacy* with Scott Nearing, and the following year founded *New Masses*. He then went to the Soviet Union, where he served for a time as a translator for the Comintern. After returning to the United States in 1927, he coauthored *Voices of October* (1930), which presented the revolutionary art and literature he had encountered in the USSR. Freeman continued to be a prominent intellectual on the Left and in the party in the first half of the thirties, but the positive view of Trotsky in his 1936 autobiography *An American Testament* put him in disfavor in the Soviet Union. At first he was simply compelled to help suppress attention for the book, but when he refused an assignment to write an article on the Moscow trials the following year, relations with the party began to deteriorate more rapidly. In 1939 *An American Testament* was attacked in the *Communist International* and Freeman was expelled. See the Introduction for further comments.

"Three Who Died"

On January 30, 1934, just outside of Moscow, the Soviet balloon Osoviakhim rose to a record height of thirteen miles on a mission to gather data on the upper atmosphere. The three crew members, Pavel Fedoseenko, Andrey Vossenko, both engineers, and Ilya Ussyskin, a young physicist and YCL member, had greetings radiogrammed to the Seventeenth Congress of the Communist Party of the Soviet Union, which was then meeting in Moscow. Unfortunately, the balloon then ran into difficulty. Forced to hover at a great height when blinding fog and mist made a safe descent impossible, the Osoviakhim may have become covered with ice. In any case, the balloon began to fall rapidly, the gondola broke away from the envelope, and the crew members fell to their death. The *Daily Worker* carried the story of the record-breaking flight in its January 31 issue and the next day reported the crash. Follow-up stories appeared on February 2 and 3, 1934. Rolfe's poem was published in the February 13 issue of *New Masses*.

"Witness at Leipzig"

Dimitroff: Georgi Mikhailovich Dimitrov (1882–1949) served as a Socialist member of the Bulgarian parliament from 1913 to 1918, helped form the Bulgarian Communist party in 1919, and then fled the country after an unsuccessful attempt to overthrow the king. In the Soviet Union he became active in the Comintern and headed its European section when he was based in Berlin from 1929 to 1933. Accused of involvement in the Reichstag fire in 1933, he and the other three defendants were tried in Leipzig and acquitted but then held incommunicado by the Nazis; he was finally deported to the USSR. There he became general secretary of the Comintern, where he was central in advocating the Popular Front and in winning support for Republican Spain.

"Poem for May First"

May 1, or May Day, was the day the nineteenth-century labor movement celebrated its revolutionary aspirations. In America, late nineteenth-century May Day celebrations often focused on the campaign for an eight-hour work day. The Communist party revived the May Day tradition in the thirties. Rolfe participated in the large May Day marches in New York in the thirties.

Haymarket: At a peaceful labor demonstration organized by anarchists in Chicago's Haymarket Square in May 1886 the police attacked the demonstrators without cause. Moments later a bomb exploded, and that started a police riot. Eight members of the International Working People's Association were then prosecuted for conspiring to murder police officers. Though there was no evidence linking them to the bomb, they were all convicted. In 1887 August Spies, Albert Parsons, George Engel, and Adolph Fischer were executed. Louis Lingg took his own life in jail.

"Wisconsin farmhouse, / barn wall sagging": See Rolfe's poem "Barn in Wisconsin."

Mendota: The University of Wisconsin campus in Madison borders Lake Mendota. Rolfe was a student in the Experimental College there from 1929 to 1930.

"Season of Death"

This poem was first published in a longer version titled "The Sixth Winter." See Appendix 1.

"Definition"

See the Introduction.

"To My Contemporaries"

Funaroff: Sol Funaroff (1911–42) was a poet whose books were *The Spider and the Clock* (1938) and *Exile from a Future Time: Posthumous Poems of Sol Funaroff* (1943). He also founded Dynamo Press, which published Rolfe's *To My Contemporaries*. Rolfe and Funaroff were close friends.

Hayes: Alfred Hayes (1911–85) was a poet whose books included *The Big Time* (1944) and *Welcome to the Castle* (1950). Although Rolfe was not as close to him as he was to Sol Funaroff and Kenneth Fearing, Hayes was among the poets on the Left who saw one another regularly in the midthirties. Hayes began to publish fiction in the forties.

Uncollected and Unpublished Poems, 1933–37

"To Those Who Fear to Join Us" is an unpublished poem. The other poems in this section were all published in journals.

"Homecoming (August 7, 1934)"

Angelo Herndon was nineteen years old in 1932 when he helped organize a peaceful hunger march in Atlanta, Georgia. He was arrested shortly thereafter, convicted of attempting to incite an insurrection, and sentenced to twenty years on a chain gang. Herndon was black and a party member, and the party's defense of him raised a number of important issues, including the constitutionality of Georgia's all-white juries and the constitutionality of the insurrection law. All this was swept aside by a racist court and jury. After extensive appeals, a bare five to four majority in the U.S. Supreme Court found the Georgia law unconstitutional in 1937. When Herndon arrived on bail in New York in 1934, Rolfe was among the crowd there to greet him. Rolfe's poem "Homecoming (August 7, 1934)" records the date and Rolfe's response to the event. The poem was published in the August 21, 1934, issue of *New Masses*. Three years later, writing from Madrid, Rolfe began an August 21, 1937, letter to Mary with the following sentences: "I've just received another letter from you—the one of July 26th, which described the arrival at Penn Station of the 4 Scottsboro boys. I would like to have been there—the memory of Herndon's arrival is still one of my most vivid." For further information see Herndon's autobiography *Let Me Live* (1937) and Rolfe's 1934 *Daily Worker* story.

"Nuthin but Brass"

Cab Calloway, extravagant singer, dancer, and band leader, was, of course, one of the notable figures of jazz's big band era and perhaps the most popular black entertainer of the thirties. "Minnie the Moocher" was his signature song, and Rolfe builds allusions to it into his poem. Thus the third verse begins "She had a dream about the King of Sweden. / He gave her things that she was need'n," while the fourth verse ends "She had a million dollars worth of nickels and dimes. / She sat around and counted them all a million times."

"Cheliuskin"

Rolfe's note after the version of the poem published in 1935 reads: "For the narratives of the voyage of the *Cheliuskin* and the rescue of the marooned crew I have followed the newspaper cables on the event, many of which I handled personally in preparing the stories for a New York daily newspaper. I am also indebted to the accounts of the members of the expedition, translated from the Russian to English by Alec Brown (*The Voyage of the Cheliuskin*—Macmillan)." Opposite the first page of the poem in the November 1935 issue of *Soviet Russia Today* is a full-page collage of arctic photographs and photographs of a ship that is presumably the *Cheliuskin*.

Some manuscript versions of the poem are titled "The Arctic," but we have used the title given to the published version. Included in the Rolfe archive is the essay "Ten Years after the Chelyuskin Rescue" by Georgi Ushakov that was distributed by the Soviet Embassy. It reads in part: "In February, 1934, the Chelyuskin, a ship of a Soviet Polar expedition headed by Professor Otto Schmidt, was crushed by ice packs, and sank in the Chukotka Sea. . . . One hundred and four seamen, scientists and Polar workers were stranded on a stretch of jagged ice 150 kilometers from the nearest section of the sparsely-inhabited tundra of the coastline. . . . Among them were nine women and two children, one of the latter an infant girl, Karina, born aboard ship in the Kara Sea. . . . Only the fascist press sneered at Soviet rescue plans. . . . One after another Soviet fliers took up the struggle against the elements. Anatoli Lypidevsky was the first to reach the arctic. . . . Through the darkness of the polar night and heavy blizzards N. Kamanin, V. Molotov, M. Vodopyanov, I. Doronin and others flew on the mission of rescue. . . . The Soviet fliers brought back all the members of the Chelyuskin expedition." At one time Rolfe planned a long poem on the arctic that was to include both "*Cheliuskin*" and "The Arctic Remembered."

We have published here a somewhat revised version from Rolfe's papers. It differs in several respects from the version of the poem published in 1935. There are a number of small rhetorical improvements and significant changes in Rolfe's historical and political references. In the 1935 version, for example, an outpost is described as a "symbol of Soviet will"; here it is a "symbol of socialist will." Following Popular Front rhetoric, this version has the expedition's commander "warmly sent off by the people." In the earlier version he was "warmly sent off by the proletariat of Leningrad, and by Soviet and Party organizations."

First Love and Other Poems

"Entry"

"Rabbi Israel's son courting the phobic maid / under a moonlit balcony near Zaragossa": These lines refer to the story told in Heinrich Heine's poem "Donna Clara," in which a young man courts the relentlessly and obsessively anti-Semitic Donna Clara. The poem ends when he declares himself to be Rabbi Israel's son. According to his wife, Mary, Rolfe often cited the poem during discussions of anti-Semitism. He owned Louis Untermeyer's translation of Heine.

"City of Anguish"

This poem is dedicated to Milton Wolff, last commander of the Lincoln Battalion.

The feeling behind the dedication may be represented most clearly by the inscription Rolfe wrote in the copy of *The Lincoln Battalion* he gave to Wolff in November 1939: "With deepest admiration and friendship. —Certain qualities remain with a man all his life: things he did, said, thought, felt. What you were and what you did in Spain, Milt, can never be lost; it remains deep in the memory and in the consciousness of all of us who at one time or other were under your command, all of us whose acts were more perfect because you were there with us, leading us. The stature you achieved there—the respect, admiration, love that we had for you, and the confidence and trust you inspired in us, will always be part of us and a part of you in our eyes." Wolff's copy of *The Lincoln Battalion* is included in his archive, which is also at the University of Illinois.

By the time Rolfe arrived in Madrid in the summer of 1937 the city, while still under siege and under bombardment, was no longer the main focus of Franco's military campaign. The poem draws on Rolfe's experience of the city in the summer and fall of 1937 to evoke the Madrid of that year and the previous year as well. In the fall of 1936 Franco sent his own troops and the German Condor Legion to take the city on the ground and break its will by artillery and air bombardment. At some points in November up to two thousand rounds of artillery were fired on Madrid each hour. As the historian Hugh Thomas wrote in *The Spanish Civil War* (1977), the German officers directing the bombardment for Franco "were interested to see the reaction of a civilian population to a carefully planned attempt to set fire to the city quarter by quarter. The bombing concentrated as far as possible on hospitals and other buildings such as the Telefónica or the war ministry, whose destruction would cause special damage" (486). Blocks of apartments were destroyed, trees were uprooted, huge bomb craters were left in the roads, fires burned regularly, and thousands of civilians were killed. But the people's will was not broken. And the city was not taken. Following the unsuccessful direct frontal assault, Franco also tried to encircle the city, first from the west and then from the east. The major battles in and around Madrid lasted from November 1936 to March 1937.

Paseo: literally, a leisurely stroll or promenade. On Sunday many people dressed up for a traditional promenade along major streets or through public squares.

Gran Via: The major east-west avenue in Madrid. It was constructed in three sections, the first of which opened in 1924. During the first months of the war, the fascist general Emilio Mola announced that he would be having coffee on the Gran Via by October 12. The general did not keep his rendezvous; thereafter a large printed reservation for him was satirically maintained on a table at the Cafe Molinero on the Gran Via. It was down the Gran Via that the International Brigades marched in November 1936 on their way to the front on the outskirts of Madrid.

Telefónica: The large modernist-style telephone building, which served as the headquarters of Spain's telecommunications company, was Madrid's highest building when it was erected in 1929. It stands on the Gran Via on the highest ground in the center of the city. Its large red clock still dominates the night skyline. During the war it was an observation post for Republican artillery, and for that reason among others it was also one of the more famous targets in Madrid. It was shelled repeatedly by the rebels and also used as a reference point to aim shells up the Gran Via.

Casa de campo: See the notes to "Elegia."

Puerta del Sol (Gateway of the Sun): The arc-shaped *plaza de la Puerta del Sol* is often considered the heart of Madrid and of Spain as well. A number of the major roads in the city have their origin there, and it is also identi-fied as "kilometer zero" for the nation's major highways. Rolfe often walked through the plaza when he was in Madrid in 1937. Both historically and during the Spanish Civil War it was the scene of major political gatherings.

Florída: This was one of two hotels in Madrid—the other being the *Gran Via* (across from the *Telefónica* building)—where journalists frequently gathered during the war. Hemingway stayed there when he was in Madrid in 1937, taking one of the large (and then inexpensive) rooms in the front that faced the fascist artillery. The *Florída* was located on the Plaza Cayou a block west of the *Telefónica* building; after the war the *Florída* was torn down to make way for a department store.

Ryan: An IRA member since 1918, Frank Ryan became the chivalrous leader of the Irish volunteers in the International Brigades. He had the rank of cap-tain and commanded the Irish company of the British Battalion. Captured by fascist forces in the spring of 1938, he was turned over to German troops and later murdered by the Gestapo. For more information see Sean Cronin, *Frank Ryan* (1980).

Pasionaria: La Pasionaria (Dolores Ibarruri Gomez) was one of the most famous figures of the Spanish Civil War. Her 1936 radio speech rallying the de-fenders of Madrid gave the republic its battle cry: "No Pasaran!" (They Shall Not Pass). She was also deeply involved in all the Spanish Communist party's political maneuvers during the war, but it is her role in the defense of Madrid that Rolfe honors here. She was born in 1895 in a small mining village and politicized by the oppressive sexism of traditional Spanish culture and by the intense poverty of her family. Four of her six children died for lack of food and medicine. Something of her impact on people is captured in this excerpt from Vincent Sheean's comments on her in his text accompanying her por-trait in Jo Davidson, *Spanish Portraits* (1938): "It was on the night of July the eighteenth, 1936, when military revolt had blazed out all over Spain, that Dolores spoke over the Madrid radio and proclaimed in her plangent, sad and magical voice, words which are Madrid's forever: 'No pasaran.' Through the long siege she was a force among the people, a force for encouragement, for organization and for hard work. The workers' militias and their successor, the popular army, the women and children of workers, and the government itself owe as much to her as to any individual element at their command. Her words found their way into every Spanish heart and imagination. 'It is better to die on your feet than to live on your knees,' she said, and millions have repeated it through these two years and a half of bitter, exhausting war. . . . She reaches those secret depths because she is herself a collective phenomenon, inseparable from the people for whom and to whom she speaks."

"Death by Water"

Malgrat is a fishing village on the Catalan coast about twenty-two miles north of Barcelona. The ship *Ciudad de Barcelona* had brought international volunteers to Spain on earlier occasions as well, often traveling a route from Marseilles to Alicante. As noted in *International Solidarity with the Spanish Republic* (1975), the ship brought 650 volunteers from many countries to Alicante on October 9, 1936; it brought another group of volunteers from Marseilles to Alicante on October 13. Abe Osheroff describes his experience as a passenger on the *City of Barcelona* when it was torpedoed by a submarine in a passage in *Our Fight: Writings by Veterans of the Abraham Lincoln Brigade* (1987): "I remember a loud, dull thud, and the whole ship sort of shuddered. In a matter of minutes, it tilted sharply and began to go down by the stern. Pandemonium followed as men raced to the very few lifeboats. I remember a loaded lifeboat crashing down on its occupants. I remember the screaming faces of seamen trapped at the portholes. And above all I remember some seamen tearing loose anything that could float and tossing it into the sea. I dived into the water and began to swim away, to avoid being pulled down by the suction. Almost immediately, I felt guilt and swam back to help with the rescue of nonswimming comrades" (85). In *The Lincoln Battalion* Rolfe quotes Sidney Shosteck: "The men died helping each other" (84). Rolfe first called the poem "City of Barcelona" and later retitled it "Death by Water." The final title is an explicit reference to the fourth section of Eliot's *The Waste Land*. In giving the poem that title Rolfe may also have had in mind his friend Sol Funaroff's poem "What the Thunder Said: A Fire Sermon," which was first published in a condensed version in *New Masses* in 1932. The full poem appeared in Funaroff's *The Spider and the Clock* (1938), which Funaroff sent to Rolfe in Spain in June of 1938.

"Catalogue"

An early draft is titled "Diary in Our Days of Grief." This is one of several manuscripts Rolfe donated to the State University of New York at Buffalo in 1952.

Roger: Rolfe describes Roger Hargrave's last day in action near Brunete in the summer of 1937 in *The Lincoln Battalion*: "Most seriously wounded of all was

Roger Hargrave, the machine-gun company's first-aid man who had dragged
the wounded Hans Amlie off the field under intense machine-gun fire, and
who had been with Ray Steele when he died. On the very last day of battle,
after he had made a number of trips out into the field of fire to bring back
the last of the wounded men, he lay down under a tree to rest. A moment
later he felt himself lifted from the ground as an artillery shell landed ten feet
away. Shrapnel tore into his body in six different places. . . . The strip of hot
steel which hit his arm gouged a chunk of muscle and bone out of his fore-
arm. Gas-gangrene was setting in as they placed him in an ambulance bound
for Madrid" (102–3). Hargrave did survive. Rolfe visited him in the hospital
when he was in Madrid in the fall of 1937. For further information on Har-
grave see the section "Iowa Farmer" in Joseph North's pamphlet *Men in the
Ranks,* published by the Friends of the Abraham Lincoln Brigade in 1939.

Robert Raven: Robert Raven, a former University of Pittsburgh student, was
blinded on March 14, 1937, when a Canadian mistakenly opened the lever
of a grenade before handing it to him to toss at a group of advancing fas-
cist troops. Rolfe tells the story in detail in *The Lincoln Battalion* (59–61).
In "The Spanish War" (*Fact,* no. 16, July 15, 1938, 19–22), Hemingway re-
ports a visit to Raven in a hospital outside Madrid: "The voice came from a
high mound covered by a shoddy grey blanket. There were two arms crossed
on top of the mound and at one end there was something that had been a
face, but now was a yellow scabby area with a wide bandage across where the
eyes had been."

"Eyes of a Blind Man"

This was dedicated to Commandante Gabriel Fort, who commanded the Sixth of
February Battalion. Seriously wounded in the Jarama campaign, he returned to
service and was blinded at Brunete in July 1937. Rolfe wrote the poem after having
lunch with Fort in Madrid on Friday, September 3, 1937. Rolfe noted in his diary
that a bullet entered one of Fort's eyes and emerged from the other.

"Casualty"

Tibidábo: This is a 532-meter-high mountain in the foothills on the outskirts
of Barcelona. It forms the northwest boundary of the city. Republican anti-
aircraft guns were placed there during the war. It is known for the fine views
of Barcelona it provides on clear days. The mountain's name is taken from
the Latin version of Satan's offer during Christ's Temptations. Satan took
him to a high place and offered everything that could be seen below: "Haec
omnia tibi dabo si cadens adoraberis me" (All these things I will give thee, if
thou wilt fall down and worship me).

"Epitaph"

This poem was originally published as "For Arnold Reid." Reid was a classmate of Rolfe's at the University of Wisconsin. Rolfe describes his death in *The Lincoln Battalion:* "On a hill adjacent to the Lincoln position another American—one of the most competent and mature and kindly of all in Spain—died as he directed the fire of a machine-gun in his company. He was Arnold Reid, a twenty-six-year-old American who had worked for many years in South and Latin America, and who had joined the Spanish battalion of the Fifteenth Brigade in order to strengthen the work of the many Latin Americans in its ranks. The Spaniards, especially the young *quintos,* had loved the quiet young man who had become commissar of their machine-gun company; who knew their language and songs and traditions as well, if not better, than any of them, who treated them like a kind and just father. The Lincolns heard of his death for the first time when Joseph North, first of the correspondents to reach the Ebro lines, visited the battalion during a momentary lull in the fighting on July 29th. The news stunned them more than the news of any death ordinarily did" (267). See the Introduction for further comments.

"Elegy for Our Dead"

See the Introduction.

"The Guerrillas"

Rolfe also wrote a substantial essay on the *guerrilleros,* those Republican soldiers who fought behind Franco's lines. Some American volunteers fought with them. The first half of the essay was published in the November 14, 1939, issue of *New Masses.* The entire essay is in the Rolfe archive.

"Night World"

This poem was written to Rolfe's wife, Mary, while they were living in New York in the thirties.

"Prophecy in Stone"

The poem is not only dedicated to Paul Strand but also, as Rolfe notes in the version published in *The Nation,* based on one of Strand's photographs. The image Rolfe had in mind was most likely Strand's 1932 photograph *Beyond Saltillo,* but Rolfe clearly drew inspiration from the rest of Strand's Mexican sequence as well, including the photographs of images of Christ. Rolfe and Strand knew one another well in the thirties. Leo Hurwitz wrote an introduction to a folio-sized album of Strand's photographs that was included in Rolfe's library.

"see Christ / in fifty different tortured poses": The following note from Rolfe's archive, written several years later, helps clarify this image: "We lifted the injured man to the stretcher; his face was the face of a wounded Christ. Not the diluted Christ of the popular chromos, but the authentic man, the Jeshua of Nazareth, the man whom all peoples everywhere see as themselves, as one of their own. Once, I remember, I saw a carved image of a Christ in Mexico, and it was the face of a Mexican peon, the hair black and matted with sweat and suffering under the thorns, the eyes dark and smouldering with pain, the mouth and the lines falling about it reflecting the simple, protracted agony of a lifetime of crucifixion in slavery, not the dramatic momentary agony of a quick crucifixion."

"Essay on Dreiser (1871–1945)"
This poem was written in Beverly Hills, California, on December 29, 1945, the day after Dreiser died.

"Postscript to a War"
This was dedicated to Michael Gordon, who was stage manager and director for the Theatre Union in New York in the thirties at the same time as Mary Rolfe was Margaret Larkin's assistant there. Larkin later became a writer and married Albert Maltz. One of the plays Gordon worked on was Maltz's *Black Pit*. Gordon then moved to the Group Theatre. He later worked on Broadway and directed over twenty films in Hollywood. Gordon appeared before HUAC as a resistant, uncooperative witness in 1951. In 1958, however, several years after Rolfe's death, he testified in secret and went through the ritual of naming names. See Victor Navasky, *Naming Names* (1980), 276–78, for details.

"Survival Is of the Essence"
Arnold: Arnold Reid. See the Introduction and the notes to "Epitaph."
Roger: Roger Hargrave. See the notes to "Catalogue."
Muriel: Muriel Rukeyser (1913–80) was a radical American poet and a friend of Rolfe's. She was in Spain to cover the antifascist Olympics when the war began and one of those foreign nationals who were evacuated from Barcelona.
Die Heimat ist weit: This is the first line of the chorus to the song "Die Thälmann-Kolonne," which was sung in Spain and published in the song books issued by the International Brigades.
"the man . . . who turned south, singing": This is Ernst Busch (1900–1980), a German actor and cabaret singer who specialized in proletarian political and protest songs. The son of a mason, he was apprenticing as a locksmith at Kiel when he became district chief of Socialist Workers' Youth in 1917. The following year he took part in the sailors' rebellion in Kiel, the same rebellion that would be the subject of one of Ernst Toller's plays. His acting career

began with a part in Toller's *Hoppla, Wir Leben* (1927), and he was in the world premier of *The Threepenny Opera* as well. He left Germany for Holland in 1933 when Hitler came to power and went to the USSR in 1935, where he worked for Radio Moscow. He was in Spain with the International Brigades from 1937 to 1939, most notably as a singer and composer. His songs indeed appear in all the song books issued by the International Brigades. In the songs he recorded in Madrid one can hear artillery fire in the background. In France after the fall of Spain, he was eventually turned over to the Gestapo and sentenced to life in prison. Freed with the defeat of the Nazis, he continued as a "worker-singer" and acted in the Deutsches-Theater and the Berliner Ensemble, taking parts in a number of Brecht plays.

"Song (3)"

"an invisible Torquemada": Thomas Torquemada (1420–98) was, of course, the head of the Spanish Inquisition, responsible for the burning of heretics and for the expulsion of the Jews from Spain. Rolfe's "invisible Torquemada" is presumably also a recurrent historical figure, both in fact and in our fears.

"north, the eagle view from Montserrat / west, the winding street behind the Tarragona cathedral": The Montserrat (or serrated mountain) is about thirty-five kilometers northwest of Barcelona. It is part of a small range of mountains (six miles long by three miles wide) that rise in almost complete isolation from the Catalonian plateau. It is topped by barren pinnacles separated by fissures, producing an effect like pointing fingers. On a good day the view to the north from Mount Montserrat stretches from the Pyrenees to the Balearic Islands. The ancient port city of Tarragona, on the Mediterranean coast about eighty kilometers south of Barcelona, was one of the places Republican soldiers retreated to in the spring of 1938. It was also a major supply point for the Ebro campaign that summer. The cathedral, on a high point at the north end of Tarragona, is at the core of the medieval section of the city; that section of the city included the Jewish quarter. Its construction over several centuries embraces both Romanesque and Gothic architecture. In Rolfe's lines the panoramic view from Montserrat is paired with its spatial opposite: the historic enclosure of the small medieval street behind the cathedral. An earlier version of the second stanza read:

> North: the eagle view of Monserrat,
> West: the slums that abut on the Burgos Cathedral,
> South: the green peace of an undiscovered ocean,
> East: the safety and strength of the Maginot mind.

"May 22nd 1939"

Toller: Ernst Toller (1893–1939) was an exiled German-Jewish dramatist and poet whom Rolfe met in Spain (*Lincoln Battalion*, 277–80). Radicalized by the experience of thirteen months in the trenches at Verdun in World War I, in which he was wounded in 1916, Toller became a committed Socialist and wrote expressionist plays of suffering and revolt against the imperial order. As a result of his role in strikes and antiwar agitation, he was imprisoned for a time. Toller was a leader in the short-lived Bavarian Soviet Republic of 1919, succeeding Kurt Eisner after his assassination. He also headed the Red Guard. When the revolution collapsed, he was imprisoned for five years. It was there that he wrote his most famous plays, including *Masses and Men*, *The Machine-Wreckers*, and *Brokenbrow*. His prison poems, first published in 1923, were translated as *The Swallow-Book* in 1924. One of his plays dramatizes the 1918 mutiny of sailors at Kiel. Exiled in 1932, his life became increasingly difficult. Despite translations of his work by Stephen Spender and W. H. Auden, he remained little-known in the English-speaking world. But it was not his career that was his main focus in those years; it was the struggle against fascism. A foe of the Nazis throughout his exile, Toller was the object of especially intense Nazi hatred. He was also deeply engaged in efforts to help the Spanish republic, and Franco's victory plunged him into despair. Toller committed suicide in New York in 1939. A fragmentary note in Rolfe's archive reads: "I never saw Toller dead. Even the photographs of his face among the flowers in his bier seemed strange. I never even remember him really as he was at the banquet. That was not the real thing either. I saw him when he was alive."

"the horizon of Nazi faces murdering Muehsam": Erich Muehsam (1878–1934) was a German-Jewish poet, dramatist, and anarchist. His work combines proletarian social critique with anarchist philosophy and expressionist technique. He published an anarchist newspaper, *Der Arme Teufel*, briefly just after the turn of the century and in 1911 founded another anarchist periodical, *Kain*, which lasted until 1919, except for several years during World War I. Muehsam helped organize a strike at the Krupp factories in Munich later in the war; he was imprisoned for his efforts. Like Toller, he was active in the overthrow of the Bavarian monarchy and a notable figure in the short-lived Bavarian Soviet Republic of April 1919. Sentenced to fifteen years in prison on its overthrow, he was released after five years. For nine years, until he was imprisoned by the Nazis in 1933, he edited *Fanal*, a monthly of anarchist philosophy. After being repeatedly tortured in several concentration camps, he was murdered by the Nazis at Oranienburg on July 9, 1934. In the light of Rolfe's own difficulties later in publishing "Elegia," it is worth noting

that Muehsam published an elegy on the death of Lenin that compared him
with Moses; the party did not care for the biblical reference.
Like Rolfe, Toller and Muehsam were both secularized Jews and writer-
revolutionaries.

"The Melancholy Comus"

For information on Rolfe's relationship with Chaplin see Cary Nelson and Jeffer-
son Hendricks, *Edwin Rolfe: A Biographical Essay and Guide to the Rolfe Archive at
the University of Illinois at Urbana-Champaign* (1990).

"Song for a Birth Day in Exile":

"Elena, daughter of José / and Evita": José Rubia Barcia is a Spanish Socialist,
scholar, and exile whom Rolfe met in Los Angeles. The U.S. Immigration
Service tried for many years to force Barcia to return to Spain, where he
would have been promptly executed. Barcia had written a book on Ramon
del Valle-Inclán, a Spanish novelist, dramatist, and poet who adopted a
distinctive discordant style in which to register social protest late in his
life. Among Valle-Inclán's works is a 1926 novel about revolution in Latin
America. Barcia translated Rolfe's "Elegia" into Spanish.
"the words that Unamuno spoke / before his heart, confused with wisdom,
broke": Miguel de Unamuno (1864–1936) was one of Spain's most notable
modern writers. When the Civil War began, he was sympathetic with the
Nationalists, but his position shifted shortly thereafter. At a ceremony held at
the University of Salamanca, in Nationalist territory within a hundred yards
of Franco's headquarters, on October 12, 1936, Unamuno dramatically criti-
cized José Millán Astray, the Nationalist general who founded the Spanish
Foreign Legion and who shared the platform with him that day. Unamuno
thereafter remained under house arrest until his death two months later. For
a detailed account of the incident see Hugh Thomas's *The Spanish Civil War*
(1977). I will, however, quote Unamuno's speech as Thomas reports it, since
it is a good, concise example of the way Rolfe often briefly alludes to a whole
complex historical context and to a historical narrative that means a great
deal to those who know its details. After several fervent pro-Franco exhor-
tations, including a murderous attack on Catalan and Basque nationalism
by Francisco Maldonado and a public proclamation of the Foreign Legion's
motto "*Viva la muerte!*" (long live death), Unamuno rose to speak:

> "All of you are hanging on my words. You all know me and are aware that
> I am unable to remain silent. At times to be silent is to lie. For silence
> can be interpreted as acquiescence. I want to comment on the speech—to
> give it that name—of Professor Moldanado. Let us waive the personal af-
> front implied in the sudden outburst of vituperation against the Basques

and Catalans. I was myself, of course, born in Bilbao. The bishop (here Unamuno indicated the quivering prelate sitting next to him), whether he likes it or not, is a Catalan, from Barcelona."

He paused. There was a fearful silence. No speech like this had been made in Nationalist Spain. What would the rector say next?

"Just now (Unamuno went on) I heard a necrophilistic and senseless cry: 'Long live death.' And I, who have spent my life shaping paradoxes which have aroused the uncomprehending anger of others, I must tell you, as an expert authority, that this outlandish paradox is repellent to me. General Millán Astray is a cripple. Let it be said without any slighting undertone. He is a war invalid. So was Cervantes. Unfortunately there are all too many cripples in Spain just now. And soon there will be even more of them, if God does not come to our aid. It pains me to think that General Millán Astray should dictate the pattern of mass psychology. A cripple who lacks the spiritual greatness of a Cervantes is wont to seek ominous relief in causing mutilation around him."

At this, Millán Astray was unable to restrain himself any longer. "Death to Intellectuals!" "*Mueran los intelectuales!*" he shouted. "Long live death." . . . But Unamuno went on:

"This is the temple of the intellect. And I am its high priest. It is you who profane its sacred precincts. You will win, because you have more than enough brute force. But you will not convince. For to convince, you need to persuade. And in order to persuade you would need what you lack: reason and right in the struggle. I consider it futile to exhort you to think of Spain. I have done." (502–3)

The legionnaires moved forward with menace. Millán Astray's bodyguard aimed his machine-gun at Unamuno. But Franco's wife escorted him off the platform.

"that other Spaniard . . . in Paris": This is, of course, Picasso, whose most famous Spanish Civil War painting is *Guernica*.

"Lanes of Death and Birth"

Stenka Razin: Stenka Razin was a seventeenth-century cossack who led an unsuccessful revolt against the czar. He became a folk hero and the hero of a Russian folk song by the same name.

"Old Black Joe in Gaul": Rolfe's reference is presumably to Stephen C. Foster's often anthologized 1860 song "Old Black Joe," the opening stanza of which is

> Gone are the days when my heart was young and gay
> Gone are my friends from the cotton fields away

Gone from the earth to a better land I know
I hear their gentle voices calling "Old Black Joe."

The chorus is "I'm coming, I'm coming, for my head is bending low / I hear those gentle voices calling 'Old Black Joe.'" In Rolfe's italicized stanza, Joe is not content to die; he reappears in another time and place—Gaul, just as the seventeenth-century cossack Stenka Razin gets to return to dance around the sombrero of the Mexican revolutionary Emiliano Zapata (1879–1919) and Christ reappears in Harlem, perhaps as the figure of the black Christ recurrent in Harlem Renaissance poetry. "Lanes of Death and Birth" is, of course, a love poem, and Rolfe is suggesting in his italicized stanza, the stanza most devoted to historical rather than personal references, that love's energy and sense of temporal possibility enables revolutionary changes and second chances. Note that the most logical pairing would have been "Old Black Joe in Harlem—Christ in Gaul," which would have had Old Black Joe reappear in another American black community and Christ in another area conquered by the Roman Empire. That was in fact what Rolfe had in another draft, but in revising the poem he exchanged the references to obtain a more radical sense of displacement, while letting the line simultaneously be destabilized by the proximity of the more logical associations.

"At the Moment of Victory"

Les hommes de bonne volonté (Men of good will): This is the overall title of a series of twenty-seven novels written by Jules Romains from 1932 to 1946. The series focuses on French history between 1908 and 1933 and emphasizes group movement and collective effort. Romains's protagonists tend to be politically committed and, at least at first, to be optimistic about their effect on history. Romains's own optimism came to an end with the rise of Nazism. Rolfe's concluding phrase, *Les hommes san volonté,* is an ironic reversal of Romains's title.

"Elegia"

See the Introduction.

Guadarrama winds: Madrid is situated on a 2,120-foot-high plateau, and it is encircled by the Guadarrama Mountains to the north. The winds that sweep down off the Guadarrama Mountains are a distinctive part of the city's climate.

"Yes, I weep with Garcilaso": Like Rolfe himself and like some of the young men in the trenches in Madrid, Garcilaso de la Vega (1501–36) was a soldier-poet. In an unpublished essay on poetics, Rolfe mentions that Garcilaso de la Vega's "First Elegy" is one of his favorite poems. His poetic output was small but highly polished, so that he became the undisputed classic poet of the Golden Age of Spanish literature. The recurrent theme in his poetry is love, and the melancholy and frustrated idealism with which it is treated no doubt owes something to his own unrequited love for Isabel Freire, a Portuguese lady-in-waiting to the empress. Rolfe's own love for Madrid here is, of course, frustrated by Franco's domination of Spain. Although the balance of the stanza is addressed to Madrid, the reference to Garcilaso continues to permeate it. The sons and daughters of the city, when they fall in love, are also figuratively children of Garcilaso's romantic poems. Finally, it is worth noting that Garcilaso was mortally wounded when leading an assault on an unimportant but well-fortified position, a story with no lack of parallels to the battles of the Spanish Civil War.

Calle de Velasquez: This is the street where the International Brigades building was located and where Rolfe edited the English-language magazine of the brigades, *Volunteer for Liberty,* from 1937 to the beginning of 1938.

"the green Retiro and its green gardens": Spread out in the middle of Madrid, the Retiro is one of Spain's most beautiful parks. It encompasses a lake and a number of distinct squares, open spaces, and formal gardens. Laid out in the seventeenth century, the park's 320 acres originally served as a royal retreat (*retiro*).

Alcalá: This is a major highway that heads east from its origin in the *Puerta del Sol.* Rolfe often walked along the Alcalá in the fall of 1937. In walking from the International Brigades Headquarters (63 Calle de Velasquez) to the old city, Rolfe would often have walked down Velasquez to Alcalá. The streets meet at the boundary of the Retiro Park, where Rolfe would have turned west and headed past the massive Puerta de la Alcalá and the Plaza de la Cibeles, past the post office building and the Ministry of Defense, and then on to *Puerta del Sol* and the old part of Madrid. In the thirties the portion of the Alcalá in the downtown area was the major cafe street in the city.

Gateway to the Sun: This is the *Puerta del Sol,* the central plaza of Madrid. See the notes to "City of Anguish."

Plaza Mayor: This is a beautifully proportioned, rectangular, seventeenth-century, cobbled, arcaded square. Some 130 yards long and 100 yards wide, it was planned by Felipe II and his architect to serve as a public meeting place for the new capital; it was finished in 1619 during the reign of Felipe III. A 1613 bronze statue of Felipe III on horseback is in the center of the square. The Plaza Mayor has been a frequent site for public spectacles—from processions of flagellants and penitents to bullfights—as well as the site of some of Spain's major public ceremonies—such as the crowning of kings—and the site, finally, of some of its more traumatic historical moments. Thus it was here that the Inquisition held its *autos-da-fé* and executed its victims. Balconies on all four sides of the square provided vantage points for spectators.

The Plaza Mayor is located off Calle Mayor a few blocks from *Puerta del Sol.* The streets of Old Madrid radiate from the Plaza Mayor.

Casa de Campo: This is a sprawling wooded park northwest of the city that was the scene of major fighting during the attacks on Madrid. Its hills and scrub brush made rapid troop movement difficult but provided excellent cover for the Nationalist troops. In the summer of 1936, when terror reigned in both Nationalist and Republican cities, the Casa de Campo was the scene of frequent summary executions.

University City: This is the hillside campus of the University of Madrid, which was the scene of dramatic fighting during the struggle for the city. Hoping to end the war quickly with one decisive stroke, Franco ordered a major assault against the Spanish capital in the fall of 1936. After being halted by the people's militias, Franco's troops were preparing additional attacks on the city when the International Brigades marched through Madrid on November 8 to take up positions in their first major battles. On November 9 International Brigade troops spearheaded a counterattack among the gum and ilex trees of the Casa de Campo. In a series of bloody bayonet charges ending in hand-to-hand combat, the Internationals helped retake portions of the park, though Nationalist troops remained entrenched there. A week later the Internationals were engaged in hand-to-hand combat in University City, much of which was reduced to rubble in the process. Buildings were sandbagged; doors and windows were barricaded. Machine guns swept all the open approaches. At one point the ground floor of one building was held by the Thaelmann battalion of the Internationals and the other floors by Franco's Moors. On another day one room in the Hall of Philosophy changed hands four times. The battle for University City continued until November 23; the fascist advance had been stopped, but University City remained divided between the opposing armies for the rest of the war. The grounds were deeply entrenched, tunnels were dug under streets exposed to fire, and various buildings remained in either Nationalist or Republican hands.

Gypsy Ballads: This refers to the *Romancero Gitano* (1928), a book of poems by Federico García Lorca that Rolfe acquired in Albacete in 1937. Lorca was murdered by Nationalist partisans just after the outbreak of the Spanish Civil War. See the final quotation in the Introduction.

Poetas en La España Leal and *Romanceros de los Soldados en las Trincheras:* These are two of a number of poetry anthologies issued in Spain by Loyalist supporters during the war. *Poetas en la España Leal,* containing forty-four poems, was published in July 1937 to honor the Second International Congress of Anti-fascist Writers, which met in Spain that year. It was compiled by the editors of the journal *Hora de España,* which had previously published most of the poems in the book. Rolfe's entry in his diary for September 11, 1937, notes that he purchased three copies of *Poetas en la España Leal* in Madrid that day. *Romanceros de los Soldados en las Trincheras* was among a number of collections devoted to poetry, prose, or graphic art by Loyalist soldiers.

"First Love"

This poem was written in 1943 while Rolfe was in training in Texas after being drafted by the U.S. Army. See the Introduction. When first published in *Yank: The Army Weekly* in 1945, Rolfe titled it "First Love (Remembering Spain)." The parenthetical addition to the title may have been intended not only to alert readers to its Spanish referent but also to allude to Louis MacNeice's poem "Remembering Spain," which has a number of points of similarity with "First Love." MacNeice, for example, remembers "fretwork that the Moor / Had chiselled for effects of sun and shadow." MacNeice's poem's final lines have since become a touchstone for the commitment to Republican Spain:

> And next day [I] took the boat
>   For home, forgetting Spain, not realizing
> That Spain would soon denote
>   Our grief, our aspirations;
> Not knowing that our blunt
>   Ideals would find their whetstone, that our spirit
> Would find its frontier on the Spanish front,
>   Its body in a rag-time army.

Uncollected and Unpublished Poems, 1937–43

"Eyes of a Boy," "Radio Madrid—1937," "Munich," and "In Time of Hesitation" are unpublished poems. The other poems in this section were published in journals. All of these poems were included in *Two Wars and Other Poems*, a book manuscript of the 1940s that evolved into *First Love and Other Poems*.

"Eyes of a Boy"

See the opening quotation in the Introduction for another reference to Hilario. Rolfe also writes about Hilario in *The Lincoln Battalion*: "Many of the young, new recruits who joined the decimated American battalion were from Valencia and Alicante. . . . Others were Catalans, schoolboys and young farm and city workers. . . . There was one particularly—Hilario was his first name, nineteen years old and a Catalan—who delighted in singing outlandish renditions of American jazz. For a while he was battalion bugler. . . . Hilario's eyes would gleam with pride and professional solidarity. . . . Hilario lived to be almost twenty years old" (231–33). Rolfe's holograph manuscript for "Eyes of a Boy," dated August 25, 1937, does not, of course, include the dedication to Hilario, which records his death in 1938. The dedication lists Hilario's age as fifteen, whereas *The Lincoln Battalion* lists it as nineteen. There are a number of possible explanations—there may have been more than one boy with the same name, Rolfe may have altered names to protect family members from fascist reprisals—but no information has been uncovered to settle the issue now.

Valentín González: Also known as "El Campesino" (the peasant). Originally a guerilla leader, he became a commander of one of the Mixed Brigades and one of the most famous officers of the Spanish Civil War. Lawrence A. Fernsworth concludes his description of González in Jo Davidson's *Spanish Portraits* (1928) as follows: "He gathered together a little company of nineteen men and led them out into the Sierra Guadarrama to hold the road to Madrid on that first day. Later he formed a battalion which made history in the Sierra, defending its position to the last inch and the last man. It was El Campesino's battalion, too, that held the trenches of Carabanchel in the defense of Madrid. His battalion has been in the bloodiest battles since—the defense of Madrid, Villavieja, Buitrago, Quijorna, Brunete, Teruel. At thirty-three he is now commander of a division—a great, black-bearded, rough, laughing, blustering soldier whose name is a word to swear by in the army of the Republic." Also see Rolfe's essay about El Campesino, "Spain's Shirt-Sleeve General," published in the December 7, 1937, issue of *New Masses,* which gives a detailed account of a day Rolfe spent with El Campesino's division in a town near Madrid. Merino and Policarpo commanded the second and first brigades under Campesino, who headed the 46th division. Policarpo Candon was a Cuban-American; his brigade was a mobile shock brigade.

"Radio Madrid—1937"

An earlier draft has the title "Voice of Spain." Rolfe arranged programs for Radio Madrid and broadcast several talks of his own in the fall of 1937. Among the people he scheduled for a broadcast and introduced was Langston Hughes. The "dearest friend" referred to in the second stanza is Leo Hurwitz. The poem may have been partly inspired by Rafael Alberti's satiric "Radio Seville," an English version of which was published in the August 9, 1937, issue of *Volunteer for Liberty*. Alberti's poem comments on the radio broadcasts of the fascist General Gonzalo Queipo de Llano, which were often delivered under the influence of alcohol and were sprinkled with profanity and remarks about his troops' sexual prowess. If Rolfe had "Radio Seville" in mind, then he has provided a moral counterexample in "Radio Madrid."

"Radio Seville" is also translated in M. J. Bernadette and Rolfe Humphries, eds.,
. . . and Spain Sings: Fifty Loyalist Ballads (1937).
> enemy moon: A full moon gave the fascist artillery increased visibility for shell-
> ing the city.
> *dinamiteros:* These are soldiers whose weapon was often the somewhat primi-
> tive can-grenades of dynamite. Lit with a fuse and thrown by hand, their use
> required getting rather close to the target. *Dinamiteros* were often specialists
> in antitank warfare.

"Not Hatred"
An earlier draft has the title "One Does Not Feel Hatred."

"Paris—Christmas 1938"
An earlier draft has the title "Lullaby."

"Munich"
See the Introduction. In *The Lincoln Battalion* Rolfe writes that "Chamberlain and
Daladier and American neutrality starved and froze the women and children of
Spain while permitting German and Italian planes to snuff out their lives" (252).
In an unpublished piece in his archive, Rolfe makes the following comments about
1938: "Most of us can see the year of our birth, or the year America was discovered,
more clearly and through less obscuring vapor than we remember 1938. That was
the year, you may recall, when heroes acted like villains and villains strutted like
heroes; when wars—and there were many wars—were trifling and unofficial, be-
cause no skin off our backs was immediately involved; when, with a few honorable
exceptions, most men and most countries we now consider good, just, righteous,
were—at worst—aiding their own enemies; at best, turning away from distant,
unpleasant sights." For Rolfe, as for many veterans of Spain, it is particularly signifi-
cant that Chamberlain was scurrying to appease Hitler at the very moment when
the soldiers of the Spanish republic and the International Brigades were putting
their lives on the line in a stand against fascism.
> "the barbarous use of a violent cathartic": Mussolini promoted a form of torture
> involving forced feeding of large quantities of castor oil.
> Blum, Léon: Blum (1872–1950) was a Socialist who headed the French Popu-
> lar Front government from June 1936 to June 1937 and again briefly in
> 1938. Blum wanted to help the Spanish government but vacillated because
> of his fears of a broader war in Europe. He also worried about whether he
> could count on his own military to act against Franco. Thus he followed an
> ambivalent policy—allowing volunteers to cross the border into Spain but
> generally supporting nonintervention. Blum was anguished, but he was also

unable successfully to resist fascist aggression. He was interned in Germany during World War II.

Bonnet, Georges Etienne: Bonnet (1889–1973) was French foreign minister at the time of the Munich crisis of 1938.

Daladier, Edouard: Daladier (1884–1970) was a French Socialist politician who served as premier in 1933 and 1934, became war minister in 1936, and premier again in 1938. He supported appeasement and signed the Munich pact. He built his support in France by exploiting anticommunism and anti-war sentiment. Although sympathetic to the Spanish republic, he was often vacillating and advocated neutrality and nonintervention. In 1940, the year after Rolfe's poem was written, he was interned by the Vichy government. Three years later he was taken to Germany, where he was imprisoned until the end of the war.

Halifax, Edward Frederick Lindley Wood: In March 1938 Halifax (1881–1959) succeeded Sir Anthony Eden as foreign secretary under British prime minister Neville Chamberlain. He helped implement Chamberlain's appeasement policy. Halifax's visit with Hitler at Berchtesgaden on November 17, 1937, was the first concrete step in putting the policy into effect, and he played a large role in negotiating the Munich pact in 1938. From 1940 to 1945 he was Britain's ambassador to the United States.

Runciman, Lord Walter: Runciman (1870–1949) was the English politician who is remembered primarily for his 1938 mission to Czechoslovakia and his efforts to persuade the Czechs to make concessions to Hitler in order to appease him. Runciman took the position that Hitler's claims against the Czechs had merit.

Schuschnigg, Kurt von: Schuschnigg (1887–1978) became Austrian chancellor after the assassination of Engelbert Dolfuss in July 1934 and served as chancellor of a somewhat fascist regime until 1938. As a nationalist, he was initially inclined to resist Hitler's effort to take control of Austria, but he was frightened by Hitler's demands for greater union between Germany and Austria at a February 1938 meeting. Forced to resign in favor of the Nazi Arthur Seyssinquart, he was arrested and imprisoned by the Nazis after Hitler occupied Austria in March 1938.

"In the Time of Hesitation"

The title is taken from William Vaughan Moody's turn-of-the-century poem against American imperialism in the Philippines, "An Ode in Time of Hesitation."

Permit Me Refuge

"A Dedication"
An earlier draft has the title "Odysseus to Penelope."

"Bequest"
An earlier draft has the title "Testament."

"Catalogue of *I*"
Rolfe is partly writing a revolutionary version of Whitman's "Song of Myself."
"the cotton-clad exile in the caves of loess": Loess is a windblown mineral deposit associated with glaciers in the Northern Hemisphere. In China, there are loess deposits that reach five hundred feet in height that include innumerable cave dwellings. Rolfe's reference is to the Chinese revolution. Under attack by Chiang Kai-shek, Mao Tse-tung was forced to abandon his people's republic in southeast China in 1934. After the arduous and epic six-thousand-mile "Long March" of 1934–35, Mao and his followers took up residence in caves of loess in Shensi province in northwest China. They were clad in native common cloth of rough cotton. Between 1937 and 1945 Mao's Communists employed mobile, rural-based guerilla warfare against the Japanese.

"Poem"
"*Consciousness*, said Don Miguel, *is a disease*": The quotation is from the first chapter of Unamuno's *The Tragic Sense of Life* (1913). Rolfe's papers include the following fragment, titled "On reading a book by M. de U.":

> Not with its sense, not with its logic,
> Nor with its sad philosophy—
> but with its dire predicament I agree.

"Vincent"
Earlier drafts are titled "Van Gogh." The Borinage is the poor mining district in Belgium where Van Gogh served as a lay minister from 1878 until he was relieved of his duties the following year. The poem includes references to a number of Van Gogh's better-known paintings, from *The Potato Eaters* in the first stanza to *Crows over a Wheatfield* and *Van Gogh's Bedroom* in the third.

"Now the Fog"
The reference to Juan Ponce de León and his 1513 voyage to the Americas in the third stanza will be recognizable to most readers. On the other hand, the his-

torical reference at issue in the image of "the colorless Pale / of a stamped official registration card" in the previous stanza may be less familiar. Rolfe is suggesting that, if we go on as we are, we will soon find the United States to be as repressive and restrictive as czarist Russia was to the Jews. The Pale of Settlement was the restricted territory where Jews were authorized to live. Even within the Pale, Jews were generally prohibited from living in rural areas. In the late nineteenth and early twentieth centuries, Jewish villages within the Pale were subjected to the pogroms. Effectively ended by population displacements during World War I, the law establishing the Pale was overturned after the 1917 revolution.

"Night World"
Compare the very different poem with the same title in *First Love*.

"The Glory Set"
The stamps were given to Rolfe by Clifford Odets. The first draft of the poem began "Dear Clifford." It was titled "Lines to a Friend."

"All Ghouls' Night"
An earlier draft is titled "Conspiracy."

"Ballad of the Noble Intentions"
This poem was written in response to hearing that his friend Clifford Odets had testified before the House Un-American Activities Committee and named names. It was first titled "Ballad of the Lost Friend." Rolfe and Odets had known one another since the 1930s.

"Idiot Joe Prays in Pershing Square and Gets Hauled in for Vagrancy"
Earlier drafts had the titles "En La Noche Oscura" and "The Prayer of Joe Blix the Anarchist."

"On Rico LeBrun's *Crucifixion*"
Rico Lebrun was an artist on the Left whom Rolfe met in Los Angeles. Lebrun's series of 206 paintings and drawings on the theme of the crucifixion was exhibited at the Los Angeles County Museum from January 27 to February 28, 1951. The poem may focus partly on the large (192-by-312-inch) triptych that opened the exhibit. The exhibit catalogue was in Rolfe's library.

"Political Prisoner 123456789"
Rolfe had in mind a reference to the Hollywood Ten, minus Edward Dmytryk, who, after initial resistance, turned and cooperated with HUAC. The ten "un-

friendly" witnesses, all Hollywood writers or film directors, who were called to testify before the House Un-American Activities Committee in Washington in October of 1947 were John Howard Lawson, Dalton Trumbo, Albert Maltz, Alvah Bessie, Samuel Ornitz, Herbert Biberman, Edward Dmytryk, Adrian Scott, Ring Lardner, Jr., and Lester Cole. They stood on their First Amendment rights to freedom of speech and association in refusing to disclose their own and other people's political associations. Cited for contempt of Congress, they lost their appeals and eventually served time in federal prison. See the Introduction for further comments on the poem. For a time Rolfe's wife, Mary, was in charge of organizing efforts for the Hollywood Ten.

"A Poem to Delight My Friends
Who Laugh at Science-Fiction"

This was inspired in part by a *New York Times* story. See the Introduction.

Uncollected and Unpublished Poems, 1947–54

Except for "The Poisoned Air Befouled the Whole Decade," all these poems were unpublished. Rolfe did not live long enough to decide whether these poems, some written in the last months of his life, should be included in the manuscript of his book in progress, *Words and Ballads,* which was published posthumously as *Permit Me Refuge.*

"Exodus 1947"

The poem in manuscript is untitled. A page of notes preceding the poem, however, has this title. "Exodus 1947," unpublished in Rolfe's lifetime, is about holocaust survivors en route to Palestine. "Exodus 1947" was the name given to a ship that carried 4,554 Jewish refugees to Palestine in 1947. The trip was organized by the *Haganah.* In any case, following a battle in which three Jews died, the ship was seized by the British near Haifa. Sent back to Europe, the passengers were forcibly removed from the ship by British soldiers. The ship's name and the poem's title, of course, refer not only to the biblical exodus from Egypt but also to the exodus as a figure for Jewish history.

In the absence of these notes, it might seem to some readers that it is also Rolfe's only poem on an explicitly Jewish theme. Actually, there are several other poems that make reference to Jewish history and anti-Semitism—including "Entry," "Song (3)," "Essay on Dreiser," "May 22 1939," and "Now the Fog"—but the references in most of these poems will not readily be recognized without the relevant background knowledge included in the relevant notes.

"Blues"

Rolfe's papers include an unused stanza for the poem in holograph:

> Got a two-headed woman
> Treats me awful nice:
> ·When I look at her one time
> She looks right back at me twice.

"The Poisoned Air Befouled the Whole Decade":

Rolfe used this title in the manuscript of *Words and Ballads*.

"Are You Now or Have You Ever Been"

The poem is typed, but the title is printed somewhat roughly in holograph.

"Letter"

The poem is untitled. It was written as a companion piece to "Are You Now or Have You Ever Been." At the bottom of the second page of the former poem Rolfe typed three asterisks and began this poem, which we have titled "Letter."

"Poem"

The poem is untitled, but it is dated Malibu, August 29, 1949.

"A Letter to the Denouncers"

There are several drafts of this poem in the archive, but this is clearly the latest version. In one draft, in an essentially private gesture of circular commemoration, Rolfe signed the poem "W. Tell." It was one of the pseudonyms he had used in high school in order to publish in *The Comet,* the school literary magazine, when he was barred from doing so as a punishment·for failing trigonometry. Here the pseudonym evokes the strategy forced by blacklisting and signals the poem's unwelcome cultural testimony.

"1949 (After Reading a News Item)"

An earlier draft has the title "1949: On Reading One News Item and Recalling Another." Pius XII became Pope in 1939 and enthusiastically celebrated Franco's victory. The previous Pope had also spoken out in support of Franco during the Spanish Civil War.

"June 19, 1953"

The poem is untitled. We gave it a dated title to make it consistent with the other quatrains involving a historical comparison. That the poem compares the U.S. Supreme Court's roles in the executions of Sacco and Vanzetti and the Rosenbergs is not in doubt. The date we assigned, however, may not be correct, since the court was also involved in the Rosenberg case the previous year (1952), when it refused to review it. It was on June 19, 1953, that the Supreme Court convened for a special session, returning from vacation for that purpose, in order to vacate a stay of execution that had been granted by Justice William O. Douglas. The Rosenbergs were executed that evening. The phrase "kills Jews today" seemed to argue for the 1953 date, which also assumes that Rolfe meant "twenty-five years ago" to be a rhetorical figure for the year (1927) when Sacco and Vanzetti were executed. In any case, the poem carries the same force whether it was written in response to the 1952 or 1953 decision.

Julius and Ethel Rosenberg were accused of passing data on the construction of the atomic bomb to the Soviet Union. Although no documentary evidence of espionage was presented at their 1951 trial, which occurred during the period of anticommunist hysteria in the United States, they were promptly convicted and sentenced to death. Some of the oral testimony against them has since been shown to have been fabricated. Whether they were guilty or innocent, therefore, it seems clear that some testimony was perjured and that the case against them did not meet the legal burden of proof.

"Little Ballad for Americans—1954"

Rolfe's title no doubt alludes ironically to Earl Robinson's famous 1939 patriotic cantata *Ballad for Americans,* which set to music John Latouche's 1935 poem of the same title. Rolfe and Robinson knew one another and collaborated on two projects. In the thirties Rolfe did the words and Robinson the music for a dance for Jane Dudley, one of Martha Graham's dancers. In 1948 Rolfe wrote the verse accompaniment and Robinson wrote the music for the Joseph Strick–Irving Lerner short film *Muscle Beach*. Robinson himself was blacklisted in the fifties. Moreover, Robinson's *Ballad for Americans* gained national fame in 1939 when it was performed on radio by Paul Robeson and then recorded and released by RCA. By the time Rolfe wrote his poem Robeson too was blacklisted in the entertainment industry, and Robeson's passport had been revoked so as to prevent him from performing abroad. Years earlier, incidentally, Rolfe was one of a group of students at the Experimental College at Wisconsin who found a place for Robeson to stay while he performed in Madison; none of the hotels would rent a room to a black man. Rolfe's poem thus resonates with intertwined personal and historical allusions; none are necessary to the poem, but they enrich its ironies and add a personal element to its composition. More broadly, the reference to Robinson's *Ballad for Americans* underlines the difference between the idealized image of America and its reality during the inquisition. *Ballad for Americans* is an inclusive, Whitmanesque celebration of all the ethnic, religious, and racial groups that make up America; during the McCarthy period the dominant culture was obsessed instead with casting people out as un-American.

Early Poems

"Where Buildings Congregate" is unpublished. The other poems in this section, all uncollected, were published in journals and newspapers

Appendix 1

"The Sixth Winter"

This poem was published in 1935. A much condensed version, "Season of Death," is included in *To My Contemporaries*. The dedication to Sol Funaroff was added to a typed version of the poem in the forties.

Books of Poems

1933   *We Gather Strength: Poems by Herman Spector, Joseph Kalar, Edwin Rolfe, Sol Funaroff.* Introduction by Mike Gold. New York: Liberal Press, 1933. The poems by Rolfe, printed on pages 37–46, are "Asbestos," "Brickyards at Beacon," "Credo," "Winds of Another Sphere," "Portrait of a Death," "Kentucky—1932," and "Homage to Karl Marx." All except "Portrait of a Death" were reprinted in *To My Contemporaries.*

Reviews

Anon. *Daily Worker,* May 30, 1933, 2.

Calmer, Alan. *Daily Worker,* Aug. 14, 1933, 5.

Kline, Herbert. "Comrade Poets." *Left Front* 1, no. 2 (Sept.–Oct. 1933): 15.

Maas, Willard. *Poetry* 44, no. 1 (1933): 50–53.

1936   *To My Contemporaries.* New York: Dynamo, 1936.

Reviews

Anon. *The Nation,* June 17, 1936, 784.

Anon. (Evaluative Notice.) *New Yorker,* Dec. 12, 1936, 110

Benet, William Rose. *Saturday Review of Literature,* Feb. 15, 1936, 26.

Fearing, Kenneth. *Daily Worker,* Jan. 23, 1936, 7.

Freeman, Joseph. *New Masses* 18, no. 11 (Mar. 10, 1936): 23–25. Also see Freeman's "What a World" column in *Daily Worker,* Nov. 17, 1933, 5.

M., J. *Enterprise* (High Point, N.C.), Mar. 22, 1936.

Rodman, Selden. *Common Sense,* Mar. 1936, 28–29 (reviewed with Kenneth Patchen's *Before the Brave*).

Rosenberg, Harold. *Partisan Review and Anvil* 3, no. 3 (Apr. 1936): 29–30.

Rukeyser, Muriel. *Book Union Bulletin.*

S., W. T. "A Poet Speaks." *Journal* (Providence, R.I.), Mar. 15, 1936.

Stone, Geoffrey. *American Review* 7 (Apr. 1936): 108.

Thornbury, Ethel. *Times* (Madison, Wisc.), May 24, 1936.

Walton, Edna Lou. "Three Young Marxist Poets." *New York Times Book Review,* June 21, 1936, 16 (reviewed with Kenneth Patchen, *Before the Brave;* Stanley Burnshaw, *The Iron Land*).

Wilson, T. C. *New Republic,* June 10, 1936, 139.

Zabel, Morton Dauwen. "Poets of Five Decades." *Southern Review* (Summer 1936): 160–86 (omnibus review of seventeen books of poetry; see 185–86 for a response to Rolfe).

1951   *First Love, and Other Poems.* Los Angeles: Larry Edmunds Book Shop, 1951. Illustrations by Lia Nickson.

Reviews

Humphries, Rolfe. "Verse Chronicle." *The Nation,* Feb. 2, 1952.

Kramer, Aaron. "New Rolfe Book." *National Guardian,* Jan. 16, 1952.

McGrath, Thomas. "Belated Recognition for a Splendid Book of Poetry." *Daily People's World,* May 12, 1954.

1955   *Permit Me Refuge.* Los Angeles: California Quarterly, 1955. Preface by Thomas McGrath. Published posthumously from a manuscript Rolfe had in progress at the time of his death.

Reviews

Bessie, Alvah. "Edwin Rolfe Says Farewell in a Moving 'First' Book of Poems." *Daily People's World,* Nov. 3, 1955, 7. Reprinted in *Daily Worker,* Nov. 10, 1955, 7.

Frumkin, Gene. *Coastlines* 1, no. 4 (Spring 1956): 30–31.

Kramer, Aaron. "A Legacy of Light: The Poems of Edwin Rolfe." *National Guardian,* Jan. 2, 1956, 10.

Rodman, Selden. "Classic and Modern." *New York Times Book Review,* Jan. 1, 1956, sect. 7, p. 4 (reviewed with Kenneth Rexroth, *One Hundred Poems from the Japanese;* Witter Bynner, *Book of Lyrics;* P. D. Cummins, *Some Phases of Love;* and Robert Conquest, *Poems*).

Weiss, Theodore. "A Neutral Platter." *Saturday Review of Literature,* June 16, 1956, 51–52.

Poems First Published in Periodicals, Newspapers, and Anthologies

Key: * previously uncollected poems
       + poems not included in the present volume

1927   + "The Ballad of the Subway Digger"
        Daily Worker, Aug. 6, 1927 (*New Magazine*), 5.
    + "Processional"
        Daily Worker, Nov. 21, 1927, 6.

1928   + "Modern Croesus"
        Daily Worker, Mar. 10, 1928, 5.
    + "John the Baptist Goes to Heaven"
        Daily Worker, Mar. 17, 1928, 5.

+ "Jonah and the Whale—1928"
  Daily Worker, Apr. 26, 1928, 6.
+ "Portrait of a Farmer"
  Cooperative Bulletin, May 3, 1928. (This is most likely a bulletin issued by the United Workers' Cooperative Association that ran the "COOPS," the progressive Bronx apartment complex where Rolfe's family moved when it opened in 1928.)
* "May Day Song"
  Daily Worker, May 5, 1928, 5.
+ "The little pigeons"
  Daily Worker, May 23, 1928, 6.
+ "Paunchy Paytriots"
  Daily Worker, May 24, 1928, 6.
+ "Eight O'clock Whistle"
  New Masses 4, no. 1 (June 1928): 18.
+ "Red Planet"
  Daily Worker, Sept. 1, 1928, 4.
  "The 100 Percenter" ["Asbestos"]
  Daily Worker, Sept. 22, 1928, 6.
* "Any Slave"
  Daily Worker, Nov. 9, 1928, 4.

1929   + "Song for Youth!"
  Daily Worker, May 29, 1929, 6.
  "Brickyards at Beacon"
  Daily Worker, June 22, 1929, 6.

1930   + "The Lake Path"
  Daily Cardinal (Madison, Wisc.), Mar. 23, 1930, 8.
+ "Beyond"
  New York Times, Sept. 11, 1930, 24. Reprinted in *Daily Cardinal,* Oct. 26, 1930, 7.
+ "In Suns More Golden"
  New York Times, Oct. 3, 1930, 26. Reprinted in *Daily Cardinal,* Oct. 18, 1930, 6.
+ "Metropolis"
  Daily Cardinal, Nov. 9, 1930, 7.
+ "The Sponge"
  Daily Cardinal, Nov. 9, 1930, 7.
+ "White-Bearded Beggar"
  Daily Cardinal, Nov. 9, 1930, 7.
+ "Clay of Life"
  New York Times, Nov. 28, 1930, 18. Reprinted in *Knickerbocker Press* (Albany, N.Y.), Nov. 30, 1930, 8; *Ottawa Journal,* Dec. 3, 1930, 6;

The Enquirer (Cincinnati), Jan. 26, 1931, 4; and *Albany Evening News,* Feb. 5, 1931, 28.

1931   + "Needless"
New York Times, Mar. 3, 1931, 28.

+ "From the Chrysler Tower"
The Left: A Quarterly Review of Radical and Experimental Art 1, no. 2 (Summer-Autumn 1931): 36.

+ "Prospectus"
Front 1, no. 4 (1931): 340.

1932   + "Eventualities"
Pagany 3, no. 1 (Jan.–Mar. 1932): 45–46.

* "Sunday Evening Revery"
Pagany 3, no. 2 (Apr.–June 1932): 16–17.

+ "Entreaty at Delphi"
Pagany 3, no. 3 (July-Sept. 1932): 88–89.

+ "Sonnet" ("Precise, the undulating mockery")
Contempo 2, no. 7 (Sept. 25, 1932): 4.

1933   "Lanes of Death and Birth"
Poetry 41 (Feb. 1933): 266–67 (not collected until *First Love and Other Poems*).

"Homage to Karl Marx"
New Masses 8, no. 8 (Apr. 1933): 9.

"Kentucky—1932"
Daily Worker, Sept. 9, 1933, 7.

* "Barn in Wisconsin"
The Anvil (Nov.–Dec. 1933): 20.

1934   * "Something Still Lives"
The Anvil (Jan.–Feb. 1934): 23.

"Three Who Died"
New Masses 10, no. 7 (Feb. 13, 1934): 6.

"Poem" ["Poem for May First"]
Partisan Review 1, no. 1 (Feb.–Mar. 1934): 32–34. Reprinted in Granville Hicks et al., *Proletarian Literature in the United States* (New York: International Publishers, 1935), 184–86.

"The Pattern of Our Lives"
Dynamo: A Journal of Revolutionary Poetry 1, no. 2 (Mar.–Apr. 1934): 13–15.

+ "First Lesson"
Daily Worker, July 3, 1934, 5.

* "Homecoming (August 7, 1934)"
New Masses 12, no. 8 (Aug. 21, 1934): 10.

"Witness at Leipzig"
New Masses 12, no. 13 (Sept. 25, 1934): 22.

* "Communists"
Magazine 2, no. 2 (Sept.–Oct. 1934): 100.

"Room with Revolutionists"
Partisan Review 1, no. 4 (Sept.–Oct. 1934): 17–18.

"These Men Are Revolution"
New Masses 13, no. 2 (Oct. 9, 1934): 20–21.

"Unit Assignment"
New Republic, Nov. 28, 1934, 76–77. Reprinted in *Daily Worker,*
Dec. 4, 1934, 5, and in Granville Hicks et al., *Proletarian Literature
in the United States* (New York: International Publishers, 1935),
187–88.

"Somebody and Somebody Else and You"
Partisan Review 1, no. 5 (Nov.–Dec. 1934): 9–10.

1935   * "Nuthin but Brass"
New Theatre 11, no. 7 (July 1935): 25.

* "The Sixth Winter" ["Season of Death" is a condensed version]
International Literature, no. 9 (Sept. 1935): 46–50.

* "Not Men Alone"
The Anvil 3, no. 13 (Oct.–Nov. 1935): 10.

* *"Cheliuskin"*
Soviet Russia Today, Nov. 1935, 65–67.

1936   "Georgia Nightmare"
New Masses 18, no. 4 (Jan. 21, 1936): 10.

"The Ship"
Poetry 48, no. 2 (May 1936): 61–62 (social poets issue, edited
by Horace Gregory; published with "Night World" as "Before
the Hour").

"Night World"
Poetry 48, no. 2 (May 1936): 62–63 (social poets issue, edited
by Horace Gregory; published with "The Ship" as "Before the
Hour").

"Prophecy in Stone"
New Republic, Sept. 16, 1936, 154.

1937   "Arctic" ["The Arctic Remembered"]
Forum and Century 97 (Feb. 1937): 116.

* "The Nine"
New Masses 22, no. 10 (Mar. 2, 1937): 8.

* "Winter's Ghost Plagues Them"
New Masses 21, no. 11 (Dec. 8, 1937): 6.

"Madrid" [Parts 4 and 5 of "City of Anguish"]
Romancero de los voluntarios de la libertad. Madrid: Ediciones del Comisariado de Las Brigadas Internacionales, 1937, 81–82.

1938   "Elegy for Our Dead"
The Volunteer for Liberty 2, no. 1 (Jan. 3, 1938): 9. Reprinted in *New Republic,* May 25, 1938, 65, in *Young Communist Review,* Feb. 1939, 10, and in *Daily Worker,* Oct. 1, 1939, 5.

1939   "No Man Knows War" [from "City of Anguish"]
New Republic, July 19, 1939, 300.

"For Arnold Reid" ["Epitaph"]
New Masses 32, no. 5 (July 25, 1939): 11.

1944   "Poems of Three Years"
New Masses 50, no. 3 (Jan. 18, 1944)
*   1. "Running from the shadow-coach" ["Entry"], 10–11.
*   2. "Nearing land, we heard the cry of gold" ["Death by Water"], 11.
*   3. "On shore later" ["Death by Water, Part II"], 12.
*   4. "One does not feel hatred" ["Not Hatred"], 12.
*   5. "You will remember, when the bombs" ["Paris—Christmas 1938"], 12.
*   6. "To say we were right is not boastful" ["Brigadas Internacionales"], 12.

1945   "Casualty"
Poetry 66, no. 1 (Apr. 1945): 12.

"Recruit"
Poetry 66, no. 1 (Apr. 1945): 15. Reprinted in *New York Times Book Review,* May 6, 1945, 2.

"Survival Is of the Essence".
Poetry 66, no. 1 (Apr. 1945): 13–14.

"To Thine Own Self"
Poetry 66, no. 1 (Apr. 1945): 12–13.

"The Guerrillas"
Saturday Review of Literature, Sept. 15, 1945, 42.

"First Love (Remembering Spain)"
Yank: The Army Weekly, Sept. 28, 1945, 21. Reprinted in *Volunteer for Liberty,* Oct. 1945.

"Song" ("There is indeed now reason for rejoicing")
Saturday Review of Literature, Oct. 13, 1945, 15.

"About Eyes"
Poetry 67, no. 3 (Dec. 1945): 135–36.

"Song (3)" ("Through all the cowering world, crouching, shrinking")
Poetry 67, no. 3 (Dec. 1945): 134–35.

1946 + "Three Sonnets" ["At the Moment of Victory"]
        Saturday Review of Literature, Mar. 23, 1946, 57.
            1. "At the moment of victory he examines his own"
            2. "He knows, at last, good will is not enough"
            3. "He remembers the fevers, the symptoms of disease"
        "Theodore Dreiser (1871–1945)"
            Poetry 68, no. 3 (June 1946): 134–36.
1947 "Two Pastorals"
        Mainstream: A Literary Quarterly 1, no. 4 (Fall 1947).
            1. "The lonely evening crouches, darkens as the hour" ["Pastoral"], 493.
            2. "Now, on this bluest of mornings, we wake" ["Pastoral (2)"], 494.
1948 "Silence Is Something Lost" ["Soledad"]
        Saturday Review of Literature, Sept. 25, 1948, 20.
1951 "The Melancholy Comus"
        Montevallo Review 1, no. 2 (Summer 1951): 35–37.
        "Sentry"
        California Quarterly 1, no. 1 (Autumn 1951): 48.
1952 "Two Mysteries"
        California Quarterly 1, no. 4 (Summer 1952): 53–54.
            1. ["Mystery"], 53.
            2. ["Mystery II"], 54.
1953 "Kill the Umpire!"
        Saturday Review of Literature, Apr. 18, 1953, 46.
        "A Poem to Delight My Friends Who Laugh at Science-Fiction"
            Poetry 82, no. 3 (June 1953): 141–42.
      + "Seascape"
        The Nation, July 18, 1953, 51.
1954 "Be Proud" ["Bequest"]
        California Quarterly 3, no. 3 (1954): 6.
        "Bon Voyage"
        California Quarterly 3, no. 3 (1954): 11.
        "Dawn Song"
        California Quarterly 3, no. 3 (1954): 9–10.
      * "Paris—Christmas 1938"
        California Quarterly 3, no. 3 (1954): 6–7.
        "In Praise Of"
        California Quarterly 3, no. 3 (1954): 8.
        "Undersea Poem"
        California Quarterly 3, no. 3 (1954): 8–9.

   "Vincent"
   California Quarterly 3, no. 3 (1954): 7–8.
1955 "Five Poems"
   Contemporary Reader 1, no. 4 (Jan. 1955): 18–20.
   * 1. "When I write, I am no longer I alone" ["Catalogue of *I*"], 18.
   * 2. "Now the fog falls on the land" ["Now the Fog"], 19.
   * 3. "The poisoned air befouled the whole decade," 20.
   * 4. "To understand the strength of those dark forces" ["In Praise Of"], 20.
   * 5. "After Tu Fu (713–770)," 20.
   "Conscript's Song"
   Coastlines 1, no. 1 (Spring 1955): 14.
   "Idiot Joe Prays in Pershing Square and Gets Hauled In for Vagrancy"
   Coastlines 1, no. 1 (Spring 1955): 14.
   "And If You Don't See What You Want Ask for It"
   Coastlines 1, no. 1 (Spring 1955): 15.
   "Poem" ["Many an outsider calls me friend"]
   Coastlines 1, no. 1 (Spring 1955): 13.

Poems Reprinted or Translated in Books, Anthologies, Pamphlets, and Newspapers

"After Tu Fu (713–770)"
 Jan Zábrana, ed. *Pátá Roční Doba: Antologie Americké Radikální Poezie*. Prague: Mladafronta, 1959. "Podle Tu Fu (713–770)," a Czech translation.
"And If You Don't See What You Want, Ask for It"
 Jan Zábrana, ed. *Pátá Roční Doba: Antologie Americké Radikální Poezie*. Prague: Mladafronta, 1959. "Co Nevidíte Ve Výloze, Žádejte Uvnitř," a Czech translation.
"The Arctic"
 Alan F. Pater, ed. *Anthology of Magazine Verse for 1937, and Yearbook of American Poetry*. New York: Paebar, 1938.
"City of Anguish"
  1. Alvah Bessie, ed. *The Heart of Spain*. New York: Veterans of the Abraham Lincoln Brigade, 1952.
  2. Jack Salzman and Leo Zanderer, eds. *Social Poetry of the 1930s*. New York: Burt Franklin, 1978.
  3. Roman Alvarez Rodriguez and Ramon Lopez Ortega, eds. *Poesia Anglo-Norteamericana de la guerra civil espanola*. Salamanca: Junta de Castilla y Leon / Consejeria de Educacion y Cultura, 1986. English reprint opposite "La ciudad de la angustia," a Spanish translation by Roman Alvarez and Francisco Fernandez Colinas.

4. Ramon Lopez Ortega and Roman Alvarez Rodriguez, eds. *Antologia de poesia inglesa siglos XVI—XX*. Salamanca: Anglo-American Studies, 1991. English reprint opposite "La ciudad de la angustia," a Spanish translation by Roman Alvarez and Francisco Fernandez Colinas.

"Death by Water"

Alvah Bessie and Albert Prago, eds. *Our Fight: Writings by Veterans of the Abraham Lincoln Brigade*. New York: Monthly Review Press, 1987.

"Definition"

1. August Derlith and Raymond E. F. Larsson, eds. *Poetry out of Wisconsin*. New York: Henry Harrison, 1937.
2. Selden Rodman, ed. *A New Anthology of Modern Poetry*. New York: Random House, 1938.
3. George K. Anderson and Eda Loy Walton, eds. *This Generation*. New York: Scott Foresman, 1939.
4. Elizabeth Selden, comp. *The Book of Friendship*. New York: Houghton Mifflin, 1947.
5. Jan Zábrana, ed. *Pátá Roční Doba: Antologie Americké Radikální Poezie*. Prague: Mladafronta, 1959. "Definice," a Czech translation.
6. Jack Salzman and Leo Zanderer, eds. *Social Poetry of the 1930s*. New York: Burt Franklin, 1978

"Elegia"

Elegia (pamphlet). (Mexico City: Talleres Gráficos de la Compañia Editora y Librera, 1949). This Spanish translation by José Rubia Barcia was the poem's first publication.

"Elegy for Our Dead"

1. Alan Calmer, ed. *Salud!: Poems, Stories, and Sketches of Spain by American Writers*. New York: International Publishers, 1939.
2. Oscar Williams, ed. *The War Poets: An Anthology of the War Poetry of the 20th Century*. New York: John Day, 1945.
3. Jan Zábrana, ed. *Pátá Roční Doba: Antologie Americké Radikální Poezie*. Prague: Mladafronta, 1959. "Elegie Za Naše Mrtvé," a Czech translation.

"Entry"

Jack Salzman and Leo Zanderer, eds. *Social Poetry of the 1930s*. New York: Burt Franklin, 1978.

"First Love"

1. Alvah Bessie, ed. *The Heart of Spain*. New York: Veterans of the Abraham Lincoln Brigade, 1952.
2. Frontispiece to Edwin Rolfe, *The Lincoln Battalion*. Reprint edition issued by the Veterans of the Abraham Lincoln Brigade, 1954.
3. Jan Zábrana, ed. *Pátá Roční Doba: Antologie Americké Radikální Poezie*. Prague: Mladafronta, 1959. "První Láska," a Czech translation.
4. Dario Puccini, ed. *Romancero della resistenza spagnola*. Milan: Feltrinelli

Editore, 1960. English reprint facing "Primo amore," an Italian translation by Stefania Piccinato.

5. Dario Puccini, ed. *Le romancero de la resistance espagnole.* Paris: Francois Maspero, 1962. English reprint facing "Premier amour," a French translation by Michele Mangin.

6. Dario Puccini, ed. *Romancero de la resistencia espanola.* Mexico City: Biblioteca ERA, 1967. English reprint facing "Primer amor," a Spanish translation by José Agustin Goytisolo.

7. Frontispiece to Arthur Landis, *Spain!: The Unfinished Revolution.* Baldwin Park, Calif.: Camelot Publishing, 1972. Special numbered edition of one thousand issued to commemorate the "volunteers of the Abraham Lincoln Brigade who gave their lives in defense of the Spanish Republic."

8. Jack Salzman and Leo Zanderer, eds. *Social Poetry of the 1930s.* New York: Burt Franklin, 1978.

9. Program for February 27, 1983, anniversary dinner of the Bay Area Post of the Veterans of the Abraham Lincoln Brigade.

10. Roman Alvarez Rodriguez and Ramon Lopez Ortega, eds. *Poesia Anglo-Norteamericana de la guerra civil espanola.* Salamanca: Junta de Castilla y Leon / Consejeria de Educacion y Cultura, 1986. English reprint opposite "Primer amor," a Spanish translation by José Manuel Cabezas Cabello.

"Kill the Umpire!"

Jan Zábrana, ed. *Pátá Roční Doba: Antologie Americké Radikální Poezie.* Prague: Mladafronta, 1959. "Zabte Rozhodčího!" a Czech translation.

"Many an Outcast"

American Journal of Psychoanalysis 37, no. 3 (Fall 1977): 252.

"The Melancholy Comus"

Cinema Nuovo, Mar. 25, 1956, 183. "L'ultima poesia su Chaplin di un pocta americano (1951)," an Italian translation by Glauco Viazzi

"Mystery"

Jan Zábrana, ed. *Pátá Roční Doba: Antologie Americké Radikální Poezie.* Prague: Mladafronta, 1959. "Tajemství," a Czech translation.

"Mystery II"

Jan Zábrana, ed. *Pátá Roční Doba: Antologie Americké Radikální Poezie.* Prague: Mladafronta, 1959. "Tajmeství II," a Czech translation.

"Night World"

Alan F. Pater, ed. *Anthology of Magazine Verse for 1936, and Yearbook of American Poetry.* New York: Poetry Digest Association, 1937.

"No Man Knows War"

1. Alan F. Pater, ed. *Anthology of Magazine Verse for 1938–1942, and Yearbook of American Poetry.* New York: Paebar, 1942.

2. Nathan and Mary Ausubel, eds. *A Treasury of Jewish Poetry*. New York: Crown, 1957.

3. Oscar Williams, ed. *The War Poets: An Anthology of the War Poetry of the 20th Century*. New York: John Day, 1945.

"Not Men Alone"

Jack Salzman and Leo Zanderer, eds. *Social Poetry of the 1930s*. New York: Burt Franklin, 1978.

"A Poem to Delight My Friends Who Laugh at Science-Fiction"

1. Rolfe Humphries, ed. *New Poems by American Poets*. New York: Ballantine, 1953.

2. Oscar Williams, ed. *The New Pocket Anthology of American Verse from Colonial Days to the Present*. Cleveland: World Publishing, 1955.

3. *Daily Worker,* Feb. 22, 1957, 6.

4. Jan Zábrana, ed. *Pátá Roční Doba: Antologie Americké Radikální Poezie*. Prague: Mladafronta, 1959. "Báseň Pro Potěchu Mých Přátel, Kteří Se Vysmívají Utopickým Románum," a Czech translation.

5. Al Hine, ed. *This Land Is Mine: An Anthology of American Verse*. Philadelphia: Lippincott, 1965.

6. Arnold Kenseth, ed. *Poems of Protest Old and New*. New York: MacMillan, 1968.

7. Paul C. Holmes and Harry E. Sauza, eds. *The Touch of a Poet*. New York: Harper and Row, 1976.

"Prophecy in Stone"

Paul Strand: A Retrospective Monograph—Volume One, the Years 1915–1946. New York: Aperture, 1972.

"Room with Revolutionists"

Jack Salzman and Leo Zanderer, eds. *Social Poetry of the 1930s*. New York: Burt Franklin, 1978.

"The Sixth Winter"

Jack Salzman and Leo Zanderer, eds. *Social Poetry of the 1930s*. New York: Burt Franklin, 1978.

"Somebody and Somebody Else and You"

Jack Salzman and Leo Zanderer, eds. *Social Poetry of the 1930s*. New York: Burt Franklin, 1978.

"Song (2): Keep the Dream Alive and Growing Always"

Nathan and Marynn Ausubel, eds. *A Treasury of Jewish Poetry*. New York: Crown, 1957.

"To My Contemporaries"

Jack Salzman and Leo Zanderer, eds. *Social Poetry of the 1930s*. New York: Burt Franklin, 1978.

"Vincent"
Daily Worker, Feb. 22, 1957, 6
"Winter's Ghost Plagues Them"
Alan F. Pater, ed. *Anthology of Magazine Verse for 1937, and Yearbook of American Poetry.* New York: Paebar, 1938.
"Words Found on a Cave's Wall"
Jan Zábrana, ed. *Pátá Roční Doba: Antologie Americké Radikální Poezie.* Prague: Mladafronta, 1959. "Slova Nalezená Na Stěně Jeskyně," a Czech translation.

Fiction–Book

1946   Edwin Rolfe and Lester Fuller, *The Glass Room.* New York: Rinehart. Reprinted, New York: Bantam, 1948; London: Sampson Low, Marston, 1948. Translated as *A Sala de Vidro,* trans. Alvaro Leopoldo e Silva, Sao Paulo, Brazil: Editora Anchieta S.A., 1947; and *Un vrai chopin!* trans. Jean Rosenthal and Janine Herisson, Paris: Gallimard, 1951.

Reviews

Anderson, Issac. *New York Times,* Nov. 17, 1946, 48.
Book Review Digest, Jan. 1947. Reprinted in *Book Review Digest: Forty-second Annual Cumulation* (1947), 696.
Boucher, Anthony. *San Francisco Chronicle,* Nov. 17, 1946, 16.
Byers, Charles. *The Enquirer* (Cincinnati), Dec. 18, 1946.
Columbus Dispatch, Nov. 18, 1946.
Cuppy, Will. *New York Herald Tribune,* Dec. 15, 1946.
Drake, Drexel. *New York World-Telegram,* Nov. 14, 1946.
The Journal (Providence, R.I.), Dec. 8, 1946.
Kirkus, Sept. 1, 1946, 437.
Lavine, Sigmund. *World in Books,* Dec. 1946.
The News (Charleston, S.C.), Nov. 17, 1946.
New York Sun, Nov. 14, 1946.
New York Times, Nov. 17, 1946, 48.
Sandoe, James. *Book Week,* Nov. 17, 1946, 12.
Saturday Review of Literature, Nov. 9, 1946, 28.
The Star (Indianapolis), Jan. 5, 1947.
The Times (Hartford, Conn.), Dec. 7, 1946.
The Times-Starr (Cincinnati), 1946.
The Tribune (Oakland, Calif.), Nov. 1946.
Tribune (El Paso, Tex.), Mar. 3, 1947.
Weekly Book Review, Dec. 15, 1946, 20.

Fiction–In Periodicals

1927   "Disorderly Conduct"
        Daily Worker, Aug. 13, 1927 (*New Magazine*), 2.
1930   "Post Mortem"
        New World Monthly 1, no. 2 (Feb. 1930): 134–42.
1945   "Nocturne"
        Antioch Review 5, no. 4 (Dec. 1945): 524–31.

Nonfiction–Book

1939   *The Lincoln Battalion: The Story of the Americans Who Fought in Spain in the International Brigades.* New York: Random House. Reprinted in 1954 by the Veterans of the Abraham Lincoln Brigade in a boxed set along with Alvah Bessie's *Men in Battle.*

Reviews

Advocate (Stamford, Conn.), Dec. 6, 1949.
"American Boys in Spain Relive Their Battles." *Post* (Milwaukee, Wisc.), Nov. 11, 1939.
Argonaut (San Francisco), Jan. 12, 1940.
Argus (Montpelier, Vt.), Nov. 11, 1939.
B., M. H. *Times* (El Paso, Tex.), Dec. 17, 1939.
Bates, Ralph. "The Last Volunteers." *New Republic,* Dec. 27, 1939, 293–94.
Booklist, Dec. 15, 1939, 147.
Books, Nov. 26, 1939, 14.
Collaci, Mario. "Heroic Mercenaries." *Boston Transcript,* Nov. 25, 1939, 1.
Collie, G. Norman. "Stirring Story of U. S. Youth with Loyalists." *Public Ledger* (Philadelphia), Dec. 20, 1939.
F., M. *News* (Charleston, S.C.), Nov. 17, 1946.
G. *Times* (Chattanooga, Tenn.), Apr. 21, 1940.
Gates, John. "Gates Lauds Rolfe's Book on Battalion." *Daily Worker,* Nov. 28, 1939.
Hamilton, Charles. "Faithful Report of Americans in Spain." *Telegram* (Worcester, Mass.), Feb. 18, 1940.
Harper's, Nov. 1939.
Herald (Syracuse, N.Y.), Dec. 3, 1939.
Journal (Corry, Pa.), Dec. 26, 1939.
Kubly, Herbert. *Sun-Telegraph* (Pittsburgh, Pa.), Feb. 18, 1940.

"Libro." *Volunteer for Liberty*, no. 11 (England, Spring 1941): 21–22.

"Lincoln Battalion in Spain: Tale of a Curious Army." *Newsweek*, Nov. 13, 1939.

M., A. *Times* (Chester, Pa.), Nov. 16, 1939.

Miller, Max. "Youth Describes Experiences of Spanish War Volunteers: Edwin Rolfe Tells of Famed Lincoln Batallion." *San Diego Union*, Nov. 19, 1939, 7-C.

New Yorker, Nov. 18, 1939, 106.

New York Times, Nov. 18, 1939, 15.

News (Birmingham, Ala.), Nov. 25, 1939.

Readers Observer, Dec. 1939.

"Record of Spain's Lincoln Battalion Is Told by Rolfe." *Star News* (Pasadena, Calif.), Nov. 25, 1939.

Republican (Phoenix, Ariz.), Jan. 21, 1940.

Rhodes, Arthur. "American Volunteers in Bloody Spain." *Brooklyn Eagle*, Nov. 7, 1939.

Romer, Samuel. *The Nation*, Nov. 18, 1939, 557.

Schurz, W. L. "Forlorn Adventure." *Post* (Washington, D.C.), Jan. 28, 1940.

"Spain's Civil War." *Journal* (Akron, Ohio), Jan. 14, 1940.

"Stirring Story of U.S. Youth with Loyalists." *Public Ledger* (Philadelphia), Dec. 20, 1939.

Sun (Washington, D.C.), Nov. 12, 1939.

Time, Nov. 20, 1939, 82–84.

"Two Writers and a War." *Philadelphia Inquirer*, Nov. 8, 1939.

W., C. "War's Futility Stressed by Boys in Spain." *Tribune* (Salt Lake City, Utah), Dec. 24, 1939.

White, David McKelvy. *Daily Worker*, Nov. 11, 1939, 4.

White, Leigh. "Faith in the Republic." *New York Herald Tribune*, Nov. 26, 1939.

Wilkins, Fred. "Part Played by American Fighters in Spanish War Told in Volume by Rolfe." *Times-Herald* (Dallas, Tex.), Nov. 12, 1939.

Yeats, John W. "Rolfe Tells of Service in Spain." *Post* (Houston, Tex.), Dec. 31, 1939.

Nonfiction–Periodicals and Newspapers

1927   "Van Loon Laments Intolerance" (review of Hendrik Willem Van Loon, *Tolerance*)

         Daily Worker, July 26, 1927, 6.

"Manias of New York" (sketch)
Daily Worker, Oct. 22, 1927, 7.
"Anachronistic Literature" (essay)
Daily Worker, Nov. 12, 1927, 8.
"Waiting for the Ashes of Two Martyrs" (sketch)
Daily Worker, Nov. 19, 1927, 4.
"Snapshots" (sketch)
Daily Worker, [c. Dec.] 1927, 6.

1928   "Factory Sketches: Slaves and Bosses" (sketch)
Daily Worker, Apr. 7, 1928, 5.
"Radicalism" (letter to the editor)
The World (New York), May 21, 1928.
"A Craftsman in Fiction of Nice Details" (review of Julian Green, *The Closed Garden*)
Daily Worker, May 26, 1928, 9.
"Muller and His Choral Society in the Factory"
Daily Worker, June 2, 1928, 5.
"Irish Guild Players Present Three Tidbits at Playhouse" (theater review)
Daily Worker, June 13, 1928, 2.
"A Novel of 'Poor Whites' by a Literary Ku Kluxer" (review of Edwin Granberry, *Strangers and Lovers*)
Daily Worker, Sept. 8, 1928, 4.
"Young Textile Striker Speaks: Figuerido Tells of Mill Struggle"
Daily Worker, Sept. 24, 1928, 1, 2.
Review of *Minor Music* by Henry Reich, Jr.
New Masses 4, no. 6 (Nov. 1928): 23.
"A Healthy Modern" (review of Glenway Wescott, *Good-bye Wisconsin*)
Daily Worker, Nov. 13, 1928, 4.
"Built on Sand" (review of Margaret Leech, *The Feathered Nest*)
New Masses 4, no. 7 (Dec. 1928): 23–24.
"Peter Pan Well-Done by Civic Repertory Players" (review of J. M. Barrie, *Peter Pan*)
Daily Worker, Dec. 4, 1928, 4.
"Old Maid Romantics" (review of Heyward Emerson Canney, *Sentry*)
Daily Worker, Dec. 22, 1928, 4.

1929   "Manicured Poetry" (review of Alice Mary Kimball, *The Devil Is a Woman,* and Carlton Kimball, *Ballyhoo for a Mendicant*)
New Masses, 4, no. 11 (Apr. 1929): 1.

"Soviet Theatre Most Vital in World, Says Dana in Interview" (no by-line)
>   *Daily Worker,* Apr. 5, 1929, 2.

"John Drinkwater Glorifies Nobility in 'Bird in Hand' " (theater review)
>   *Daily Worker,* Apr. 13, 1929, 4.

" 'Marching Guns' Embryo of Real U. S. Workers Theatre" (theater review)
>   *Daily Worker,* Apr. 18, 1929, 4.

" 'The Adventures of Maya' Is Instructive, Enjoyable Film" (unsigned review)
>   *Daily Worker,* Apr. 24, 1929, 4.

"Widow of Killed Building Worker Left Destitute"
>   *Daily Worker,* Apr. 24, 1929.

"Only Flowers for Widow of Crash Victim"
>   *Daily Worker,* Apr. 25, 1929, 1, 5.

"Revolutionary Anthology Is Excellent Work, Despite Faults" (review of Marcus Graham, ed. *An Anthology of Revolutionary Poetry*)
>   *Daily Worker,* May 25, 1929, 4.

"Life without Ecstasy" (review of Gertrude Diamant's *Labyrinth*)
>   *New Masses,* 5, no. 1 (June 1929): 20.

"A Reformed Crook Gets Religion" (review of Kane O'Dore, *Philosophy of the Dusk*)
>   *New Masses,* 5, no. 3 (Aug. 1929): 21.

1930   Review of Margery Latimer, *This Is My Body.*
>   *Hillel Review* (Madison, Wisc.), Feb. 15, 1930.

Review of Altalena, *Judge and Fool.*
>   *Hillel Review,* Mar. 1, 1930.

"A Humanist Estimates America's Literature"
>   *Daily Cardinal* (Madison, Wisc.), Mar. 2, 1930.

Review of George Sylvester Viereck and Paul Eldridge, *My First Two Thousand Years.*
>   *Hillel Review,* Mar. 15, 1930.

Review of Michael Gold, *Jews without Money.*
>   *Hillel Review,* Mar. 29, 1930.

Review of Malcolm Cowley, *Blue Juniata.*
>   *Hillel Review,* Apr. 26, 1930.

Review of Ludwig Lewisohn, *Stephen Escott.*
>   *Hillel Review,* May 10, 1930.

Review of e. e. cummings, *The Enormous Room.*
>   *Hillel Review,* May 17, 1930.

Review of Joseph Wood Krutch, *Edgar Allan Poe*.
  Hillel Review, May 24, 1930.
Review of Victoria Sackville-West, *The Edwardians*.
  Hillel Review, Oct. 10, 1930.
Review of Gorham Munson, *The Dilemna of the Liberated*.
  Hillel Review, Oct. 17, 1930.
"Raids, Redskins—a Gallop for Life and Other Book Notes" (review of
Frank Harris, *My Reminiscences as a Cowboy,* and Victoria Sackville-West,
The Edwardians)
  Daily Cardinal, Oct. 18, 1930, 7, 10.
"'Pure Young Man'—A Winner" (review of Irving Fineman, *This Pure
Young Man*)
  Daily Cardinal, Nov. 2, 1930, 7.
"On Recent War Novels" and Review of Conrad Aiken, *John Deth and
Other Poems*
  Daily Cardinal, Nov. 9, 1930, 6, 10.

1931   Review of Joseph Van Raalte, *The Vice Squad*.
          New Masses 7, no. 7 (Dec. 1930): 25.

1932   "Jacob Burck—Graphic Historian of the Class Struggle"
          Daily Worker, Jan. 18, 1932, 4.
        [Letter to the editor in "The Bear Garden"]
          New York Sun, Jan. 23, 1932.
        "A Hunger-and-War Olympics"
          Daily Worker, Feb. 12, 1932, 4.
        "Contra la olimpiada de los imperialistas la olimpiada de los obreros"
          Mundo obrero, Mar. 1932, 15, 22.
        "The Olympics and Tom Mooney"
          The New Sport and Play: An Illustrated Labor Sports Magazine, May
          1932, 4.
        "Apoyemos el mitin atletico internacional obrero de Chicago"
          Mundo obrero, June 1932, 10–11.
        "Literary Forms" (letter to the editor in "The Bear Garden")
          New York Sun, June 27, 1932.
        Review of Whittaker Chambers, *Can You Hear Their Voices?*
          New Masses 8, no. 3 (Sept. 1932): 24.
        "Walcott—Former Negro Boxer Sent to Bellevue"
          Young Worker, Sept. 1932, 3.
        "Kentucky and the Intellectual." Review of *Harlan Miners Speak*.
          Contempo, 2, no. 4 (July 5, 1932): 3, 5.

1933   "God's Little Acre" (review of Erskine Caldwell, *God's Little Acre*)
        New Masses 8, no. 7 (Feb. 1933): 26.
        "For Worker's Children—and Adults" (review of *The New Pioneer*)
        Daily Worker, Feb. 17, 1933, 4.
        "Factory Sketches: 'Bertie's' Costume" (sketch, unsigned)
        Daily Worker, Apr. 11, 1933, 4.
        "Threaten to Fire Negro Teacher Who Defended Colleague"
        Daily Worker, June 12, 1933, 2.
        "Disabled Vet Tells What Roosevelt's 'New Deal' Did for Him"
        Daily Worker, June 27, 1933, 4.
        "Farrell's Progress" (review of James T. Farrell, *Gas-House McGinty*)
        New Masses 8, no. 11 (July 1933): 29.
        "A Tired Tory" (review of Norman Douglas, *Looking Back: An Autobiographical Excursion*)
        New Masses 8, no. 11 (July 1933): 27.
        "A Novel of German Life before Hitler" (review of Hans Falada, *Little Man What Now*)
        Daily Worker, July 8, 1933, 5.
        "What Happened at the Daily Worker after the First Six Page Issue Came off the Press"
        Daily Worker, Aug. 15, 1933, 5.
        "Red Press" (review of *The Voice of the West End*)
        Daily Worker, Sept. 2, 1933, 7.
        "What a World" (on Horace Gregory and revolutionary poetry) (substituting for Mike Gold)
        Daily Worker, Oct. 13, 1933, 5.
        "Sergei Radamsky Describes Soviet Music World in Interview"
        Daily Worker, Dec. 28, 1933, 5.

1934   "Farrell's New Novel Portrays Chicago Life" (review of *The Young Manhood of Studs Lonigan*.)
        Daily Worker, Feb. 3, 1934, 7.
        "It May Have Been Cold—But Not for Everybody"
        Daily Worker, Feb. 14, 1934, 5.
        "East Side Fire Snuffs Out Lives of Eight Workers and Kids"
        Daily Worker, Feb. 20, 1934, 2.
        "Upstate Decay" (review of Howard Coxe, *First Love and Last*)
        New Masses, 10, no. 8 (Feb. 20, 1934): 26–27.
        "A College Girl Writes about Western Pennsylvania Miners" (review of Lauren Gilfillan, *I Went to College*)
        Daily Worker, Mar. 3, 1934, 7.

"Nationalistic and Jingoistic Speakers in Demagogic Mock Trial of Hitler Anti-Semitism at Madison Square Garden: Cahan, Matthew Wall, American Legionnaire among Speakers"
Daily Worker, Mar. 9, 1934, 2.
"Fusion and Real Estate Owners Seek Huge Federal Subsidies to Reap Profits in Tenement Repairs"
Daily Worker, Mar. 12, 1934, 3.
"New Masses Quarterly Is Real Advance"
Daily Worker, Apr. 4, 1934, 5.
"Three New Trade Union Papers Make First Appearance"
Daily Worker (New York Trade Union Section), May 28, 1934, 3.
"Hounded by Georgia Terror, Don West Fights for Herndon and Atlanta Six"
Daily Worker, June 11, 1934, 1, 2.
"With the Trade Union Papers"
Daily Worker (New York Trade Union Section), June 11, 1934, 3.
"The LaGuardia-O'Ryan Regime Openly Launches Violence against the Workers of New York City"
Daily Worker, June 13, 1934, 1, 2.
"With the Trade Union Papers"
Daily Worker (New York Trade Union Section), June 18, 1934, 3.
"Fight of Sharecroppers in Black Belt against NRA Described by Leader"
Daily Worker, July 6, 1934, 3.
"Alabama Sharecroppers Fight Onslaughts of NRA"
Daily Worker, July 7, 1934, 3.
"With the Trade Union Papers"
Daily Worker (New York Trade Union Section), July 9, 1934, 3.
"Change the World" (on Langston Hughes)
Daily Worker, July 10, 1934, 5.
"Mayor LaGuardia Reports 'To the People'—Conveniently Ignores His Reign of Terror against Labor—Slurs Over 'Economy' Program That Slashed City Wages"
Daily Worker, July 12, 1934, 3.
"Reporters Hold Picket Line Solid at Long Island Press"
Daily Worker, July 13, 1934, 2.
"U.S. Labor History Shows Onward March of Strike Struggles of American Workers: Great Railroad Struggles of 1877; Four-Day General Strike in Seattle in 1919; Many Others, Were Prelude to Frisco in 1934"
Daily Worker, July 17, 1934, 5.
"Seattle General Strike Terror in 1919 Shows How Labor Can Defeat It—Five Years of Crisis Make Workers Wary of 'Red Scare' Ballyhoo"
Daily Worker, July 19, 1934, 5.

"Ten Thousand Cheering Negro and White Workers Take Over Terminal as Herndon Arrives"
Daily Worker, Aug. 9, 1934, 2.
"Farrell's Fourth Book Collects Short Stories Written in Last Seven Years" (review of James T. Farrell, *Calico Shoes and Other Stories*)
Daily Worker, Oct. 8, 1934, 5.
"The Second Macaulay Strike"
New Masses 13, no. 4 (Oct. 23, 1934): 20–21.
"Stimulating Material on Theatre-Arts Front in Current New Theatre" (review of *New Theatre Magazine*)
Daily Worker, Nov. 30, 1934, 7.

1935   "Exiled Spanish Writers Here to Speak for Literary Groups" (on Rafael Alberti and Maria Teresa Leon)
Daily Worker, Mar. 18, 1935, 5.
"Poetry" (essay)
Partisan Review 2, no. 7 (Apr.–May 1935): 32–42.
"Progress or Retrogression" (review of Erskine Caldwell, *Kneel to the Rising Sun and Other Stories*)
Partisan Review 2, no. 8 (July-Aug. 1935): 61–63.

1936   "Poet's First Flight" (review of Muriel Rukeyser, *Theory of Flight*)
Daily Worker, Jan. 9, 1936, 7.
"Still Ten Years Old" (review of Nathalia Crane, *Swear by the Night*)
Daily Worker, Mar. 31, 1936, 7.

1937   "What Is Happening behind Franco's Lines"
Volunteer for Liberty 1, no. 15 (Sept. 20, 1937): 1, 4–5.
"A Year of the International Brigades"
Volunteer for Liberty 1, no. 18 (Oct. 1, 1937): 2–3.
"Franco's Captive: A Catholic Loyalist Was Captured by Italian and German Fascists in Spain. He Escaped to Tell His Story."
Daily Worker (Sunday Magazine), Oct. 17, 1937, 4.
"Hidden Treasures: The Spanish Loyalists Have Secreted the Priceless Heritage of the Centuries far from the Sight of Fascist Bombers"
Daily Worker (Sunday Magazine), Nov. 21, 1937, 5.
"Spain's Shirt-Sleeve General" (El Campesino)
New Masses 25, no. 11 (Dec. 7, 1937): 13–14.

1938   "Little Spanish Town"
Daily Worker (Sunday Magazine), Mar. 6, 1938, 4.